# GARFIELD™

## FULLY CAFFEINATED

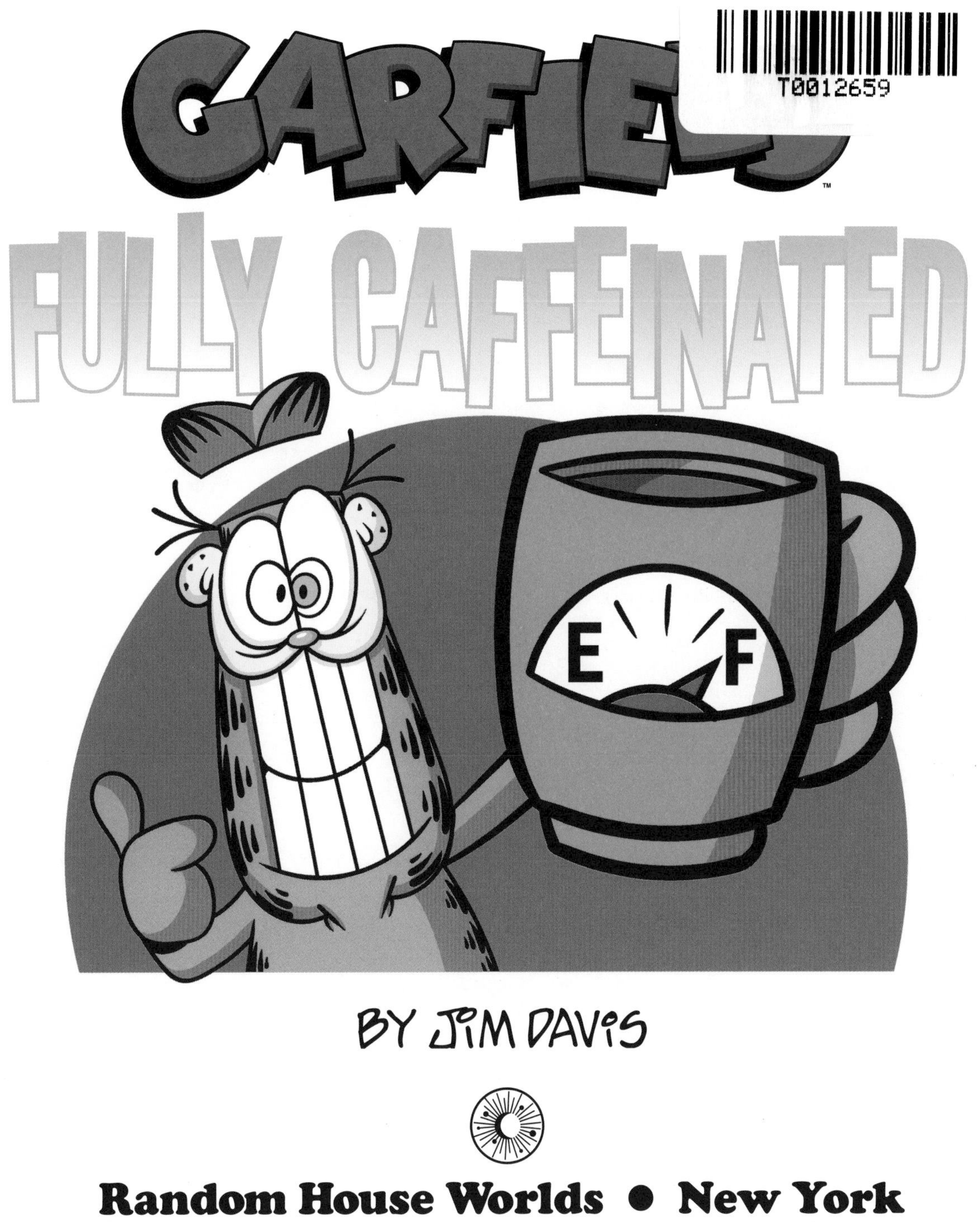
E
F

BY JIM DAVIS

Random House Worlds • New York

Published in the United States by Random House Worlds, an imprint of Random House, a division of Penguin Random House LLC, New York.

RANDOM HOUSE is a registered trademark, and RANDOM HOUSE WORLDS and colophon are trademarks of Penguin Random House LLC.

All of the comics in this work have been previously published.

ISBN 978-0-593-59921-1
Ebook ISBN 978-0-593-59922-8

Printed in China on acid-free paper

randomhousebooks.com

9 8 7 6 5 4 3 2

# WHO WANTS COFFEE?

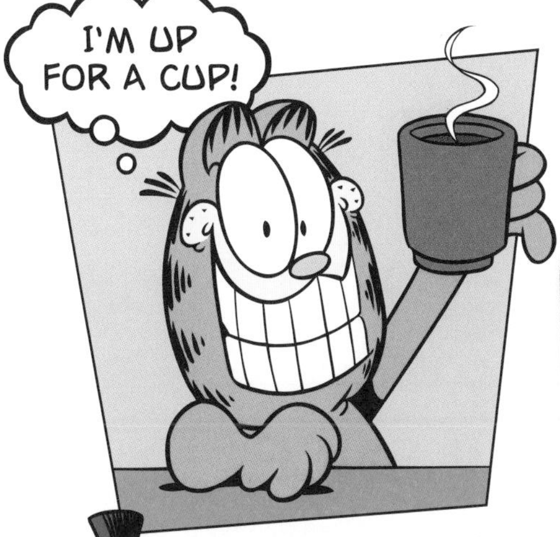
I'M UP FOR A CUP!

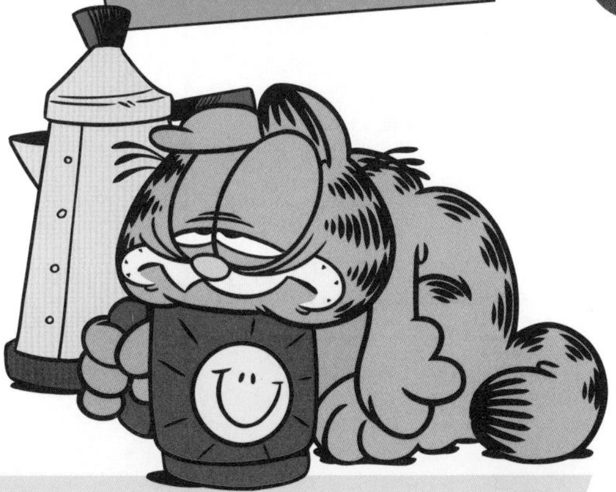

THE EYELIDS GO UP WHEN THE COFFEE GOES DOWN.

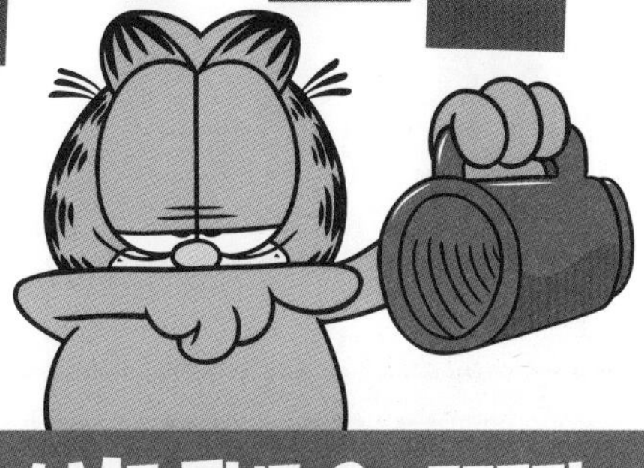

SHOW ME THE COFFEE!

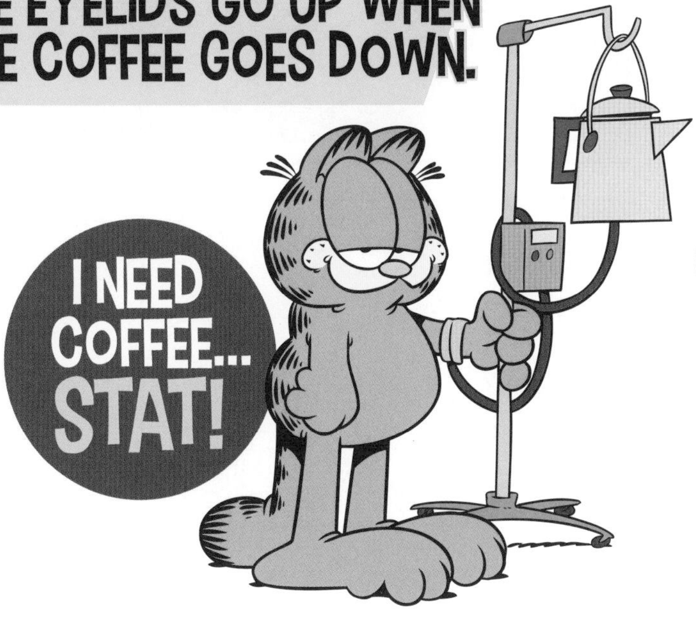
I NEED COFFEE... STAT!

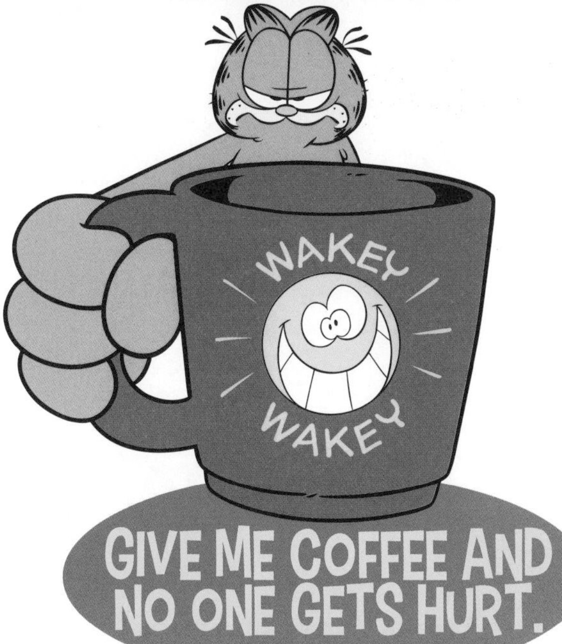
WAKEY
WAKEY

GIVE ME COFFEE AND NO ONE GETS HURT.

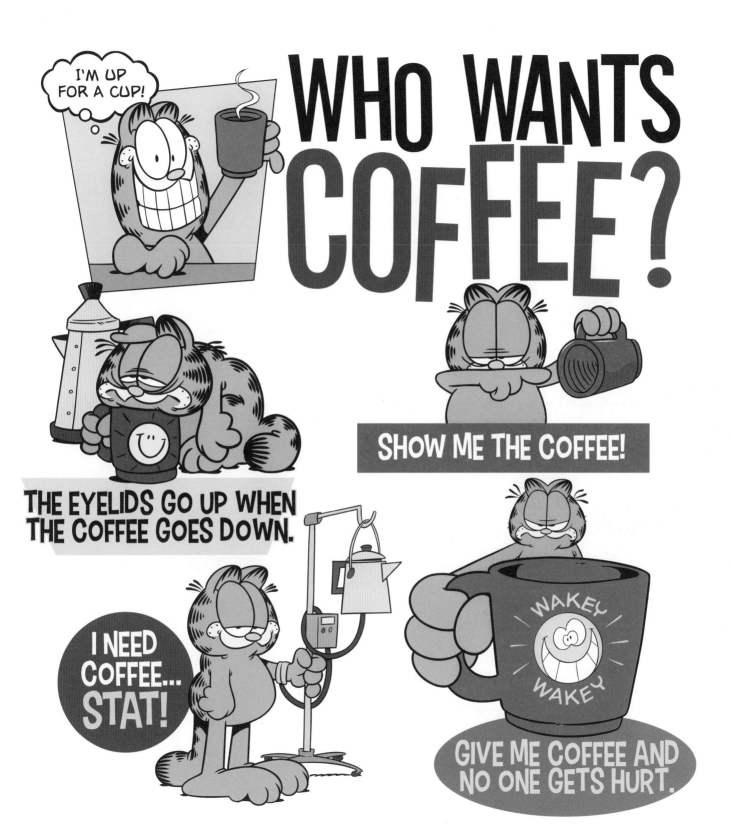

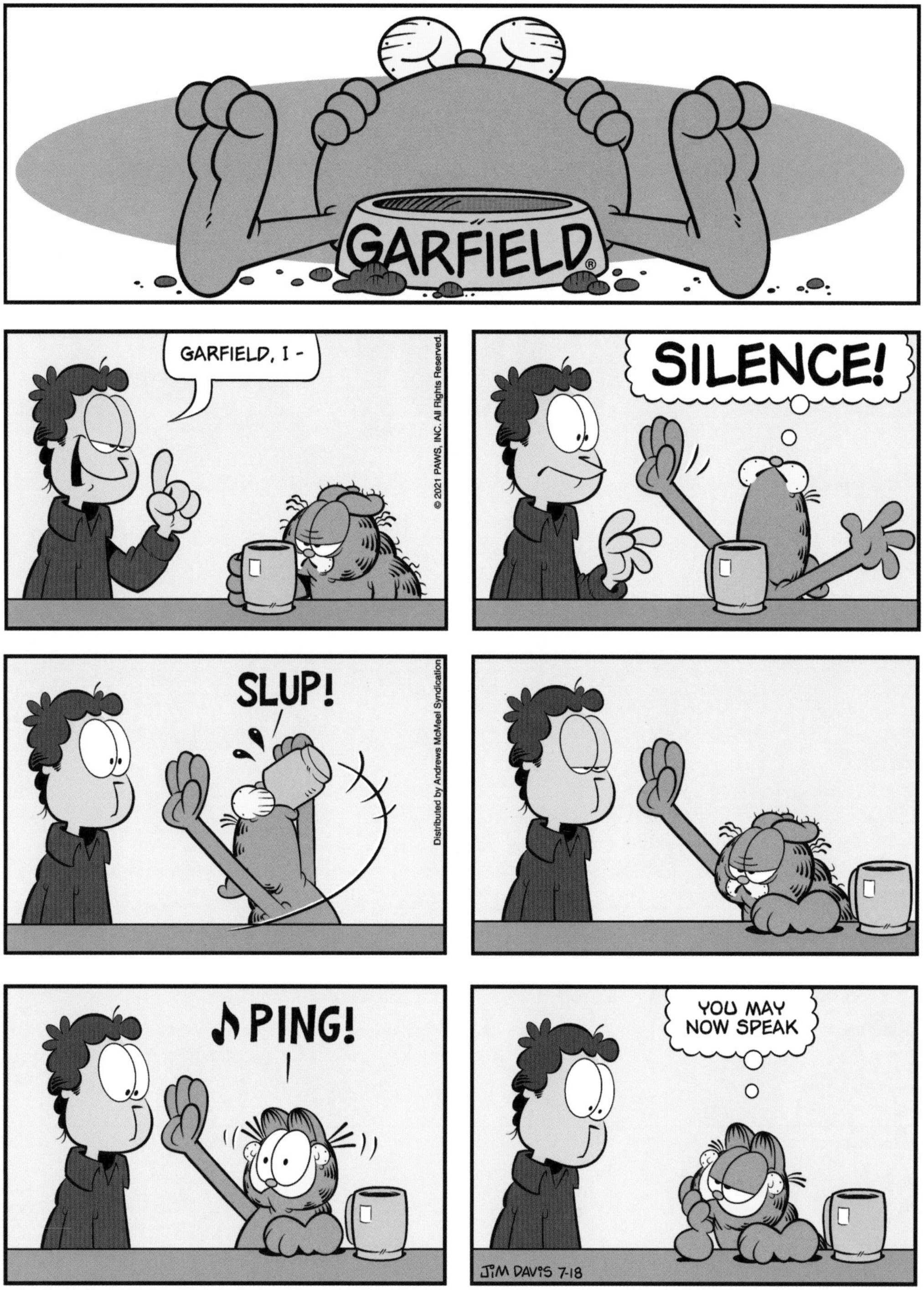
GARFIELD®
GARFIELD, I -
© 2021 PAWS, INC. All Rights Reserved.
SILENCE!
SLUP!
Distributed by Andrews McMeel Syndication
♪PING!
YOU MAY NOW SPEAK
JIM DAVIS 7-18

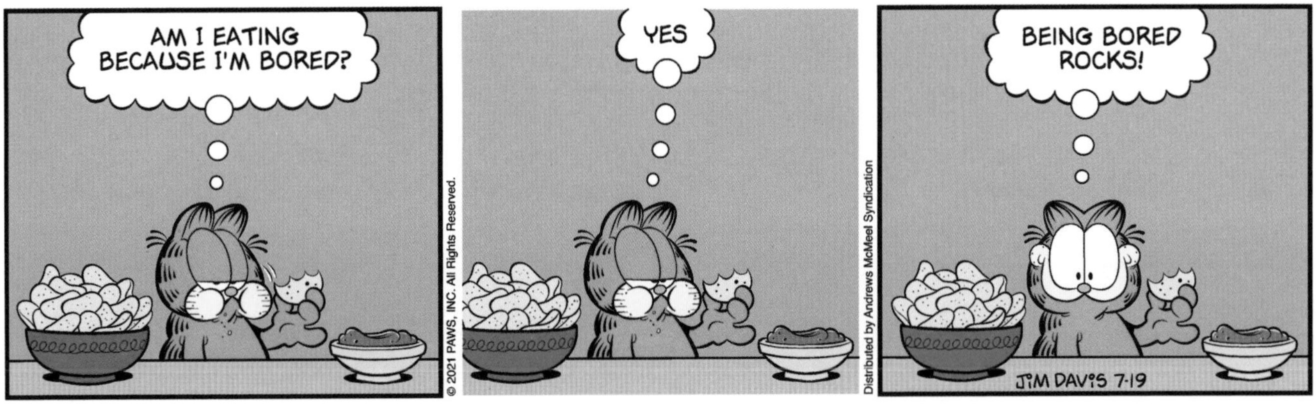
AM I EATING BECAUSE I'M BORED?
© 2021 PAWS, INC. All Rights Reserved.
YES
Distributed by Andrews McMeel Syndication
BEING BORED ROCKS!
JIM DAVIS 7-19

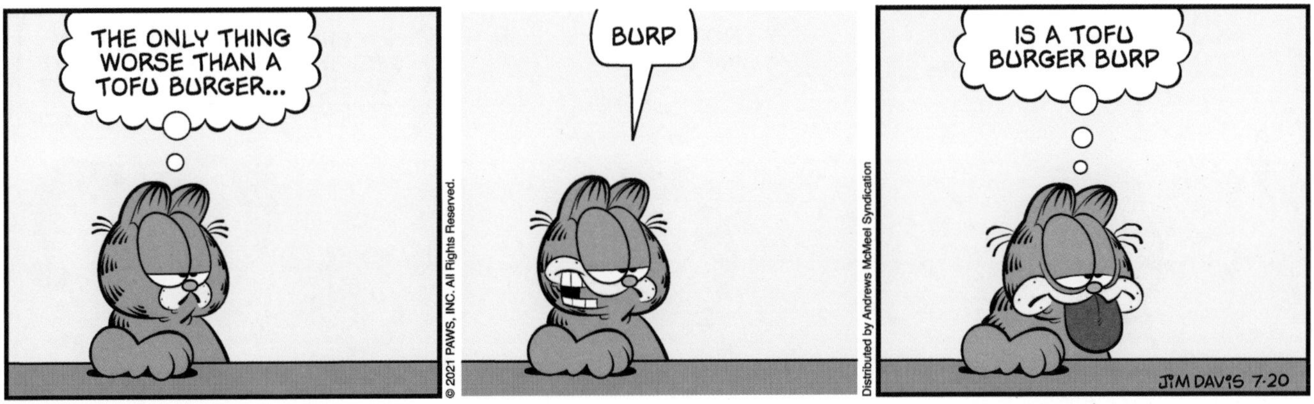
THE ONLY THING WORSE THAN A TOFU BURGER...
© 2021 PAWS, INC. All Rights Reserved.
BURP
Distributed by Andrews McMeel Syndication
IS A TOFU BURGER BURP
JIM DAVIS 7-20

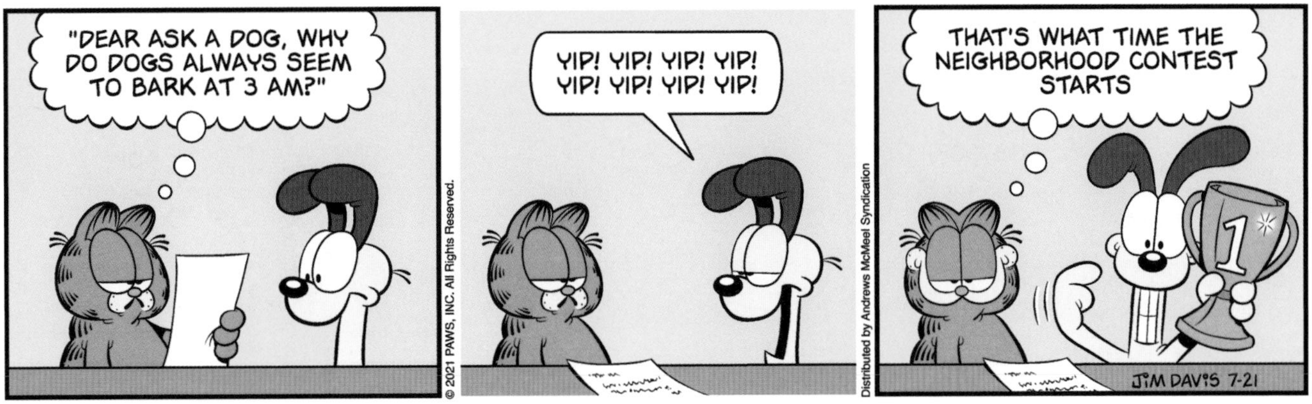
"DEAR ASK A DOG, WHY DO DOGS ALWAYS SEEM TO BARK AT 3 AM?"
© 2021 PAWS, INC. All Rights Reserved.
YIP! YIP! YIP! YIP! YIP! YIP! YIP! YIP!
Distributed by Andrews McMeel Syndication
THAT'S WHAT TIME THE NEIGHBORHOOD CONTEST STARTS
1
JIM DAVIS 7-21

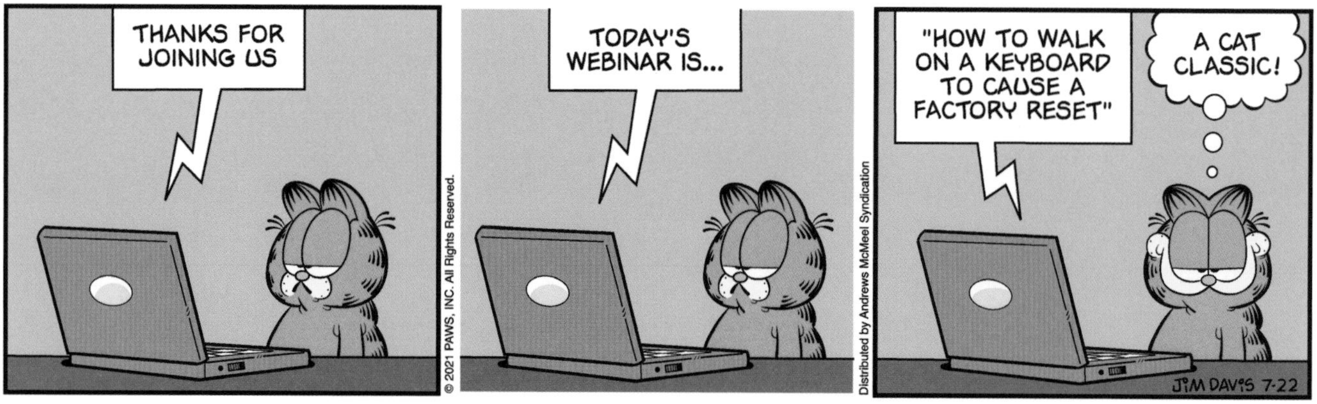
THANKS FOR JOINING US
TODAY'S WEBINAR IS...
"HOW TO WALK ON A KEYBOARD TO CAUSE A FACTORY RESET"
A CAT CLASSIC!
JIM DAVIS 7-22
© 2021 PAWS, INC. All Rights Reserved.
Distributed by Andrews McMeel Syndication

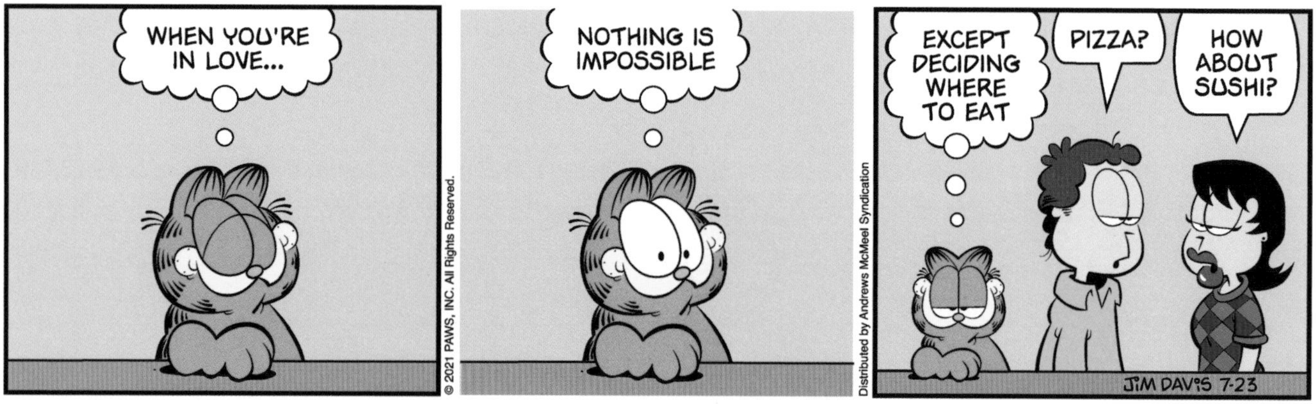
WHEN YOU'RE IN LOVE...
NOTHING IS IMPOSSIBLE
EXCEPT DECIDING WHERE TO EAT
PIZZA?
HOW ABOUT SUSHI?
JIM DAVIS 7-23
© 2021 PAWS, INC. All Rights Reserved.
Distributed by Andrews McMeel Syndication

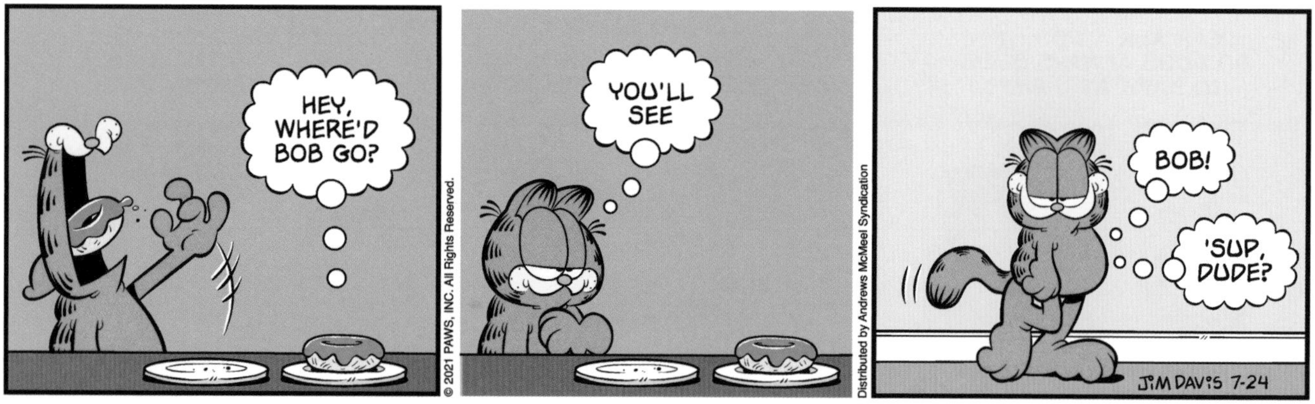
HEY, WHERE'D BOB GO?
YOU'LL SEE
BOB!
'SUP, DUDE?
JIM DAVIS 7-24
© 2021 PAWS, INC. All Rights Reserved.
Distributed by Andrews McMeel Syndication

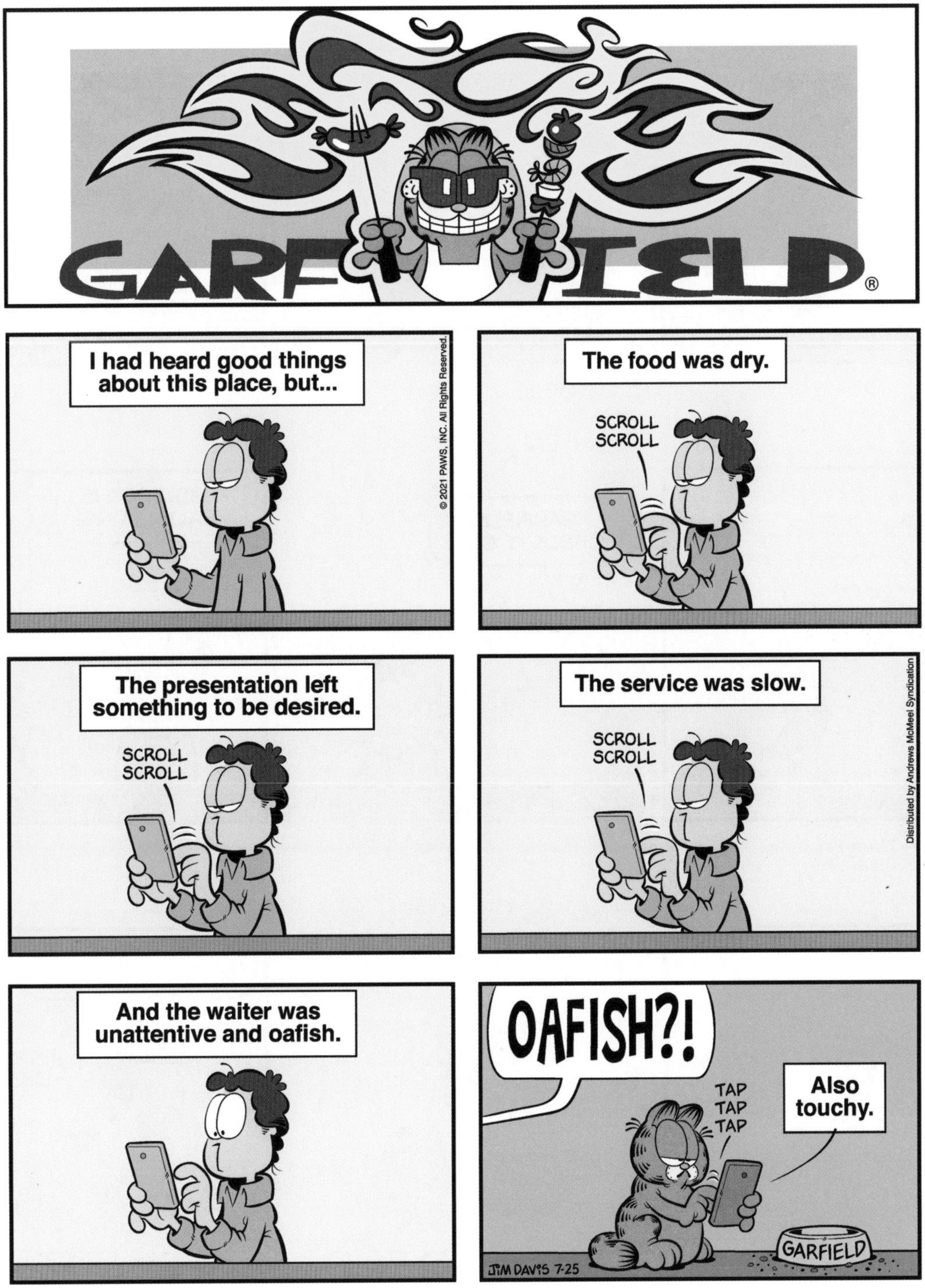
GARFIELD®
© 2021 PAWS, INC. All Rights Reserved.
I had heard good things about this place, but...
The food was dry.
SCROLL SCROLL
The presentation left something to be desired.
SCROLL SCROLL
The service was slow.
SCROLL SCROLL
Distributed by Andrews McMeel Syndication
And the waiter was unattentive and oafish.
OAFISH?!
TAP TAP TAP
Also touchy.
GARFIELD
JIM DAVIS 7-25

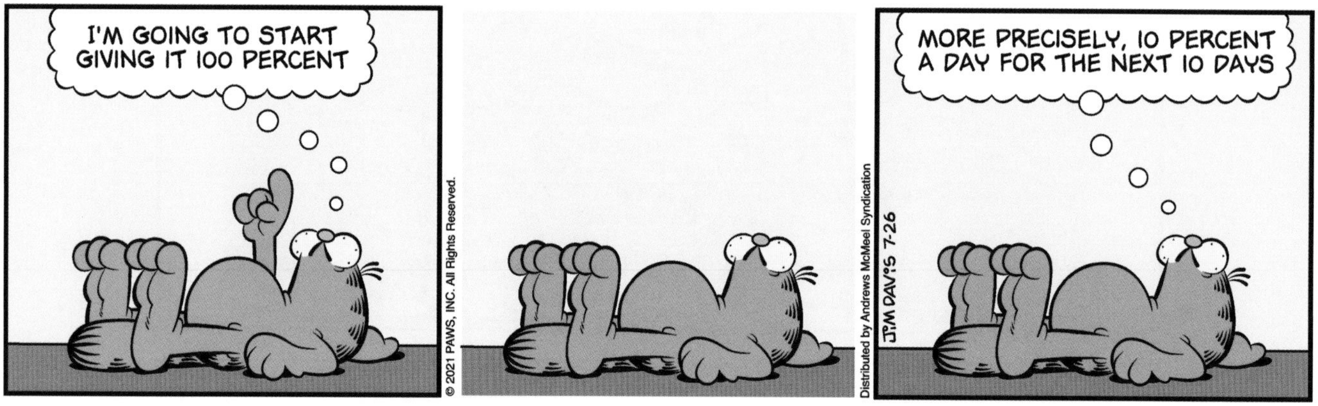
I'M GOING TO START GIVING IT 100 PERCENT
MORE PRECISELY, 10 PERCENT A DAY FOR THE NEXT 10 DAYS
© 2021 PAWS, INC. All Rights Reserved.
Distributed by Andrews McMeel Syndication
JIM DAVIS 7-26

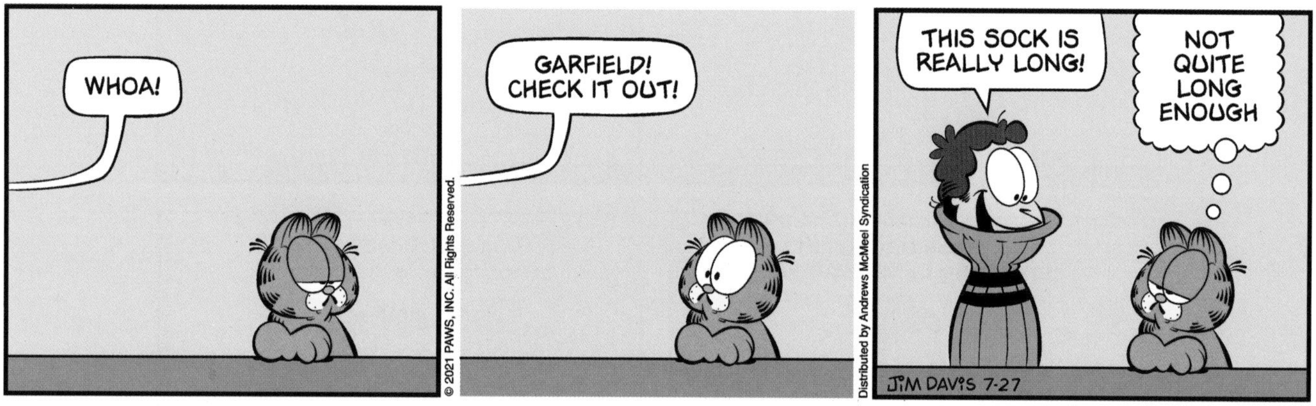
WHOA!
GARFIELD! CHECK IT OUT!
THIS SOCK IS REALLY LONG!
NOT QUITE LONG ENOUGH
© 2021 PAWS, INC. All Rights Reserved.
Distributed by Andrews McMeel Syndication
JIM DAVIS 7-27

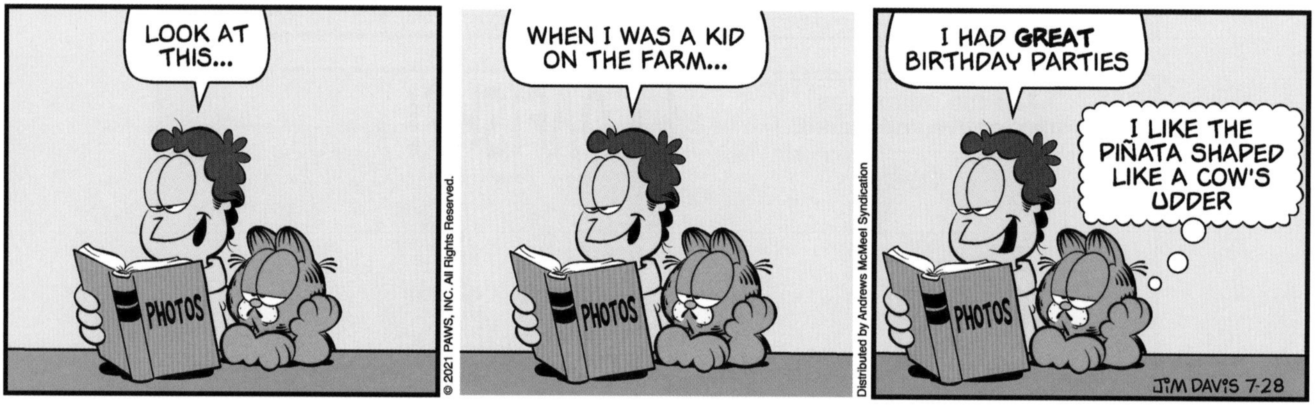
LOOK AT THIS...
PHOTOS
WHEN I WAS A KID ON THE FARM...
PHOTOS
I HAD **GREAT** BIRTHDAY PARTIES
I LIKE THE PIÑATA SHAPED LIKE A COW'S UDDER
PHOTOS
© 2021 PAWS, INC. All Rights Reserved.
Distributed by Andrews McMeel Syndication
JIM DAVIS 7-28

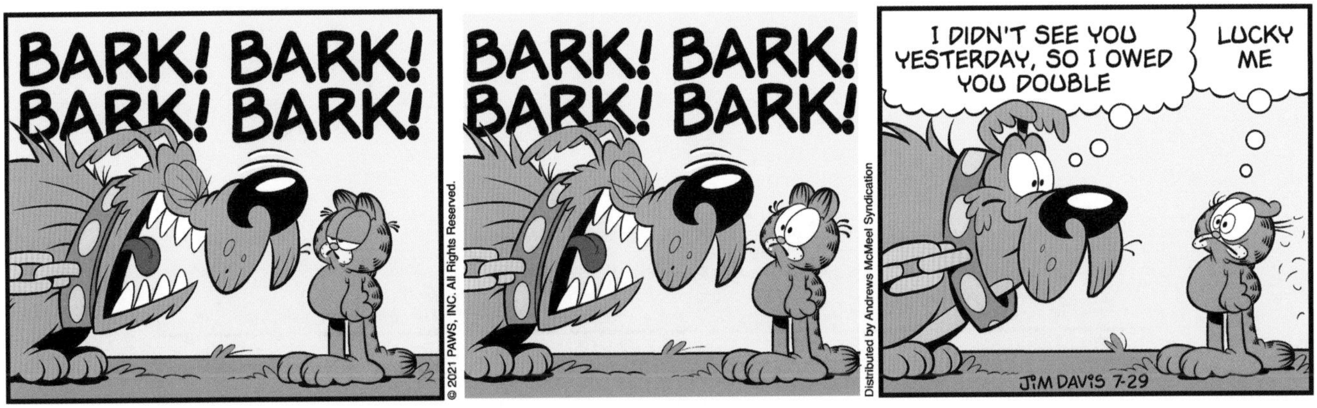
BARK! BARK! BARK! BARK!
BARK! BARK! BARK! BARK!
I DIDN'T SEE YOU YESTERDAY, SO I OWED YOU DOUBLE
LUCKY ME
© 2021 PAWS, INC. All Rights Reserved.
Distributed by Andrews McMeel Syndication
JIM DAVIS 7-29

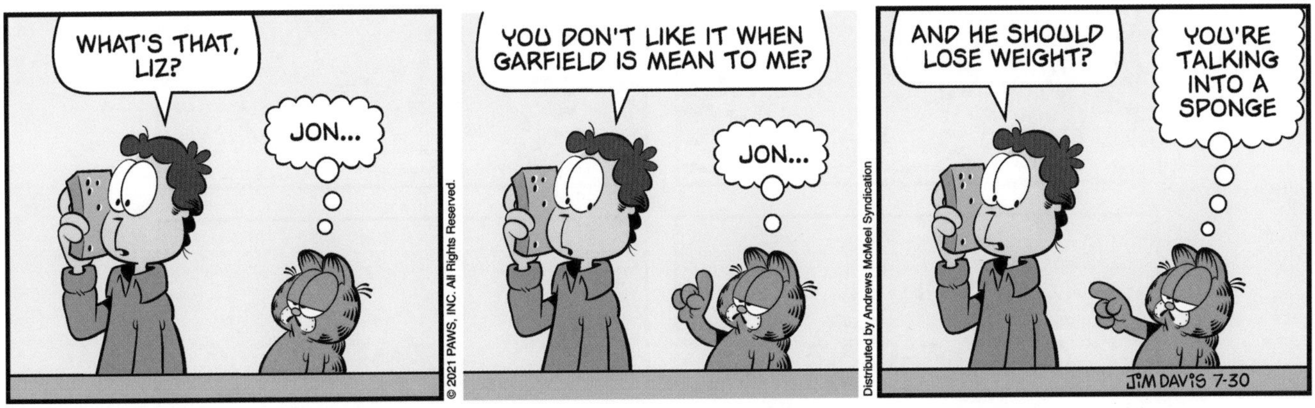
WHAT'S THAT, LIZ?
JON...
YOU DON'T LIKE IT WHEN GARFIELD IS MEAN TO ME?
JON...
AND HE SHOULD LOSE WEIGHT?
YOU'RE TALKING INTO A SPONGE
© 2021 PAWS, INC. All Rights Reserved.
Distributed by Andrews McMeel Syndication
JIM DAVIS 7-30

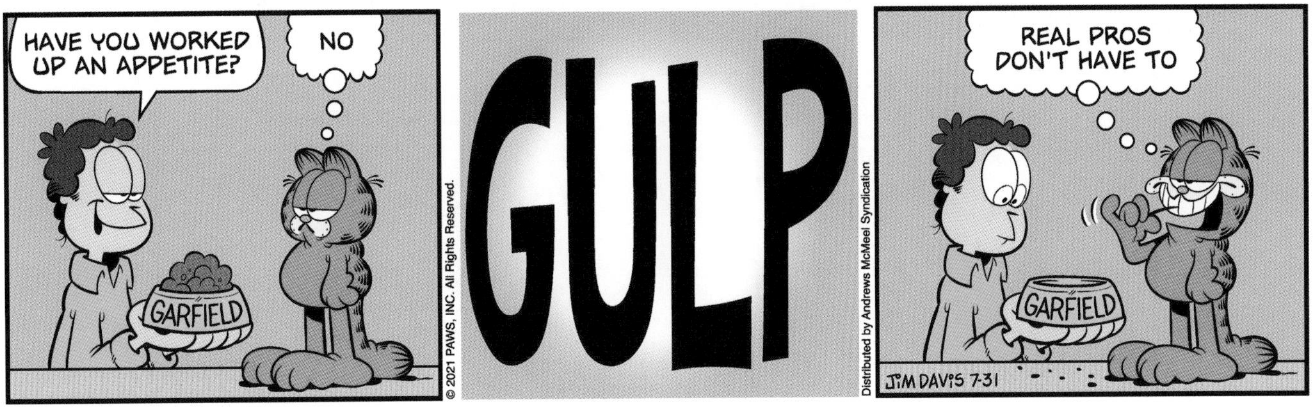
HAVE YOU WORKED UP AN APPETITE?
NO
GARFIELD
GULP
REAL PROS DON'T HAVE TO
GARFIELD
© 2021 PAWS, INC. All Rights Reserved.
Distributed by Andrews McMeel Syndication
JIM DAVIS 7-31

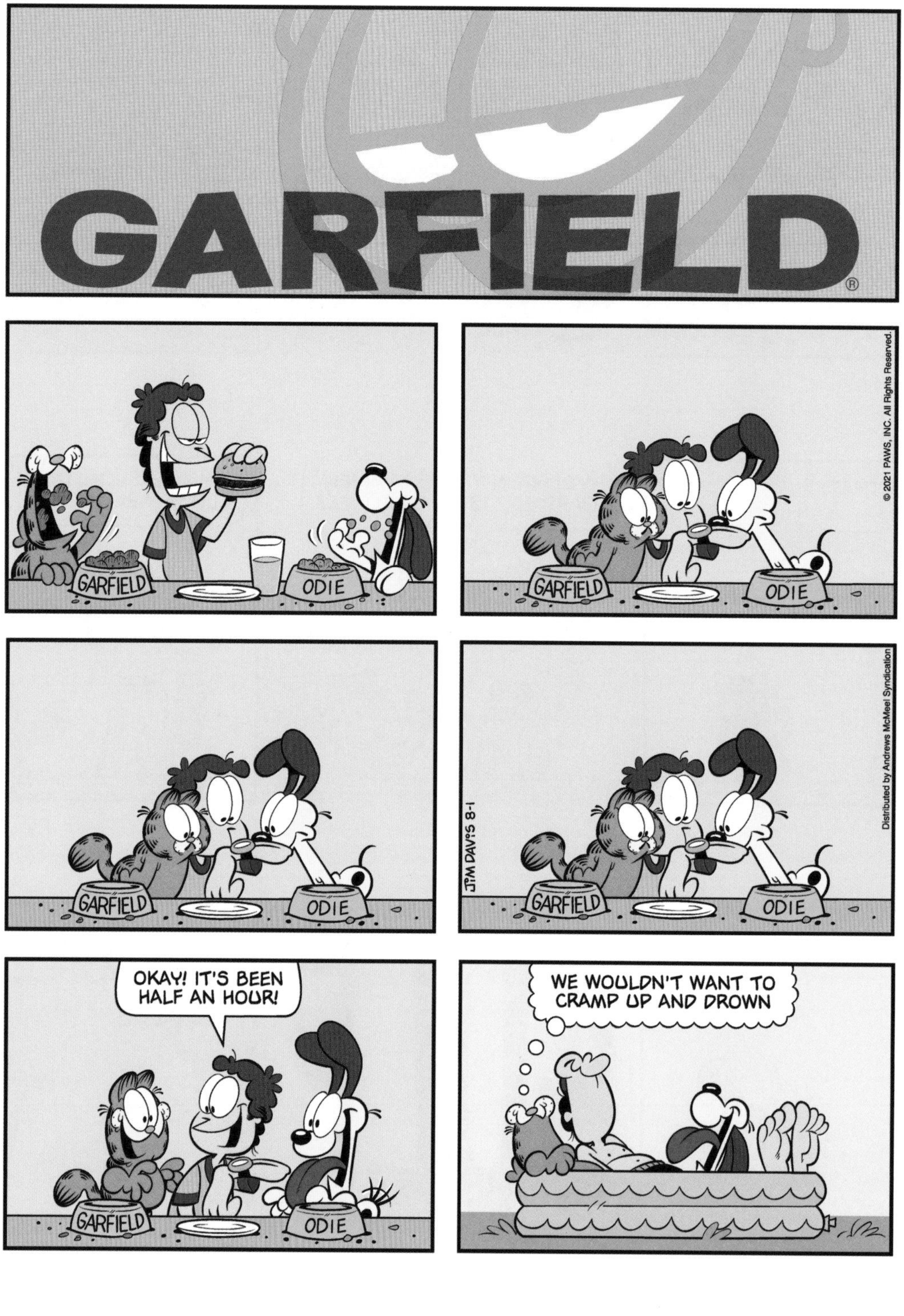
GARFIELD®
GARFIELD
ODIE
© 2021 PAWS, INC. All Rights Reserved.
JIM DAVIS 8-1
Distributed by Andrews McMeel Syndication
OKAY! IT'S BEEN HALF AN HOUR!
WE WOULDN'T WANT TO CRAMP UP AND DROWN

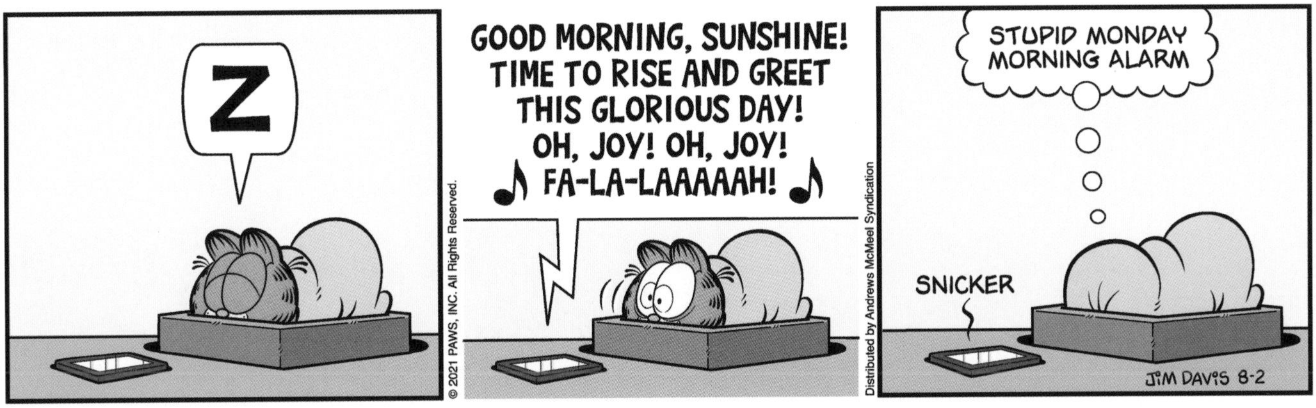
Z
GOOD MORNING, SUNSHINE! TIME TO RISE AND GREET THIS GLORIOUS DAY! OH, JOY! OH, JOY! FA-LA-LAAAAAH!
STUPID MONDAY MORNING ALARM
SNICKER
JIM DAVIS 8-2


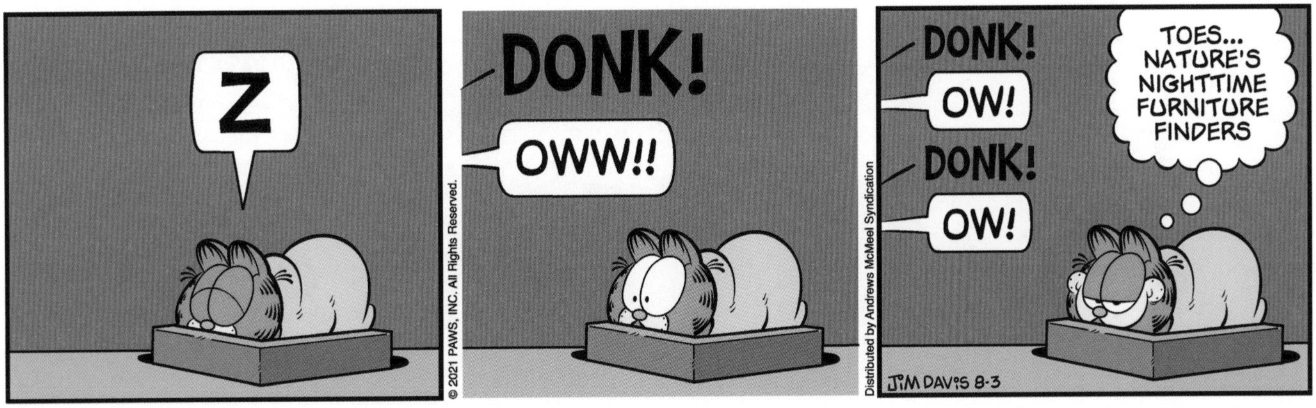
Z
DONK!
OWW!!
DONK!
OW!
DONK!
OW!
TOES... NATURE'S NIGHTTIME FURNITURE FINDERS
JIM DAVIS 8-3


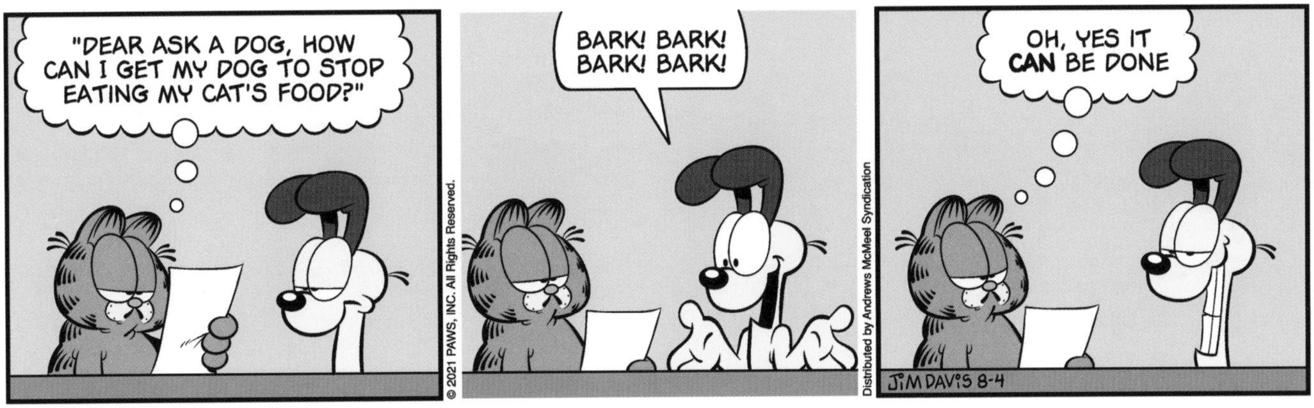
"DEAR ASK A DOG, HOW CAN I GET MY DOG TO STOP EATING MY CAT'S FOOD?"
BARK! BARK! BARK! BARK!
OH, YES IT **CAN** BE DONE
JIM DAVIS 8-4

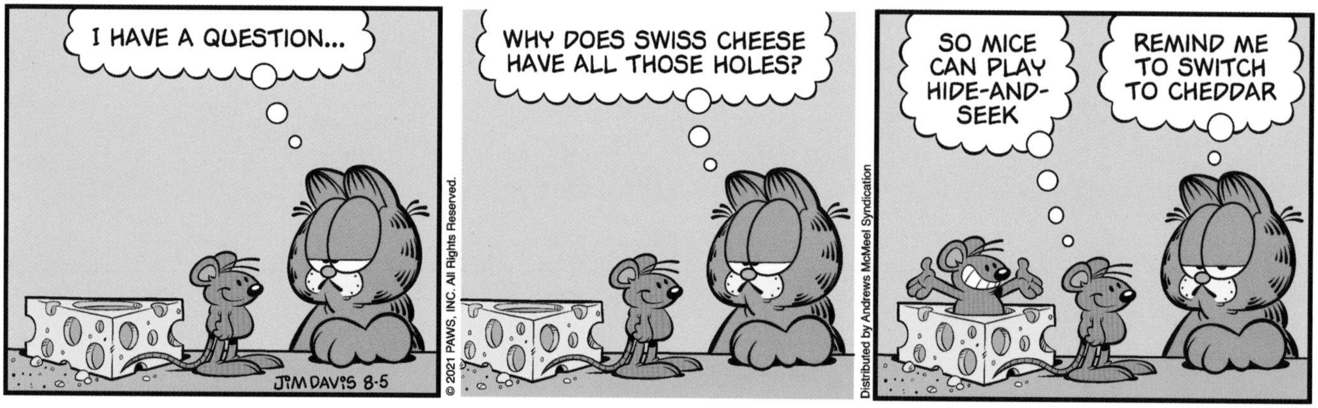
I HAVE A QUESTION...
WHY DOES SWISS CHEESE HAVE ALL THOSE HOLES?
SO MICE CAN PLAY HIDE-AND-SEEK
REMIND ME TO SWITCH TO CHEDDAR
JIM DAVIS 8-5



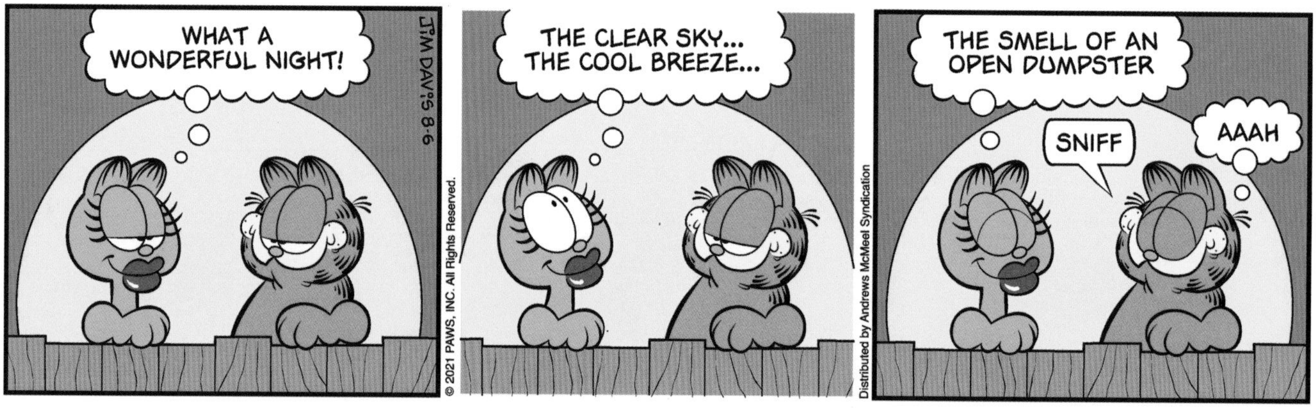
WHAT A WONDERFUL NIGHT!
JIM DAVIS 8-6
THE CLEAR SKY... THE COOL BREEZE...
THE SMELL OF AN OPEN DUMPSTER
SNIFF
AAAH



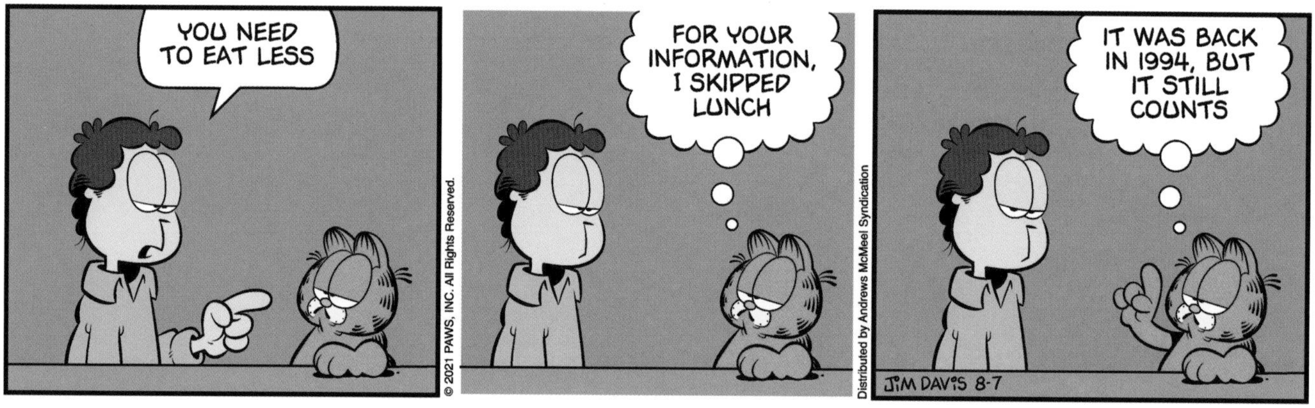
YOU NEED TO EAT LESS
FOR YOUR INFORMATION, I SKIPPED LUNCH
IT WAS BACK IN 1994, BUT IT STILL COUNTS
JIM DAVIS 8-7

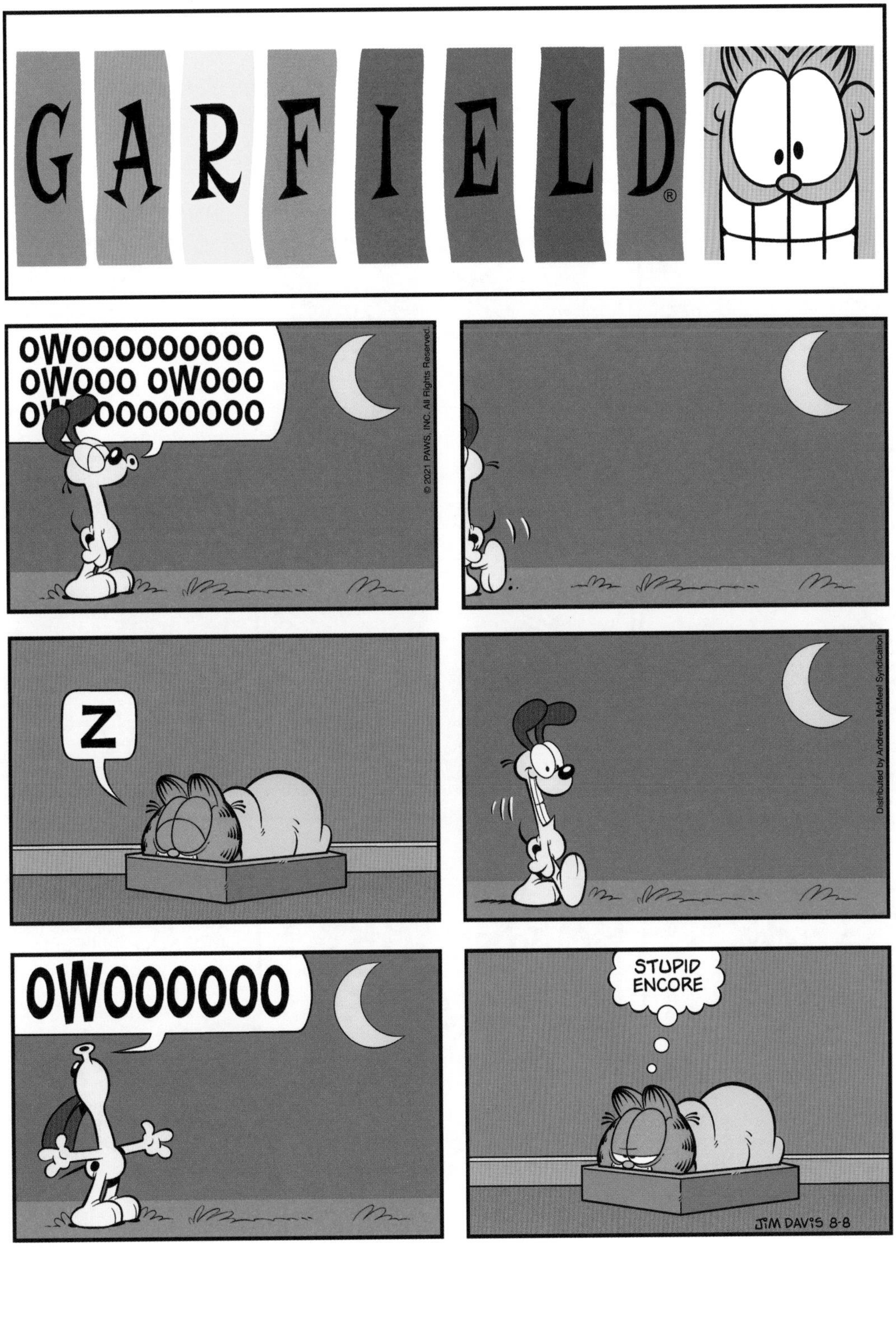
GARFIELD®
OWOOOOOOOOOO
OWOOO OWOOO
© 2021 PAWS, INC. All Rights Reserved.
Z
Distributed by Andrews McMeel Syndication
OWOOOOOO
STUPID ENCORE
JIM DAVIS 8-8

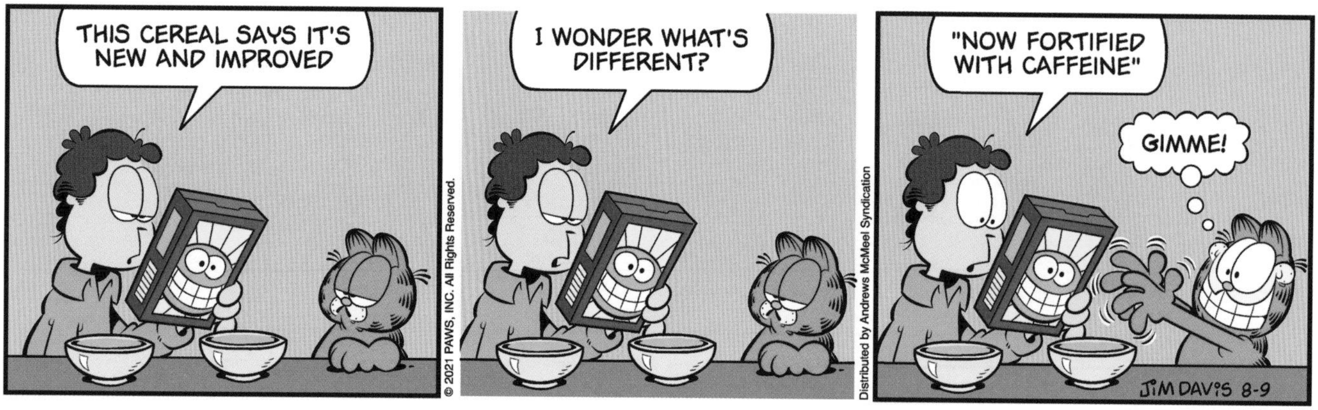
THIS CEREAL SAYS IT'S NEW AND IMPROVED
© 2021 PAWS, INC. All Rights Reserved.
I WONDER WHAT'S DIFFERENT?
Distributed by Andrews McMeel Syndication
"NOW FORTIFIED WITH CAFFEINE"
GIMME!
JIM DAVIS 8-9

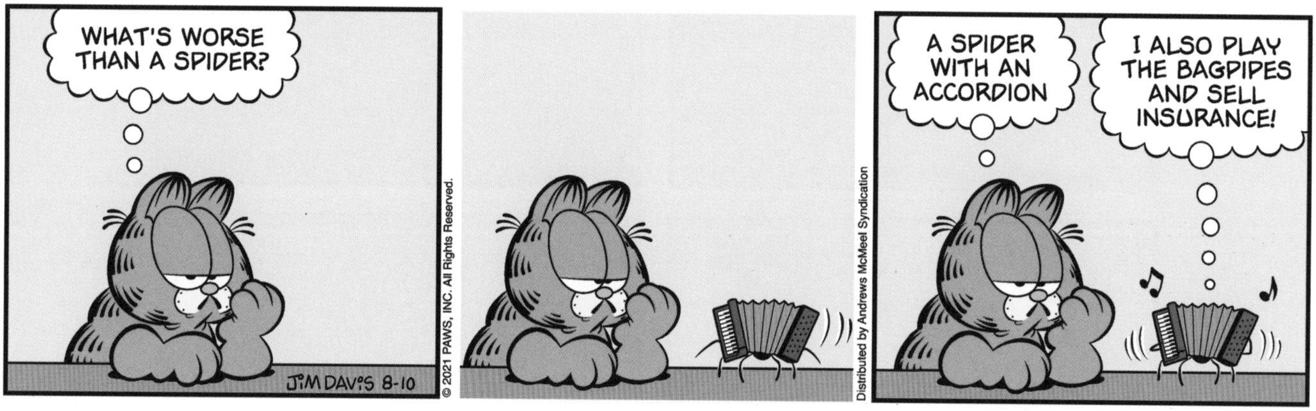
WHAT'S WORSE THAN A SPIDER?
JIM DAVIS 8-10
© 2021 PAWS, INC. All Rights Reserved.
Distributed by Andrews McMeel Syndication
A SPIDER WITH AN ACCORDION
I ALSO PLAY THE BAGPIPES AND SELL INSURANCE!

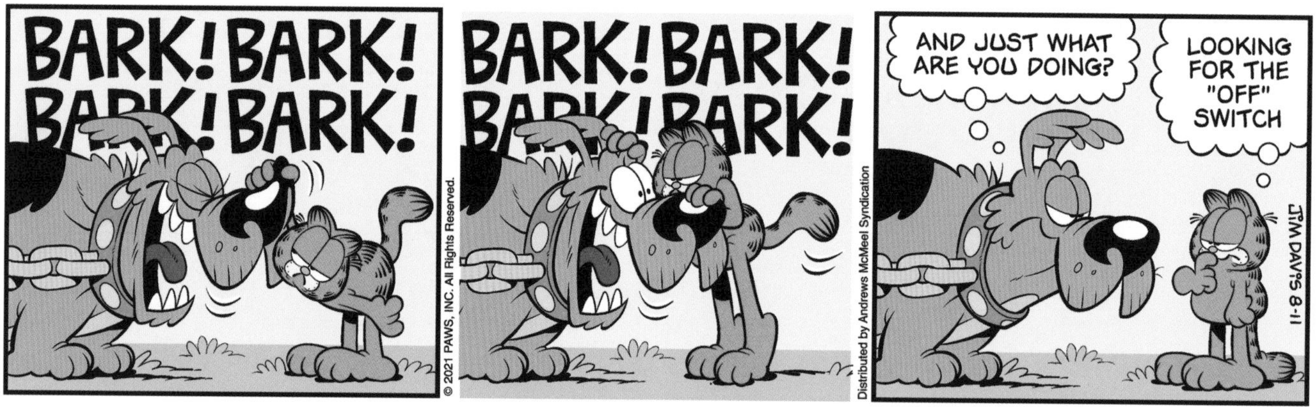
BARK! BARK! BARK! BARK!
© 2021 PAWS, INC. All Rights Reserved.
BARK! BARK! BARK! BARK!
Distributed by Andrews McMeel Syndication
AND JUST WHAT ARE YOU DOING?
LOOKING FOR THE "OFF" SWITCH
JIM DAVIS 8-11

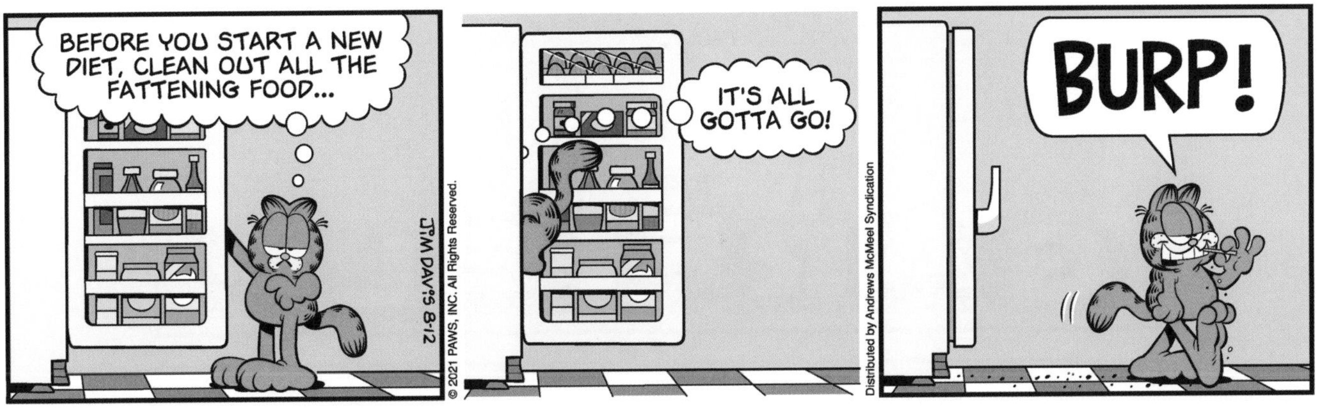
BEFORE YOU START A NEW DIET, CLEAN OUT ALL THE FATTENING FOOD...
JIM DAVIS 8-12
IT'S ALL GOTTA GO!
© 2021 PAWS, INC. All Rights Reserved.
Distributed by Andrews McMeel Syndication
BURP!

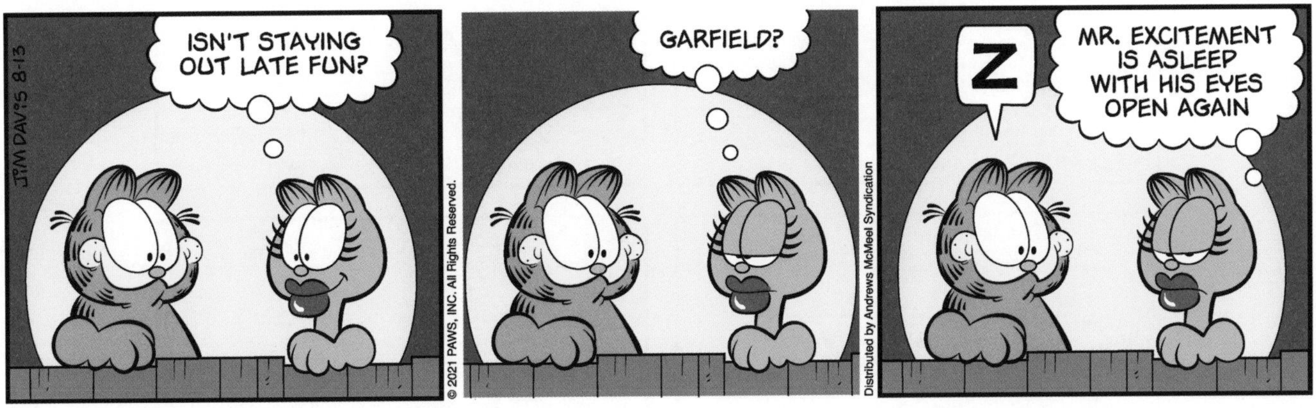
JIM DAVIS 8-13
ISN'T STAYING OUT LATE FUN?
© 2021 PAWS, INC. All Rights Reserved.
GARFIELD?
Distributed by Andrews McMeel Syndication
Z
MR. EXCITEMENT IS ASLEEP WITH HIS EYES OPEN AGAIN

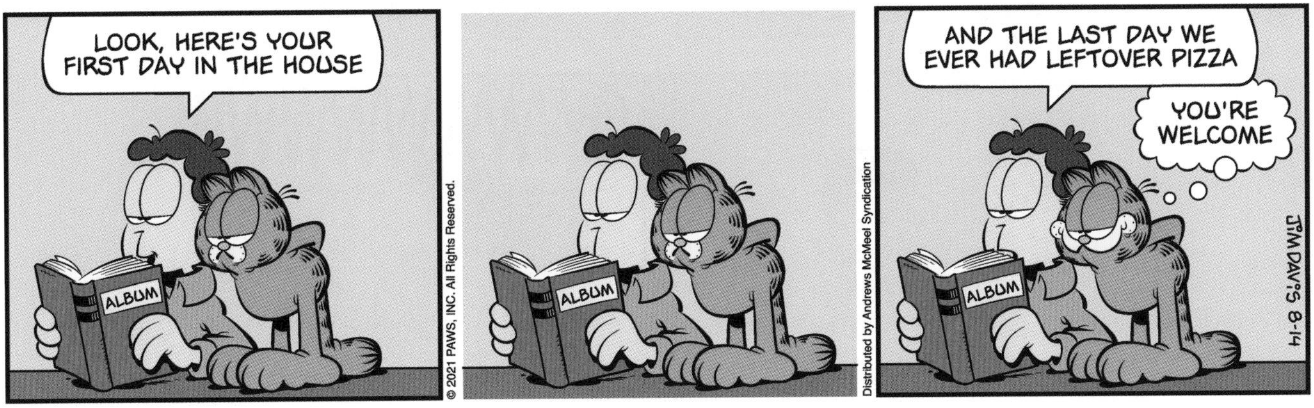
LOOK, HERE'S YOUR FIRST DAY IN THE HOUSE
ALBUM
© 2021 PAWS, INC. All Rights Reserved.
ALBUM
Distributed by Andrews McMeel Syndication
AND THE LAST DAY WE EVER HAD LEFTOVER PIZZA
YOU'RE WELCOME
ALBUM
JIM DAVIS 8-14

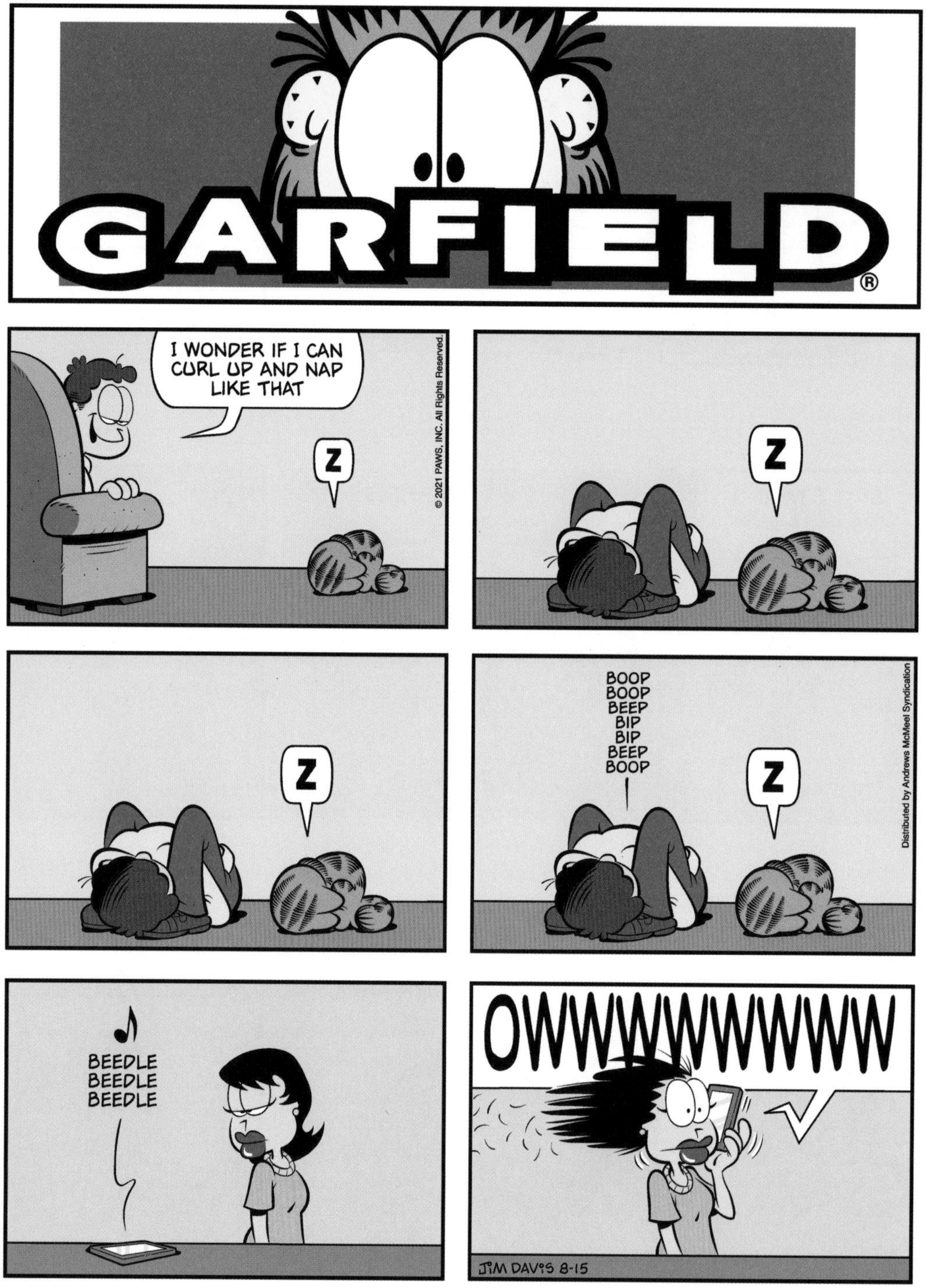
GARFIELD®
I WONDER IF I CAN CURL UP AND NAP LIKE THAT
Z
© 2021 PAWS, INC. All Rights Reserved.
Z
Z
BOOP BOOP BEEP BIP BIP BEEP BOOP
Z
Distributed by Andrews McMeel Syndication
BEEDLE BEEDLE BEEDLE
OWWWWWWWWW
JIM DAVIS 8-15

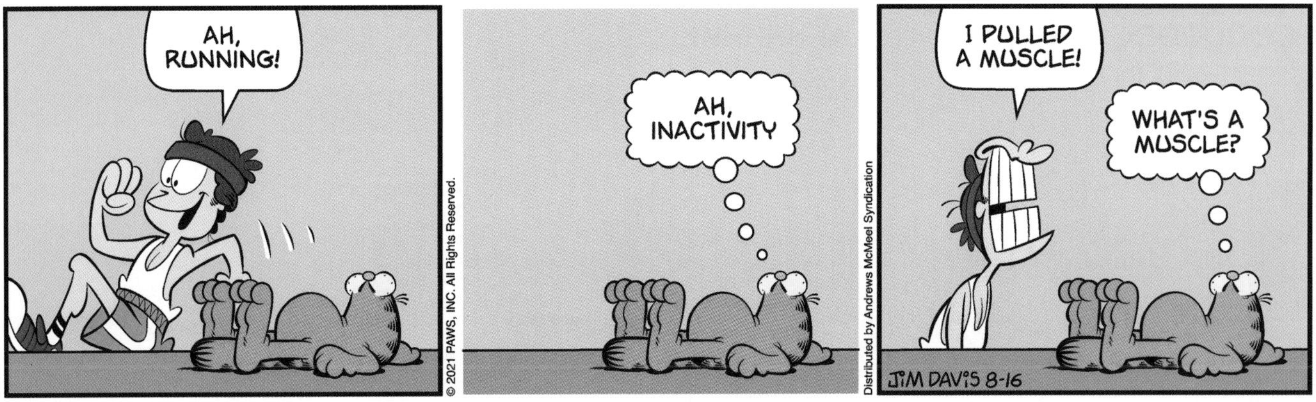
AH, RUNNING!
AH, INACTIVITY
I PULLED A MUSCLE!
WHAT'S A MUSCLE?
JIM DAVIS 8-16


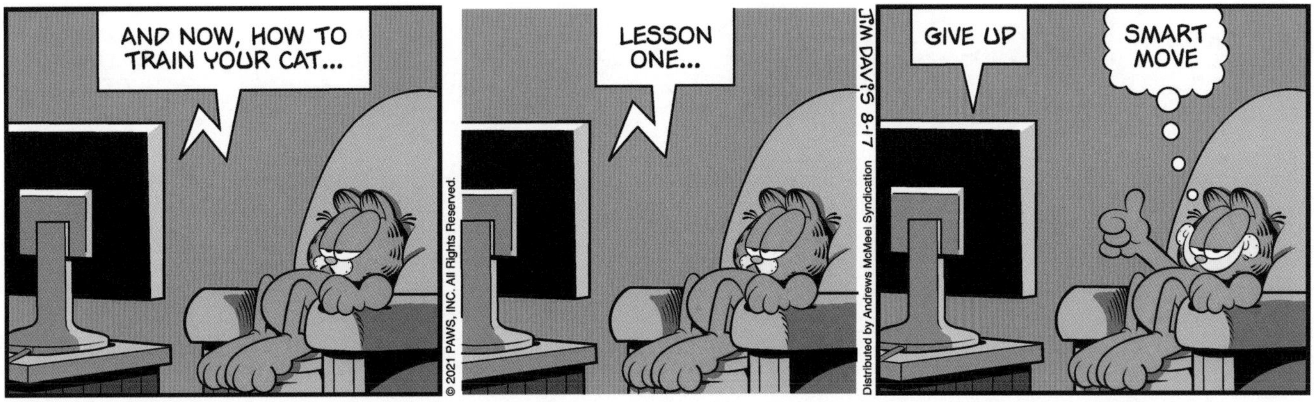
AND NOW, HOW TO TRAIN YOUR CAT...
LESSON ONE...
JIM DAVIS 8-17
GIVE UP
SMART MOVE


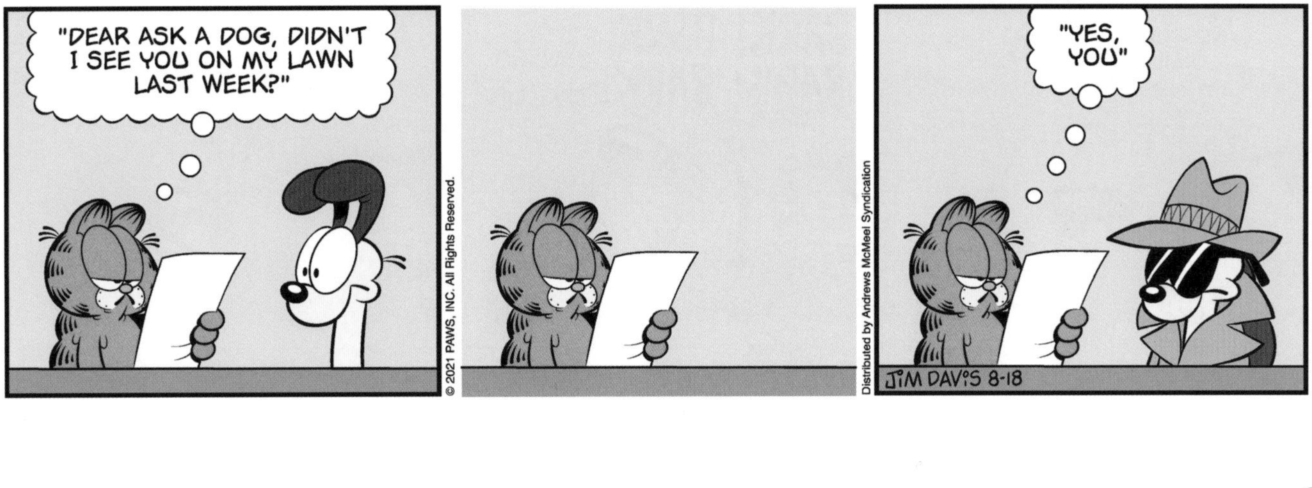
"DEAR ASK A DOG, DIDN'T I SEE YOU ON MY LAWN LAST WEEK?"
"YES, YOU"
JIM DAVIS 8-18

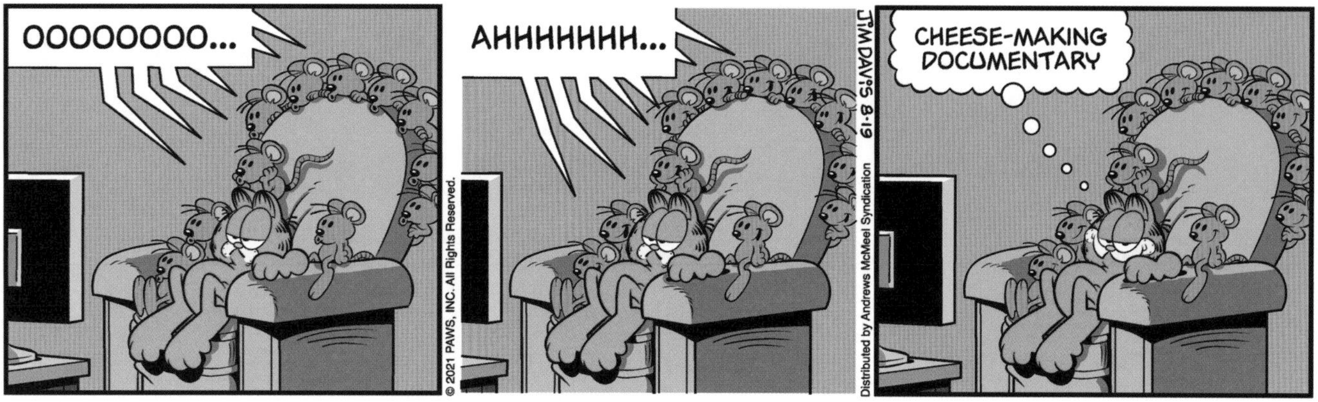
OOOOOOOO...
AHHHHHHH...
CHEESE-MAKING DOCUMENTARY
JIM DAVIS 8-19
© 2021 PAWS, INC. All Rights Reserved.
Distributed by Andrews McMeel Syndication

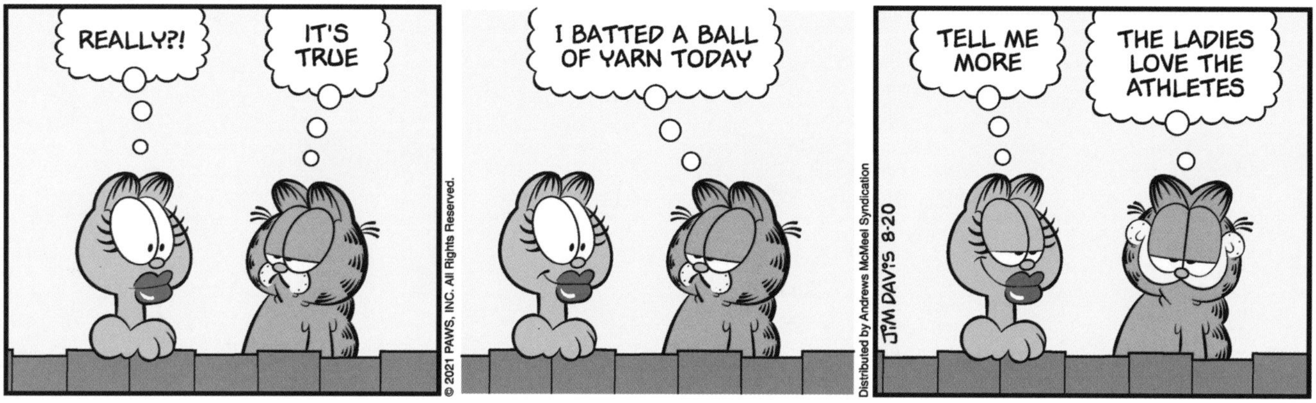
REALLY?!
IT'S TRUE
I BATTED A BALL OF YARN TODAY
TELL ME MORE
THE LADIES LOVE THE ATHLETES
JIM DAVIS 8-20
© 2021 PAWS, INC. All Rights Reserved.
Distributed by Andrews McMeel Syndication

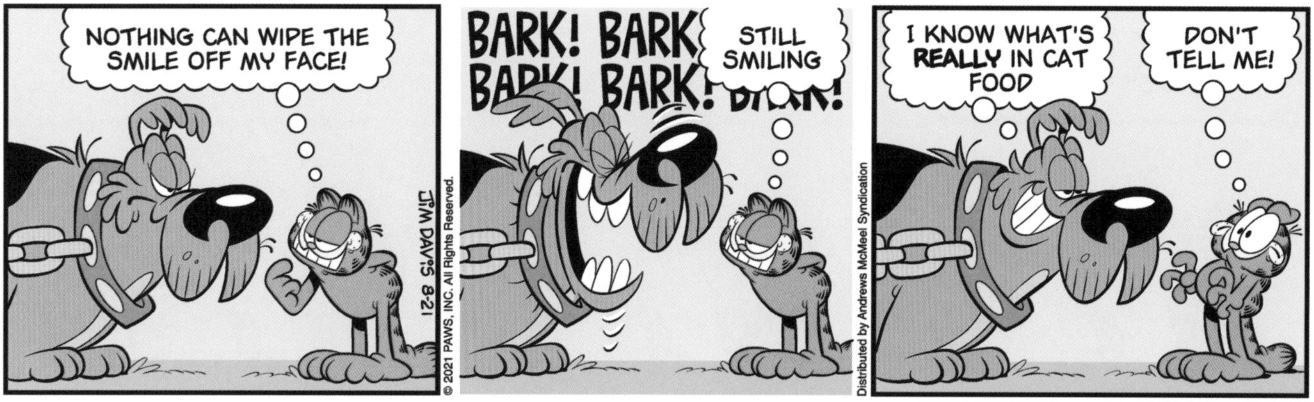
NOTHING CAN WIPE THE SMILE OFF MY FACE!
BARK! BARK
BARK! BARK!
STILL SMILING
I KNOW WHAT'S **REALLY** IN CAT FOOD
DON'T TELL ME!
JIM DAVIS 8-21
© 2021 PAWS, INC. All Rights Reserved.
Distributed by Andrews McMeel Syndication

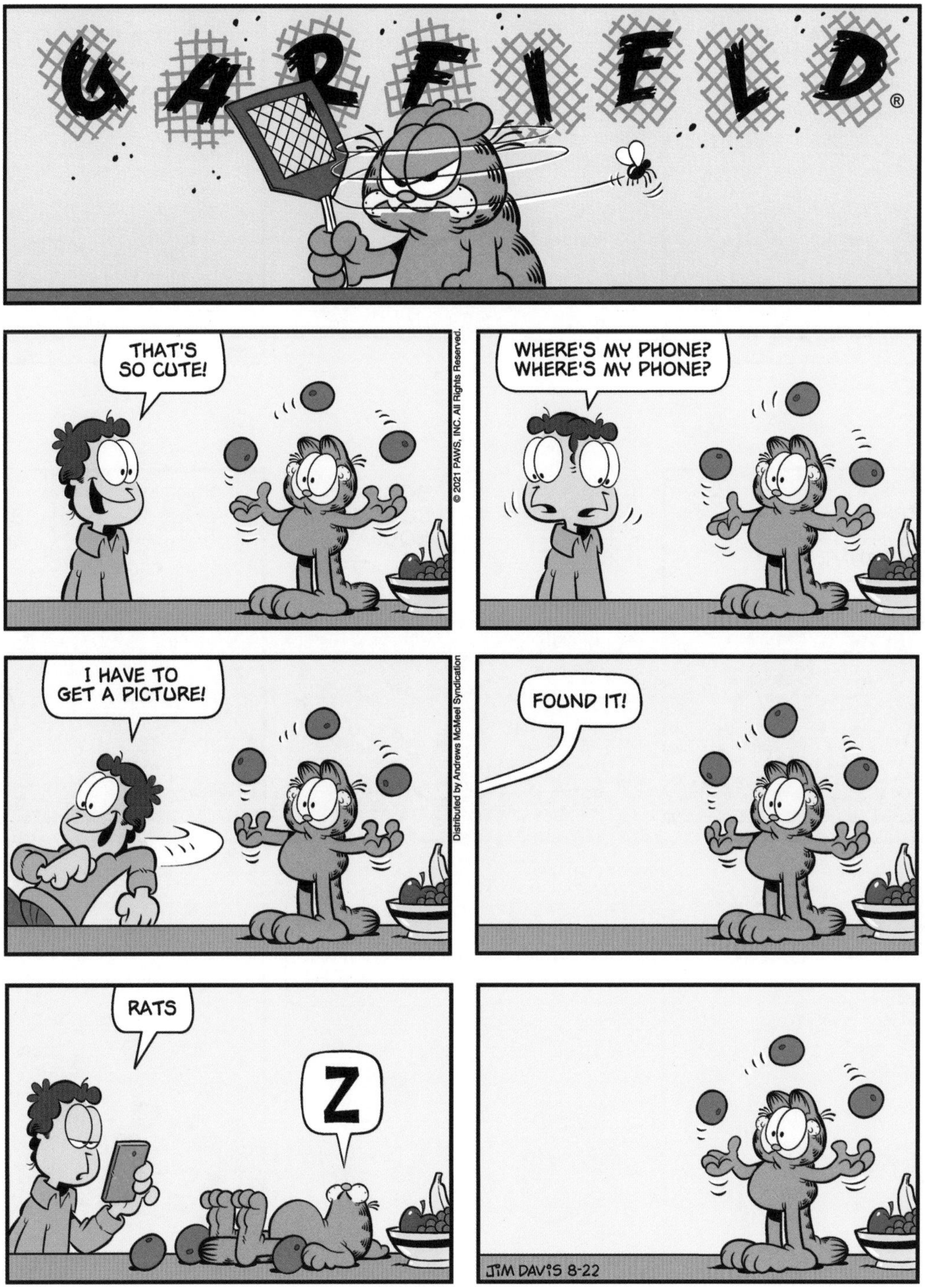
GARFIELD®
THAT'S SO CUTE!
WHERE'S MY PHONE? WHERE'S MY PHONE?
I HAVE TO GET A PICTURE!
FOUND IT!
RATS
Z
© 2021 PAWS, INC. All Rights Reserved.
Distributed by Andrews McMeel Syndication
JIM DAVIS 8-22

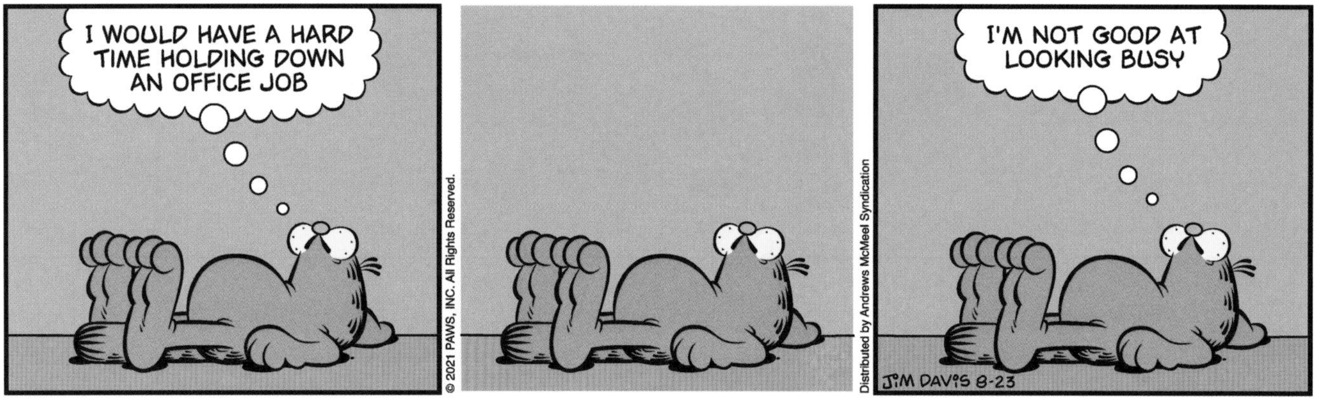
I WOULD HAVE A HARD TIME HOLDING DOWN AN OFFICE JOB
I'M NOT GOOD AT LOOKING BUSY
© 2021 PAWS, INC. All Rights Reserved.
Distributed by Andrews McMeel Syndication
JIM DAVIS 8-23

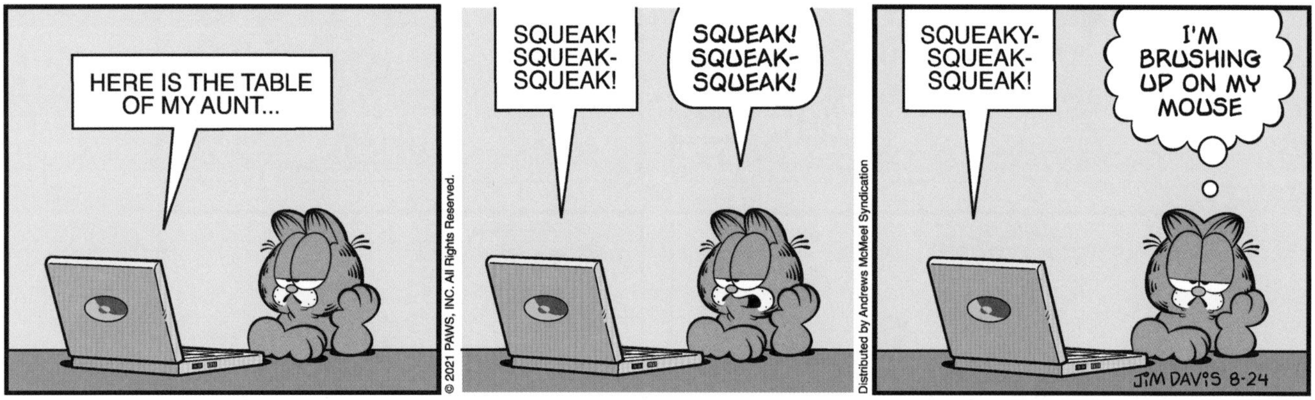
HERE IS THE TABLE OF MY AUNT...
SQUEAK! SQUEAK-SQUEAK!
SQUEAK! SQUEAK-SQUEAK!
SQUEAKY-SQUEAK-SQUEAK!
I'M BRUSHING UP ON MY MOUSE
© 2021 PAWS, INC. All Rights Reserved.
Distributed by Andrews McMeel Syndication
JIM DAVIS 8-24

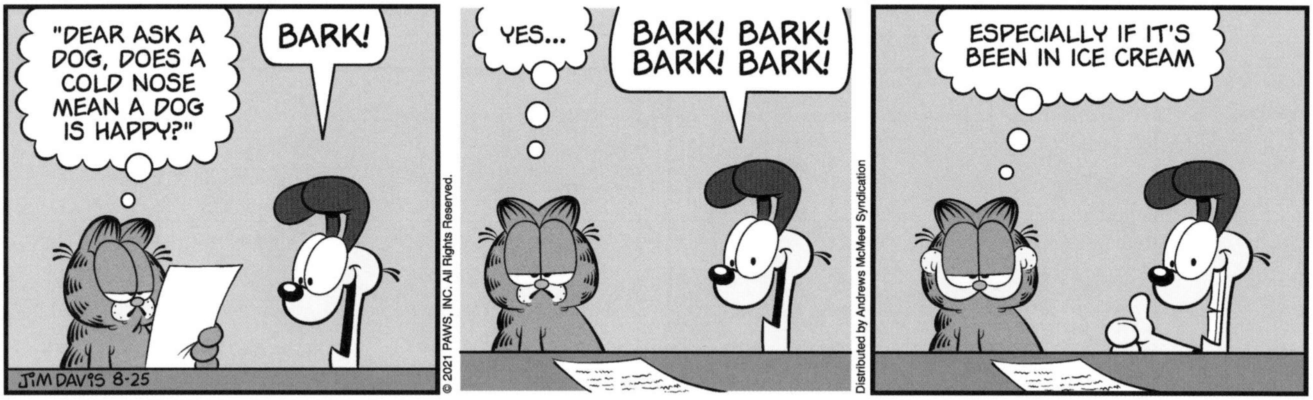
"DEAR ASK A DOG, DOES A COLD NOSE MEAN A DOG IS HAPPY?"
BARK!
YES...
BARK! BARK! BARK! BARK!
ESPECIALLY IF IT'S BEEN IN ICE CREAM
© 2021 PAWS, INC. All Rights Reserved.
Distributed by Andrews McMeel Syndication
JIM DAVIS 8-25

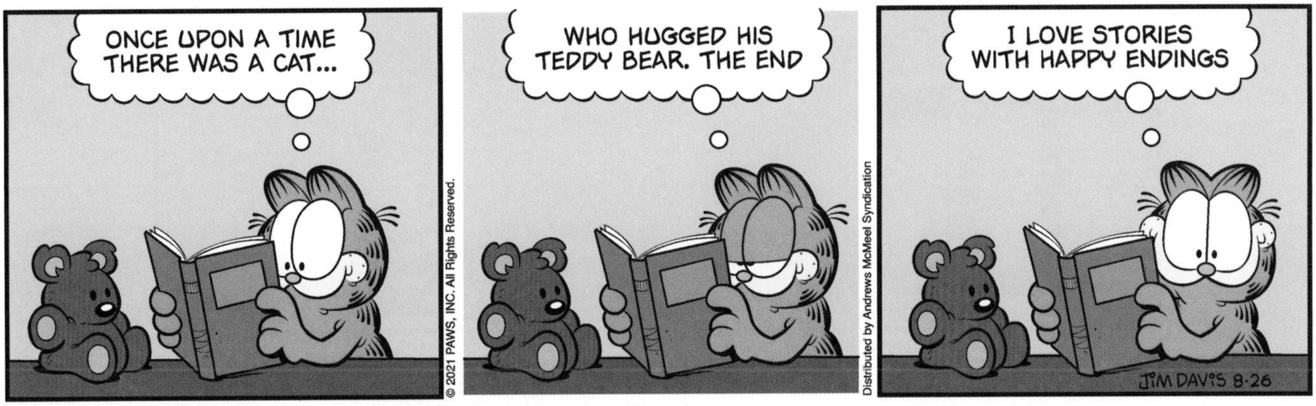
ONCE UPON A TIME THERE WAS A CAT...
WHO HUGGED HIS TEDDY BEAR. THE END
I LOVE STORIES WITH HAPPY ENDINGS
JIM DAVIS 8-26
© 2021 PAWS, INC. All Rights Reserved.
Distributed by Andrews McMeel Syndication

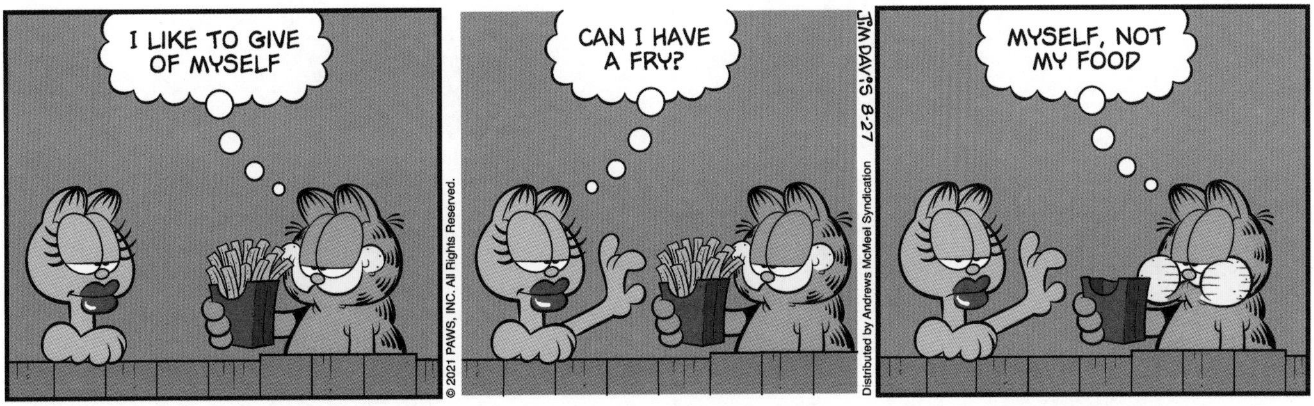
I LIKE TO GIVE OF MYSELF
CAN I HAVE A FRY?
MYSELF, NOT MY FOOD
JIM DAVIS 8-27
© 2021 PAWS, INC. All Rights Reserved.
Distributed by Andrews McMeel Syndication

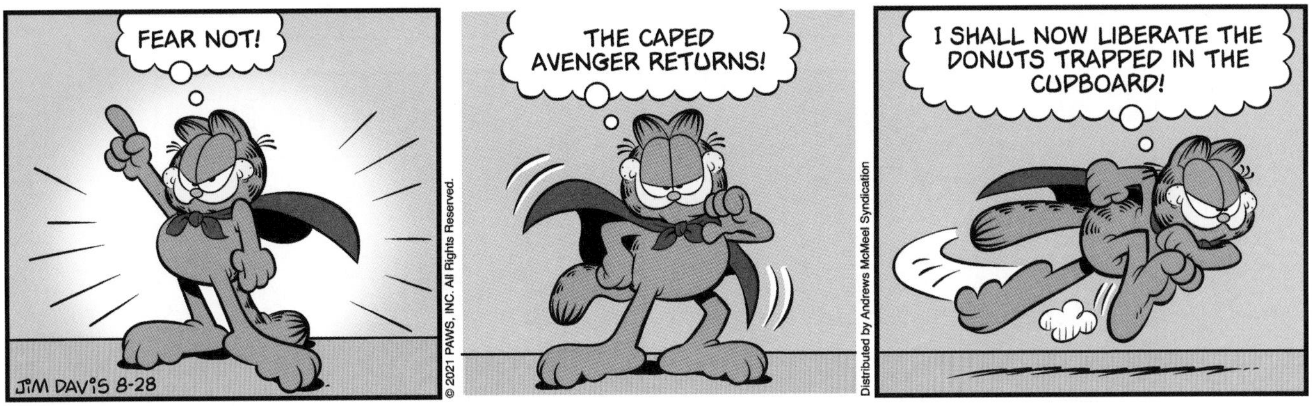
FEAR NOT!
THE CAPED AVENGER RETURNS!
I SHALL NOW LIBERATE THE DONUTS TRAPPED IN THE CUPBOARD!
JIM DAVIS 8-28
© 2021 PAWS, INC. All Rights Reserved.
Distributed by Andrews McMeel Syndication

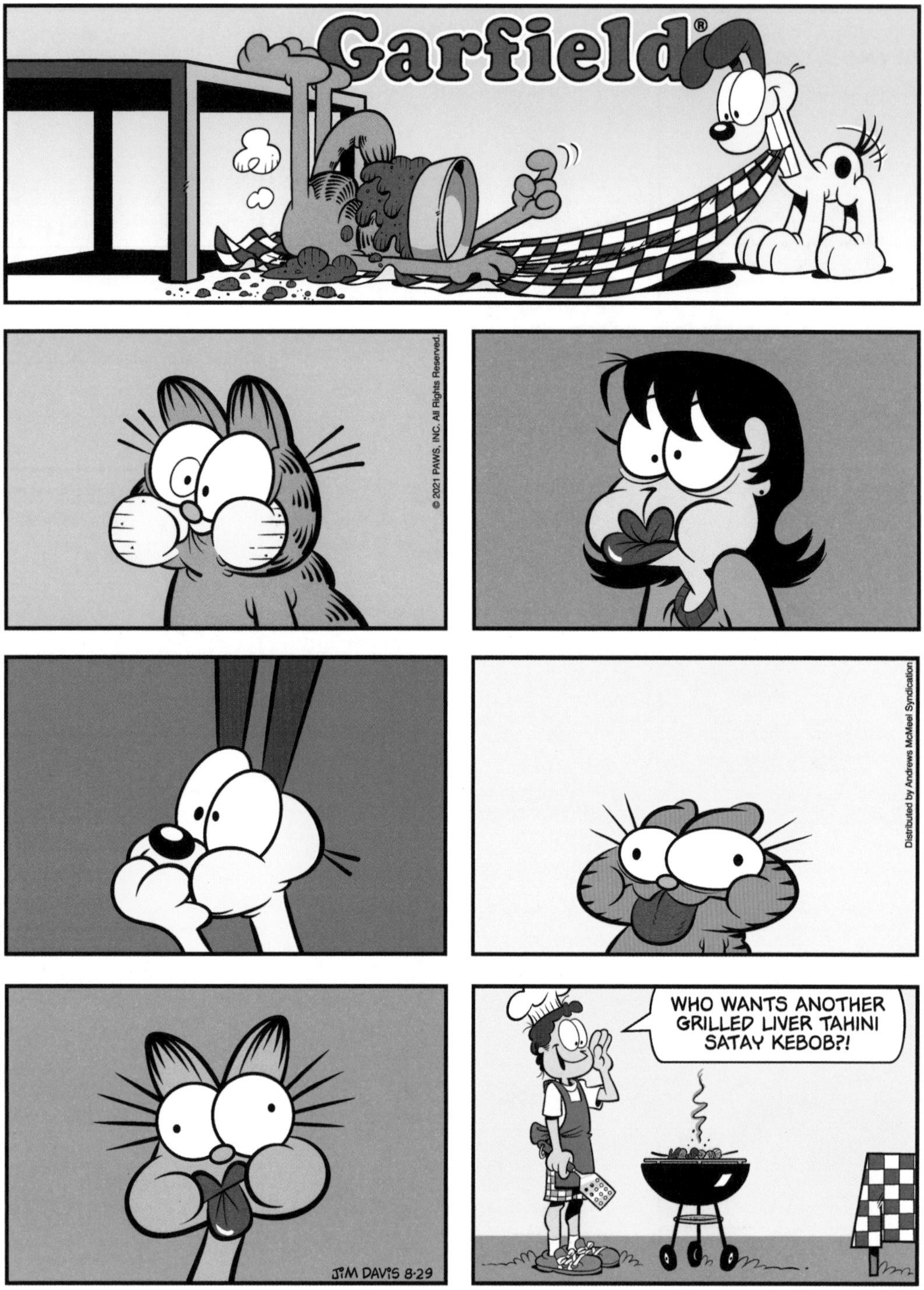
Garfield®
© 2021 PAWS, INC. All Rights Reserved.
Distributed by Andrews McMeel Syndication
WHO WANTS ANOTHER GRILLED LIVER TAHINI SATAY KEBOB?!
JIM DAVIS 8-29

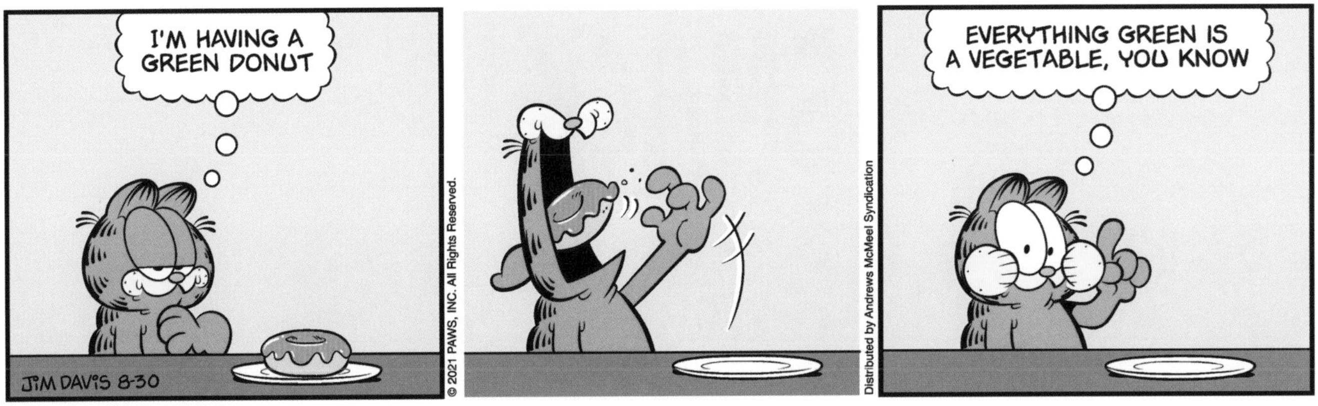
I'M HAVING A GREEN DONUT
EVERYTHING GREEN IS A VEGETABLE, YOU KNOW
JIM DAVIS 8-30
© 2021 PAWS, INC. All Rights Reserved.
Distributed by Andrews McMeel Syndication

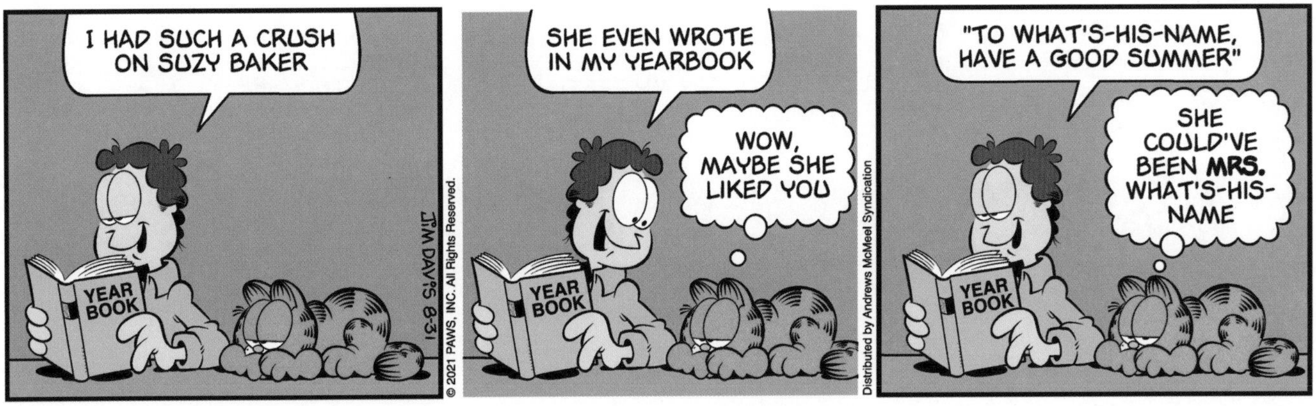
I HAD SUCH A CRUSH ON SUZY BAKER
YEAR BOOK
JIM DAVIS 8-31
© 2021 PAWS, INC. All Rights Reserved.
SHE EVEN WROTE IN MY YEARBOOK
WOW, MAYBE SHE LIKED YOU
YEAR BOOK
Distributed by Andrews McMeel Syndication
"TO WHAT'S-HIS-NAME, HAVE A GOOD SUMMER"
SHE COULD'VE BEEN **MRS.** WHAT'S-HIS-NAME
YEAR BOOK

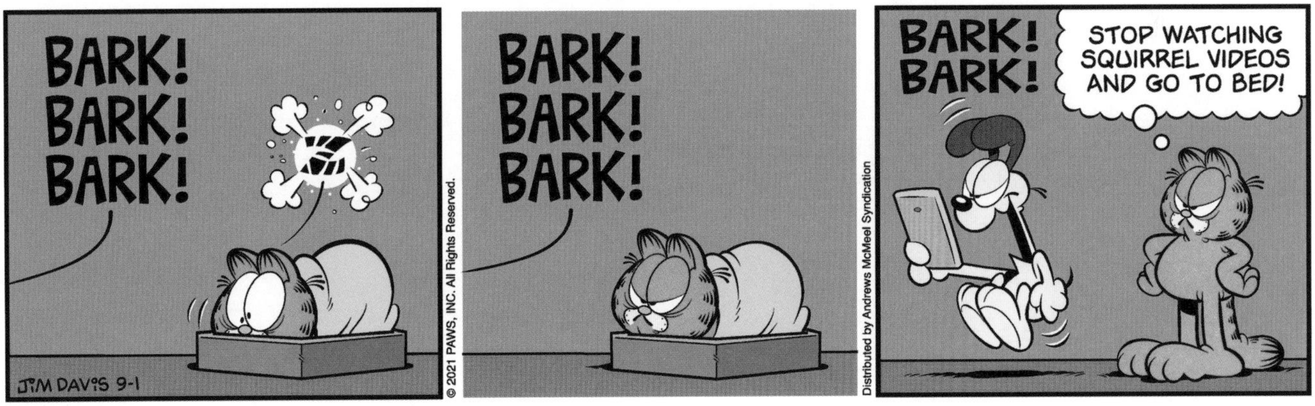
BARK! BARK! BARK!
JIM DAVIS 9-1
© 2021 PAWS, INC. All Rights Reserved.
BARK! BARK! BARK!
Distributed by Andrews McMeel Syndication
BARK! BARK!
STOP WATCHING SQUIRREL VIDEOS AND GO TO BED!

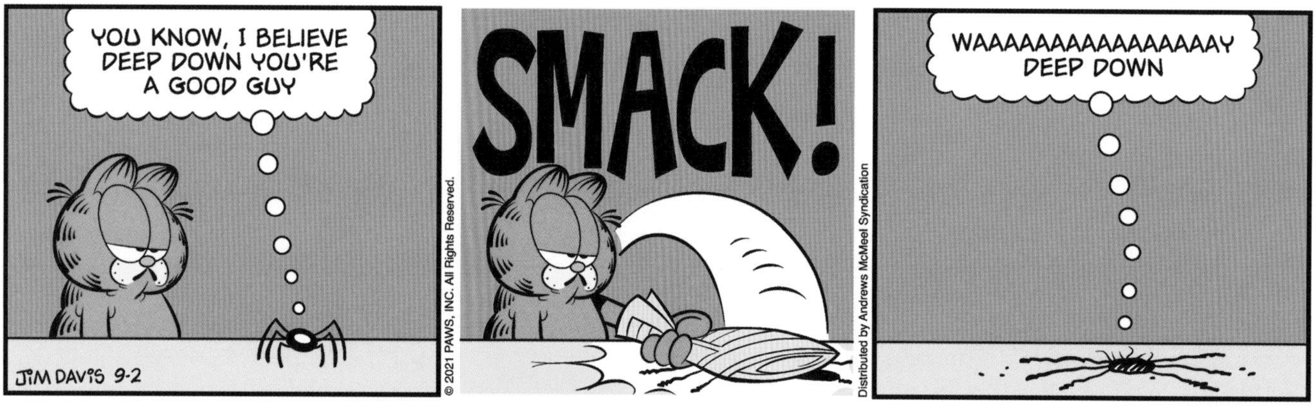
YOU KNOW, I BELIEVE DEEP DOWN YOU'RE A GOOD GUY
JIM DAVIS 9-2
SMACK!
WAAAAAAAAAAAAAAAAY DEEP DOWN
© 2021 PAWS, INC. All Rights Reserved.
Distributed by Andrews McMeel Syndication

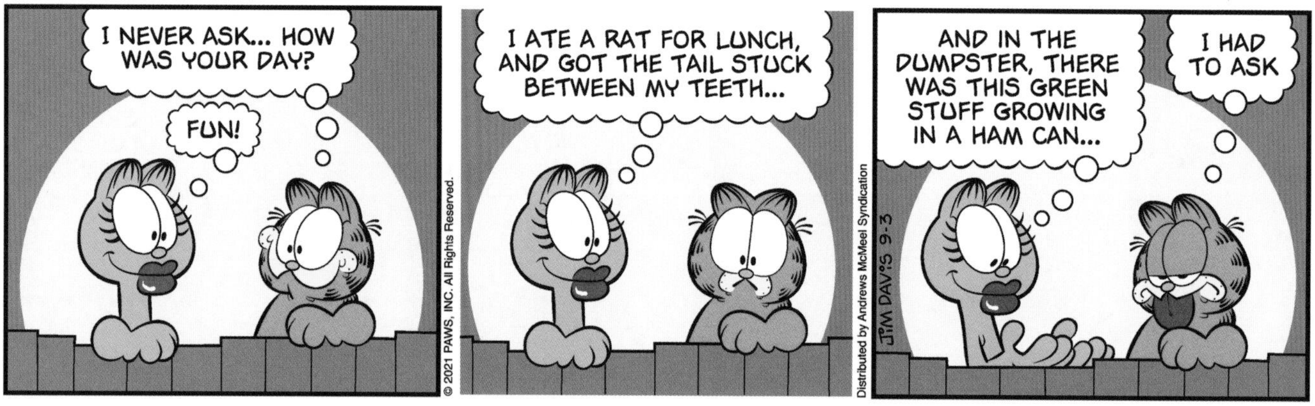
I NEVER ASK... HOW WAS YOUR DAY?
FUN!
I ATE A RAT FOR LUNCH, AND GOT THE TAIL STUCK BETWEEN MY TEETH...
AND IN THE DUMPSTER, THERE WAS THIS GREEN STUFF GROWING IN A HAM CAN...
I HAD TO ASK
JIM DAVIS 9-3
© 2021 PAWS, INC. All Rights Reserved.
Distributed by Andrews McMeel Syndication

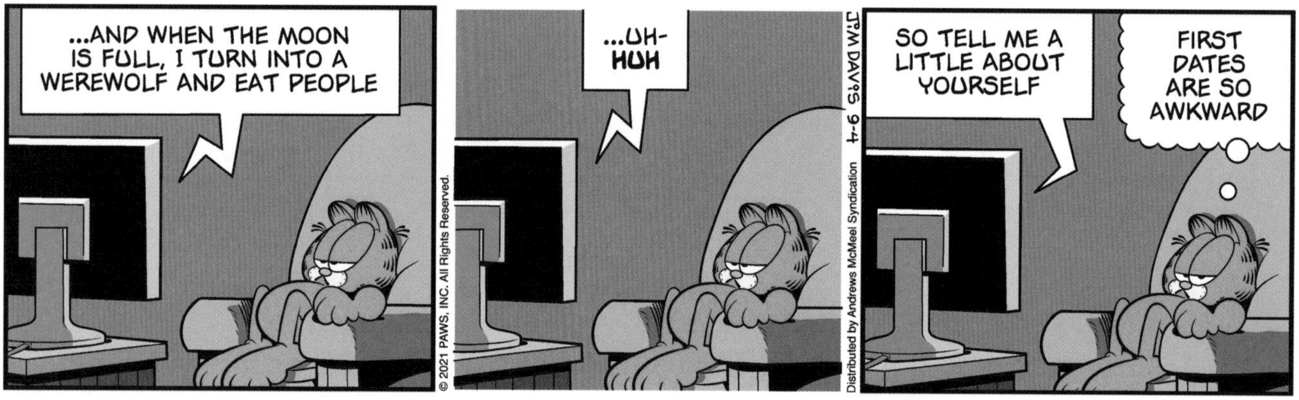
...AND WHEN THE MOON IS FULL, I TURN INTO A WEREWOLF AND EAT PEOPLE
...UH-HUH
JIM DAVIS 9-4
SO TELL ME A LITTLE ABOUT YOURSELF
FIRST DATES ARE SO AWKWARD
© 2021 PAWS, INC. All Rights Reserved.
Distributed by Andrews McMeel Syndication

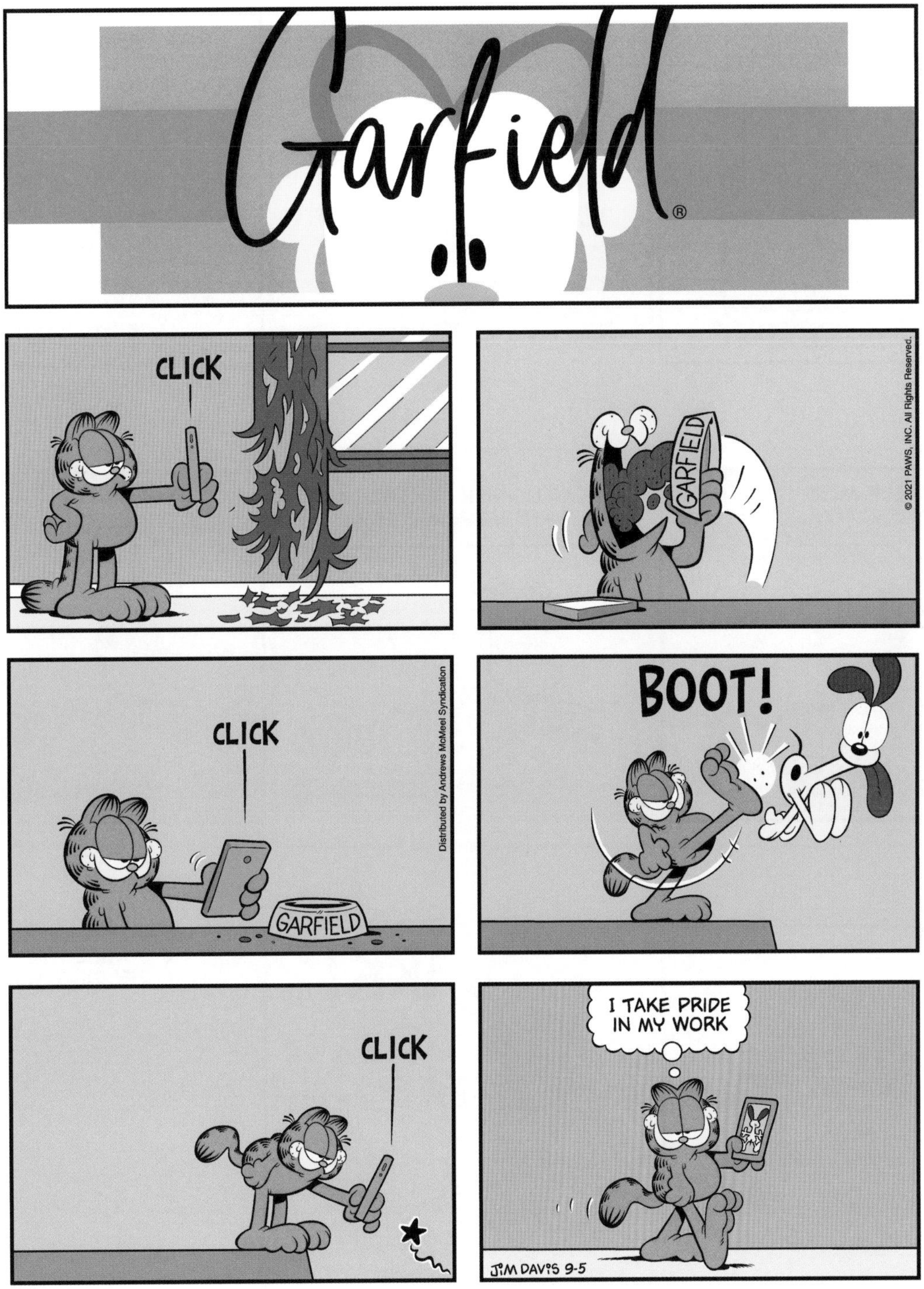

Garfield®
CLICK
GARFIELD
© 2021 PAWS, INC. All Rights Reserved.
CLICK
GARFIELD
Distributed by Andrews McMeel Syndication
BOOT!
CLICK
I TAKE PRIDE IN MY WORK
JIM DAVIS 9-5

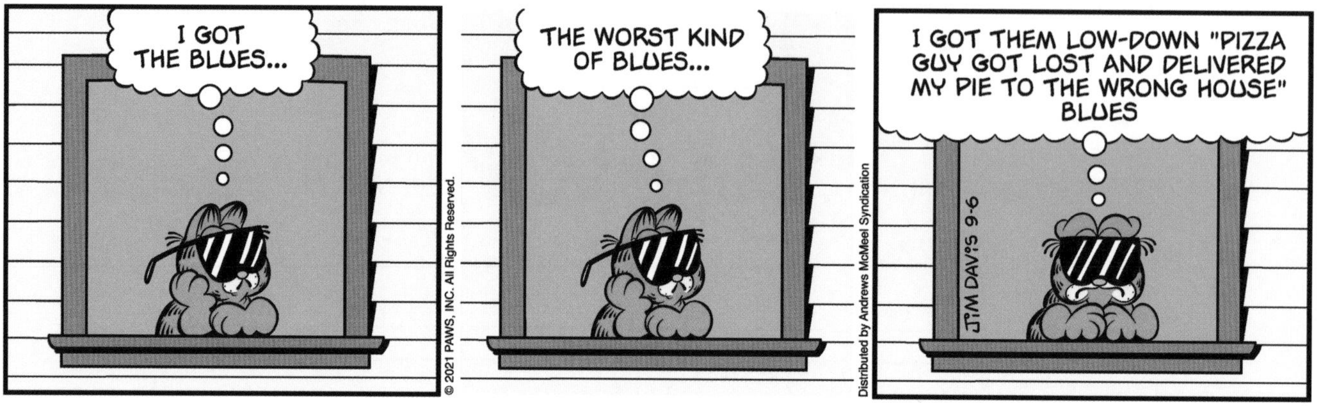
I GOT THE BLUES...
THE WORST KIND OF BLUES...
I GOT THEM LOW-DOWN "PIZZA GUY GOT LOST AND DELIVERED MY PIE TO THE WRONG HOUSE" BLUES
© 2021 PAWS, INC. All Rights Reserved.
Distributed by Andrews McMeel Syndication
JIM DAVIS 9-6

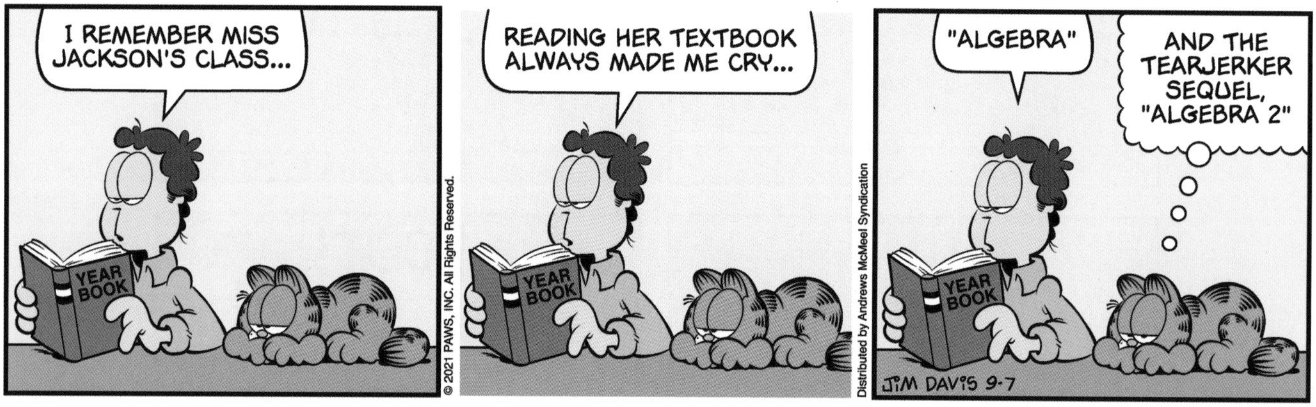
I REMEMBER MISS JACKSON'S CLASS...
YEAR BOOK
READING HER TEXTBOOK ALWAYS MADE ME CRY...
"ALGEBRA"
AND THE TEARJERKER SEQUEL, "ALGEBRA 2"
© 2021 PAWS, INC. All Rights Reserved.
Distributed by Andrews McMeel Syndication
JIM DAVIS 9-7

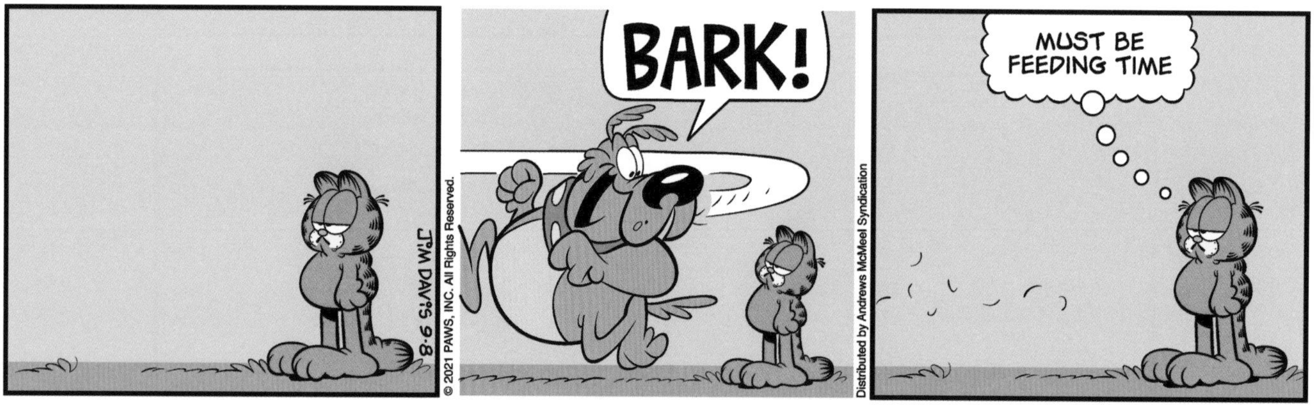
JIM DAVIS 9-8
BARK!
MUST BE FEEDING TIME
© 2021 PAWS, INC. All Rights Reserved.
Distributed by Andrews McMeel Syndication

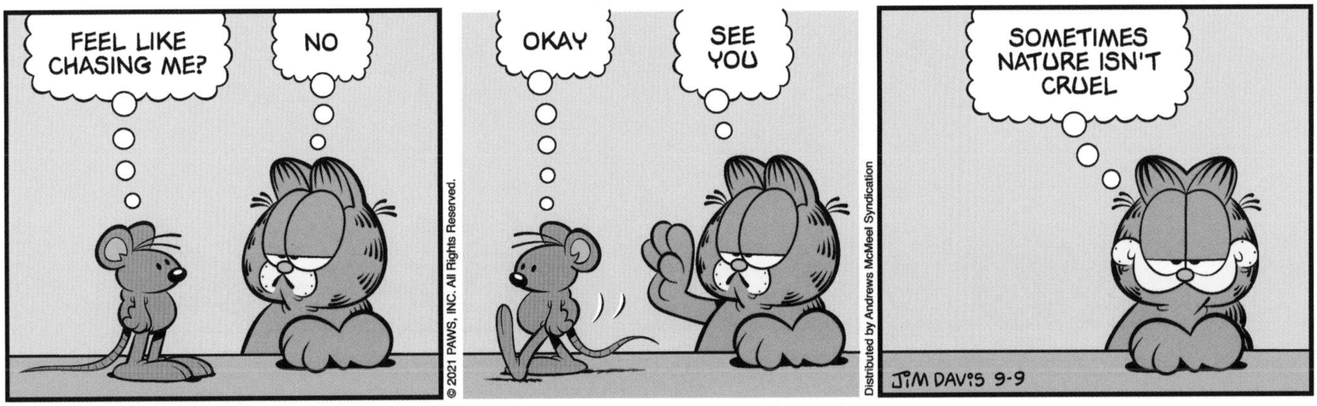
FEEL LIKE CHASING ME?
NO
© 2021 PAWS, INC. All Rights Reserved.
OKAY
SEE YOU
Distributed by Andrews McMeel Syndication
SOMETIMES NATURE ISN'T CRUEL
JIM DAVIS 9-9

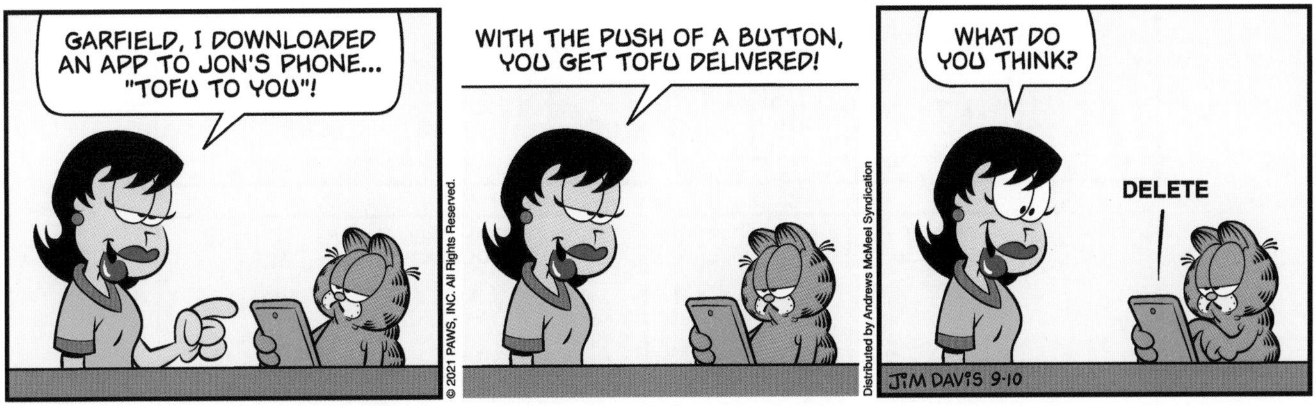
GARFIELD, I DOWNLOADED AN APP TO JON'S PHONE... "TOFU TO YOU"!
© 2021 PAWS, INC. All Rights Reserved.
WITH THE PUSH OF A BUTTON, YOU GET TOFU DELIVERED!
Distributed by Andrews McMeel Syndication
WHAT DO YOU THINK?
DELETE
JIM DAVIS 9-10

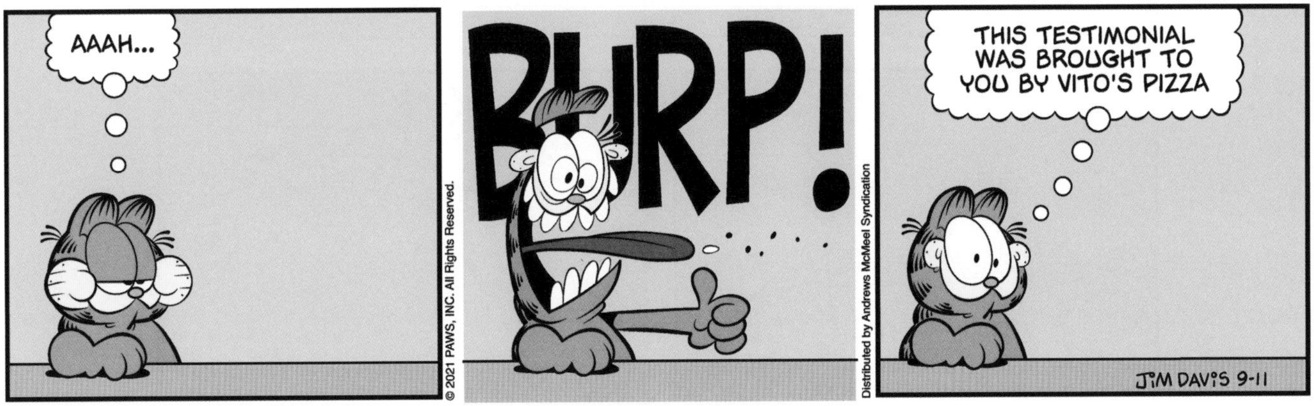
AAAH...
© 2021 PAWS, INC. All Rights Reserved.
BURP!
Distributed by Andrews McMeel Syndication
THIS TESTIMONIAL WAS BROUGHT TO YOU BY VITO'S PIZZA
JIM DAVIS 9-11

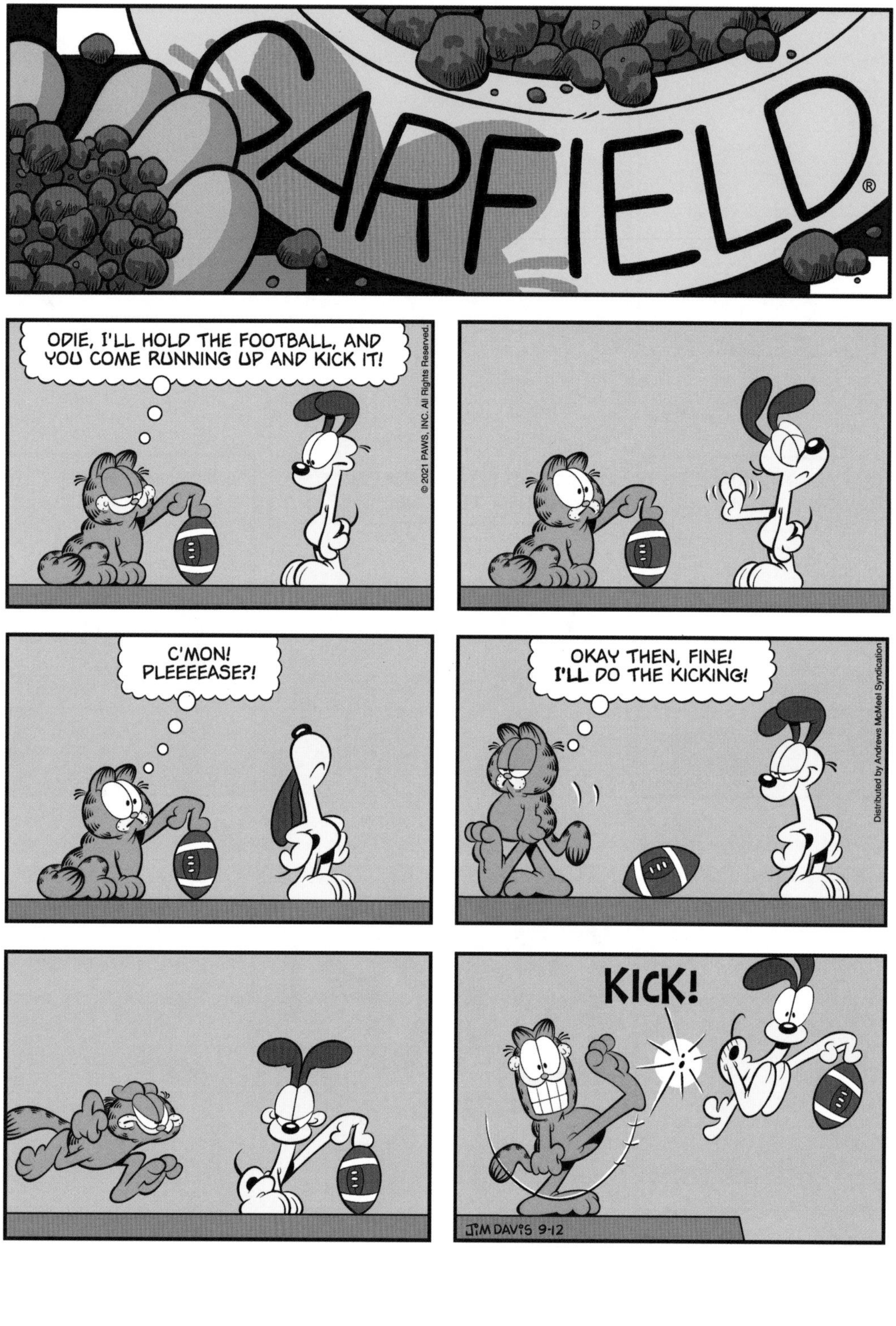
GARFIELD®
© 2021 PAWS, INC. All Rights Reserved.
ODIE, I'LL HOLD THE FOOTBALL, AND YOU COME RUNNING UP AND KICK IT!
C'MON! PLEEEEASE?!
Distributed by Andrews McMeel Syndication
OKAY THEN, FINE! I'LL DO THE KICKING!
KICK!
JIM DAVIS 9-12

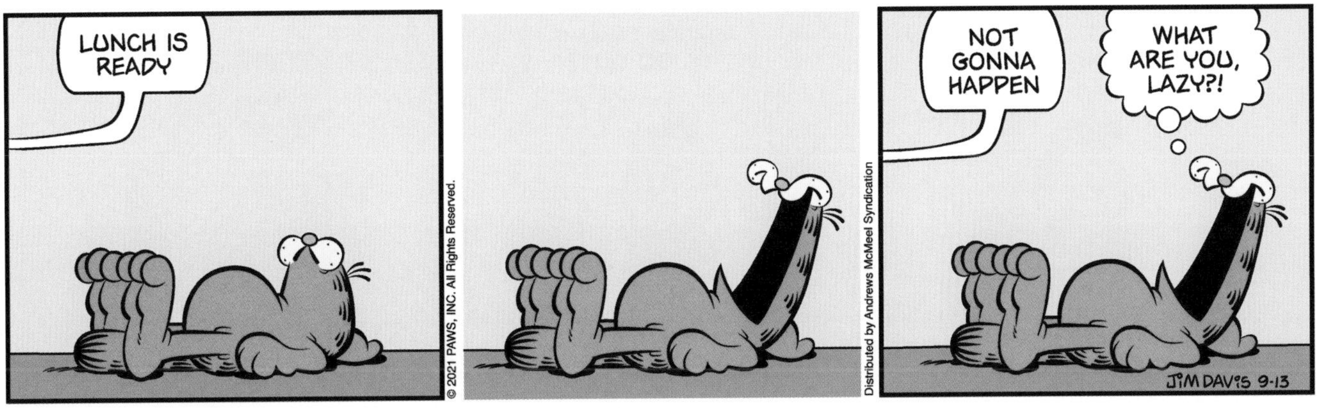
LUNCH IS READY
© 2021 PAWS, INC. All Rights Reserved.
Distributed by Andrews McMeel Syndication
NOT GONNA HAPPEN
WHAT ARE YOU, LAZY?!
JIM DAVIS 9-13

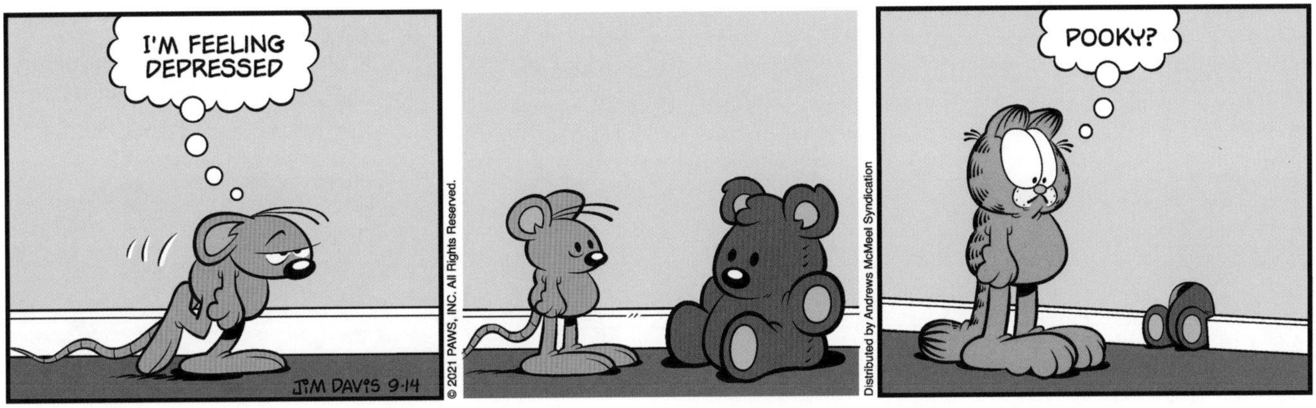
I'M FEELING DEPRESSED
JIM DAVIS 9-14
© 2021 PAWS, INC. All Rights Reserved.
Distributed by Andrews McMeel Syndication
POOKY?

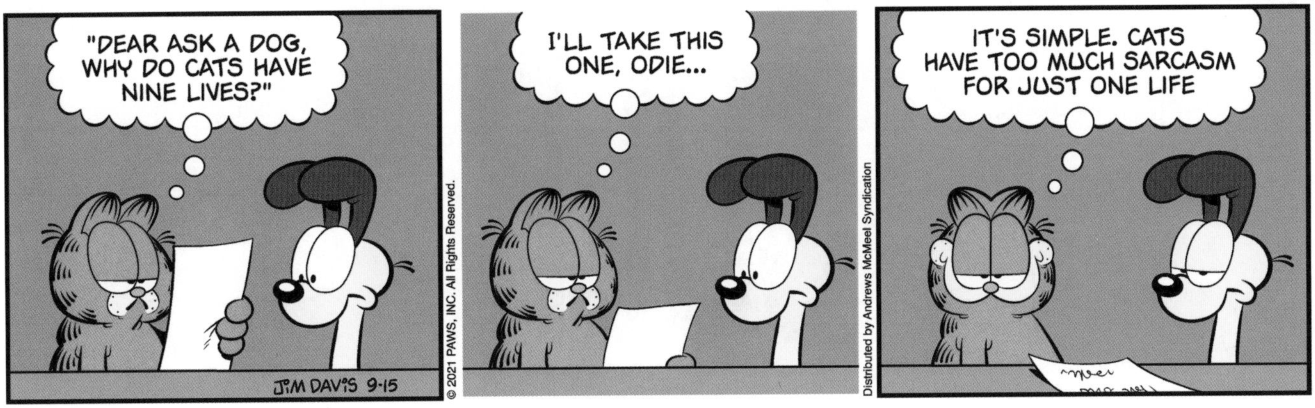
"DEAR ASK A DOG, WHY DO CATS HAVE NINE LIVES?"
JIM DAVIS 9-15
© 2021 PAWS, INC. All Rights Reserved.
I'LL TAKE THIS ONE, ODIE...
Distributed by Andrews McMeel Syndication
IT'S SIMPLE. CATS HAVE TOO MUCH SARCASM FOR JUST ONE LIFE

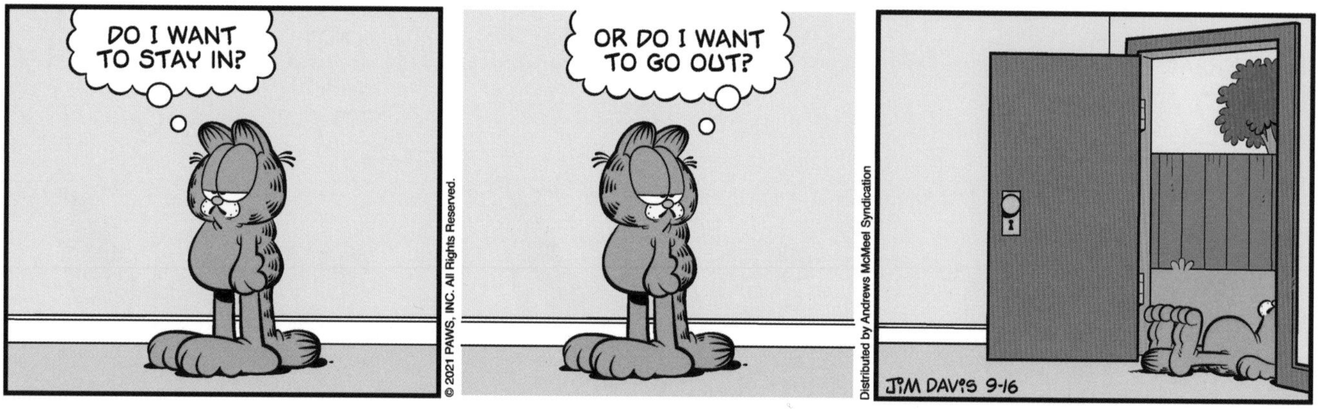
DO I WANT TO STAY IN?
OR DO I WANT TO GO OUT?
© 2021 PAWS, INC. All Rights Reserved.
Distributed by Andrews McMeel Syndication
JIM DAVIS 9-16

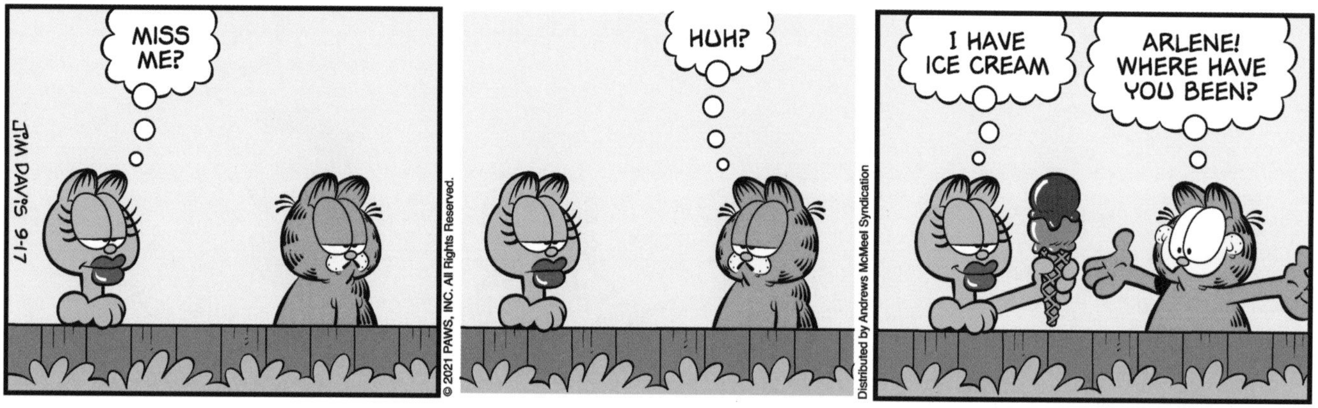
MISS ME?
JIM DAVIS 9-17
HUH?
© 2021 PAWS, INC. All Rights Reserved.
Distributed by Andrews McMeel Syndication
I HAVE ICE CREAM
ARLENE! WHERE HAVE YOU BEEN?

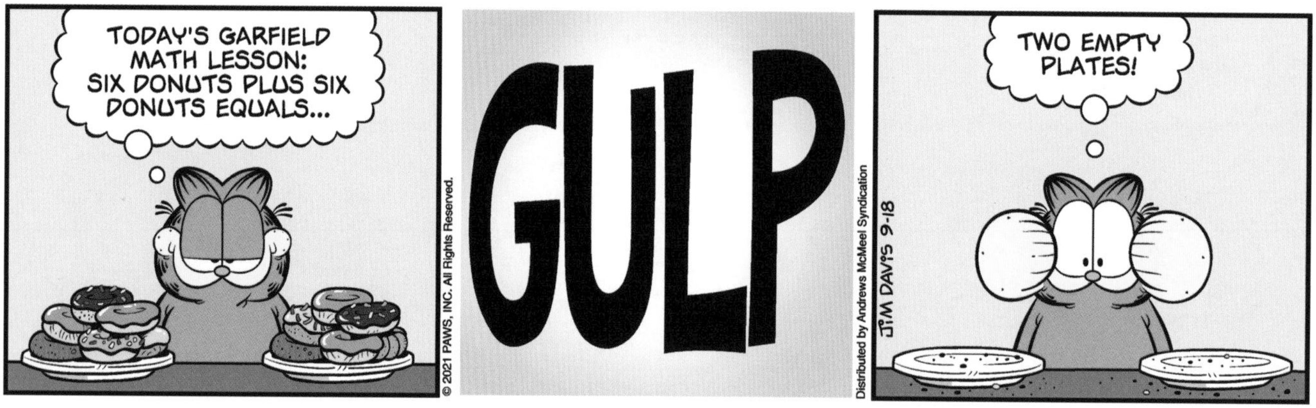
TODAY'S GARFIELD MATH LESSON: SIX DONUTS PLUS SIX DONUTS EQUALS...
© 2021 PAWS, INC. All Rights Reserved.
GULP
Distributed by Andrews McMeel Syndication
JIM DAVIS 9-18
TWO EMPTY PLATES!

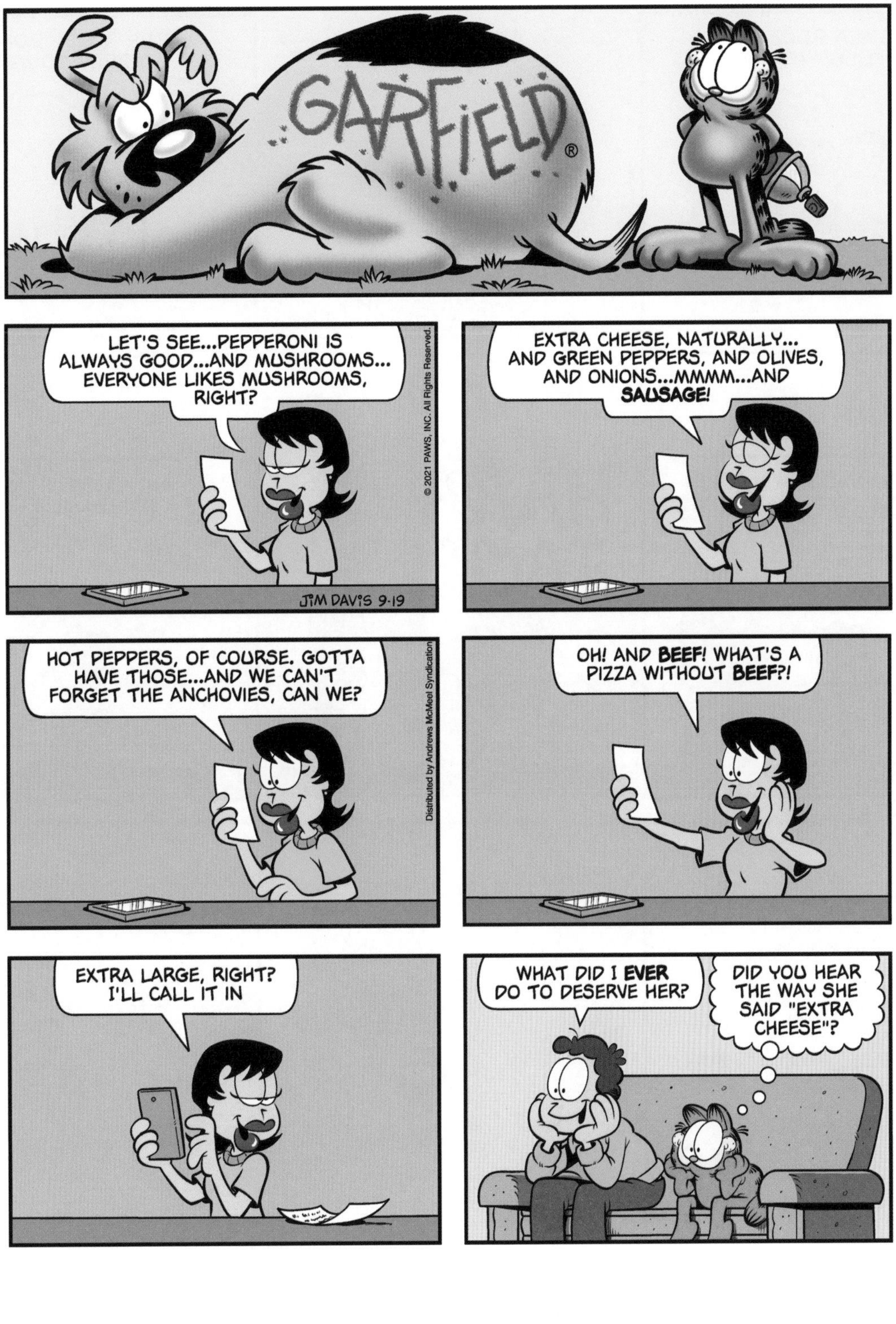
GARFIELD®
LET'S SEE...PEPPERONI IS ALWAYS GOOD...AND MUSHROOMS... EVERYONE LIKES MUSHROOMS, RIGHT?
© 2021 PAWS, INC. All Rights Reserved.
JIM DAVIS 9-19
EXTRA CHEESE, NATURALLY... AND GREEN PEPPERS, AND OLIVES, AND ONIONS...MMMM...AND **SAUSAGE**!
HOT PEPPERS, OF COURSE. GOTTA HAVE THOSE...AND WE CAN'T FORGET THE ANCHOVIES, CAN WE?
Distributed by Andrews McMeel Syndication
OH! AND **BEEF**! WHAT'S A PIZZA WITHOUT **BEEF**?!
EXTRA LARGE, RIGHT? I'LL CALL IT IN
WHAT DID I **EVER** DO TO DESERVE HER?
DID YOU HEAR THE WAY SHE SAID "EXTRA CHEESE"?

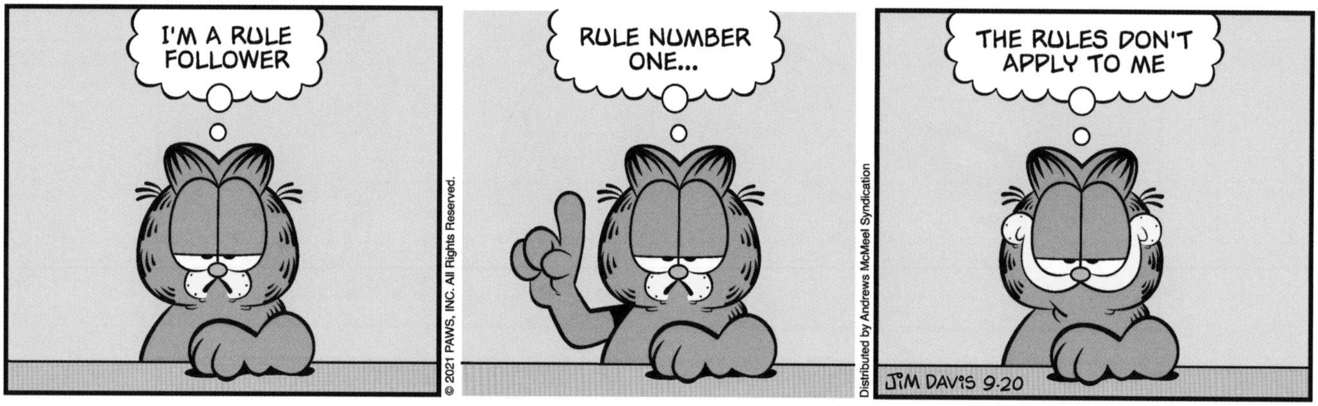
I'M A RULE FOLLOWER
RULE NUMBER ONE...
THE RULES DON'T APPLY TO ME
JIM DAVIS 9-20
© 2021 PAWS, INC. All Rights Reserved.
Distributed by Andrews McMeel Syndication

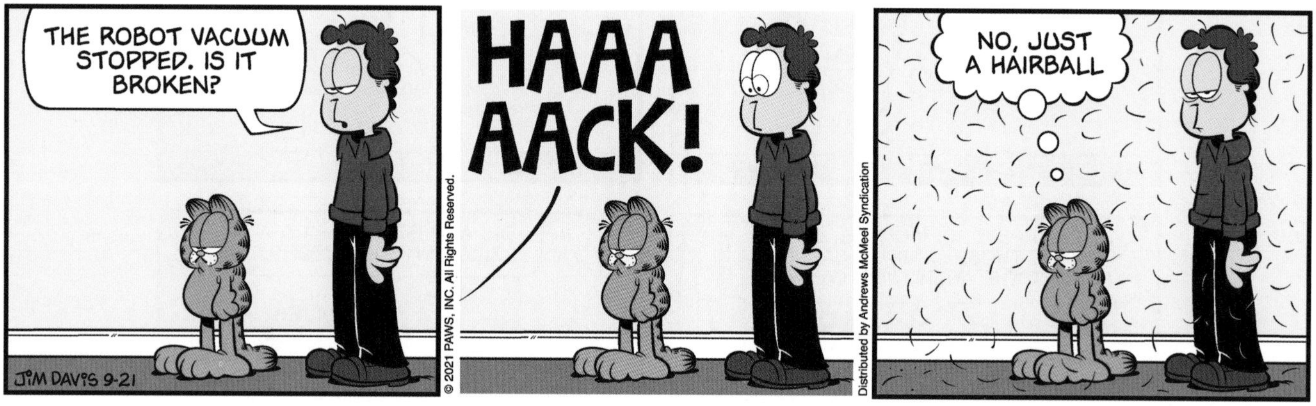
THE ROBOT VACUUM STOPPED. IS IT BROKEN?
HAAA AACK!
NO, JUST A HAIRBALL
JIM DAVIS 9-21
© 2021 PAWS, INC. All Rights Reserved.
Distributed by Andrews McMeel Syndication

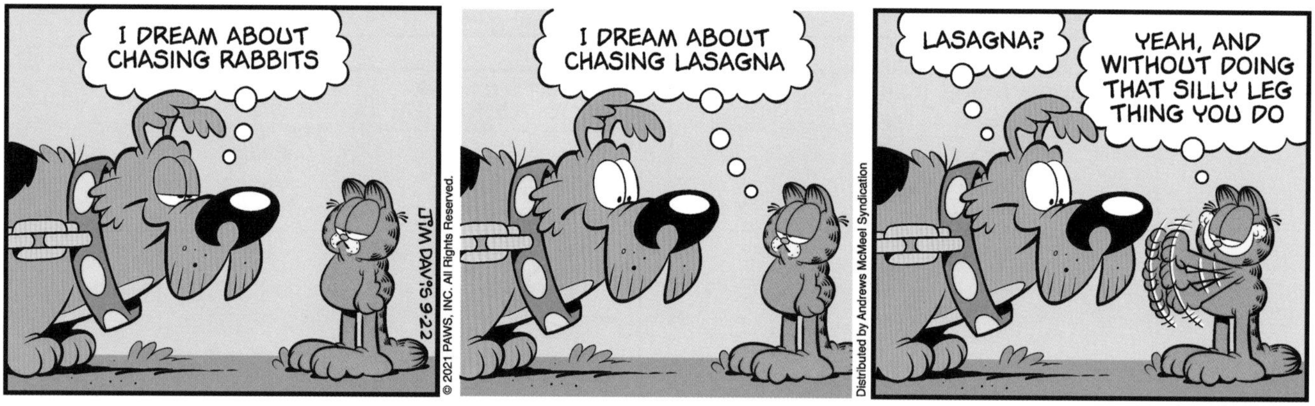
I DREAM ABOUT CHASING RABBITS
I DREAM ABOUT CHASING LASAGNA
LASAGNA?
YEAH, AND WITHOUT DOING THAT SILLY LEG THING YOU DO
JIM DAVIS 9-22
© 2021 PAWS, INC. All Rights Reserved.
Distributed by Andrews McMeel Syndication

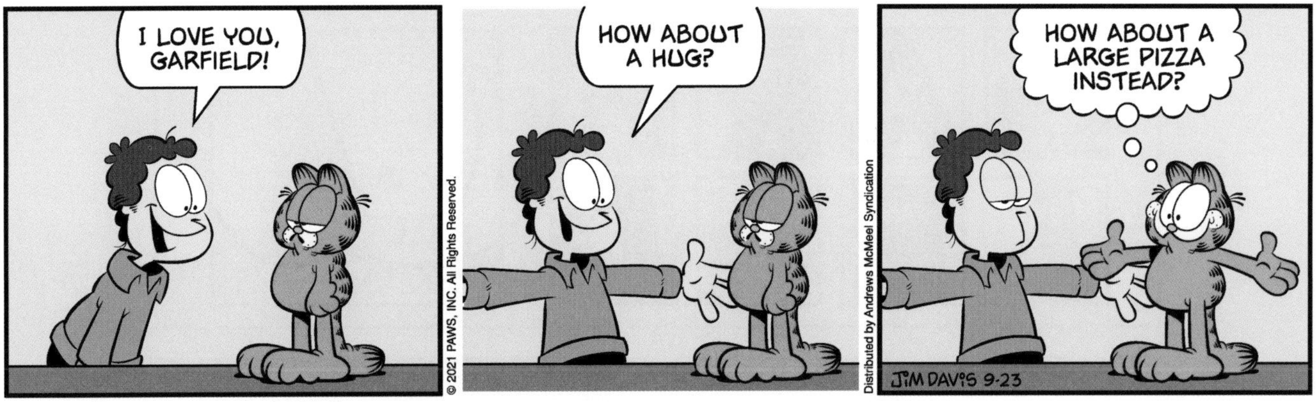
I LOVE YOU, GARFIELD!
© 2021 PAWS, INC. All Rights Reserved.
HOW ABOUT A HUG?
Distributed by Andrews McMeel Syndication
HOW ABOUT A LARGE PIZZA INSTEAD?
JIM DAVIS 9-23

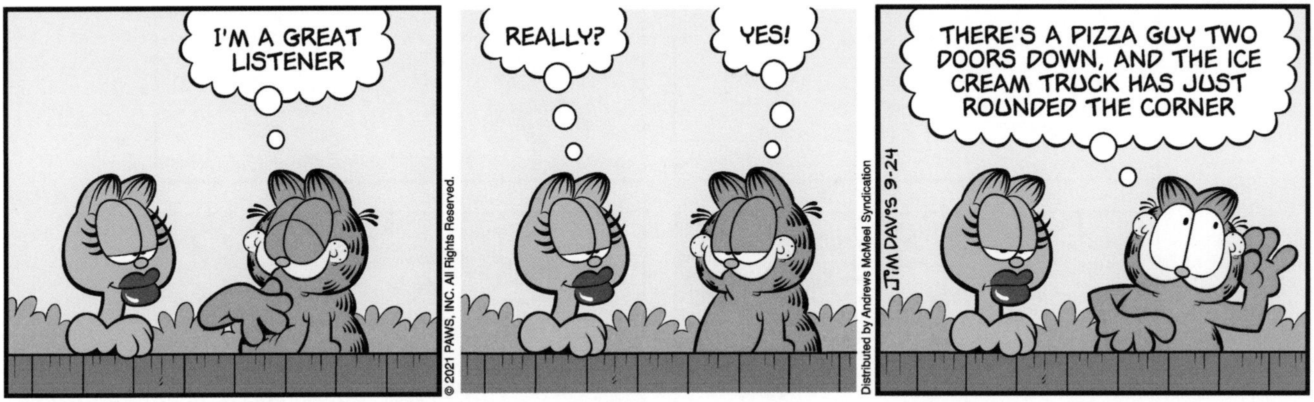
I'M A GREAT LISTENER
© 2021 PAWS, INC. All Rights Reserved.
REALLY?
YES!
Distributed by Andrews McMeel Syndication
JIM DAVIS 9-24
THERE'S A PIZZA GUY TWO DOORS DOWN, AND THE ICE CREAM TRUCK HAS JUST ROUNDED THE CORNER

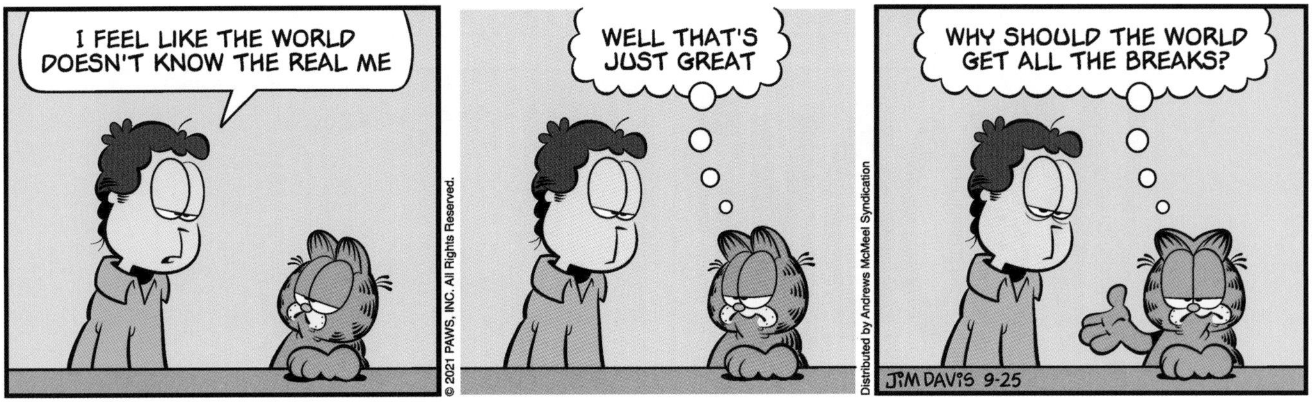
I FEEL LIKE THE WORLD DOESN'T KNOW THE REAL ME
© 2021 PAWS, INC. All Rights Reserved.
WELL THAT'S JUST GREAT
Distributed by Andrews McMeel Syndication
WHY SHOULD THE WORLD GET ALL THE BREAKS?
JIM DAVIS 9-25

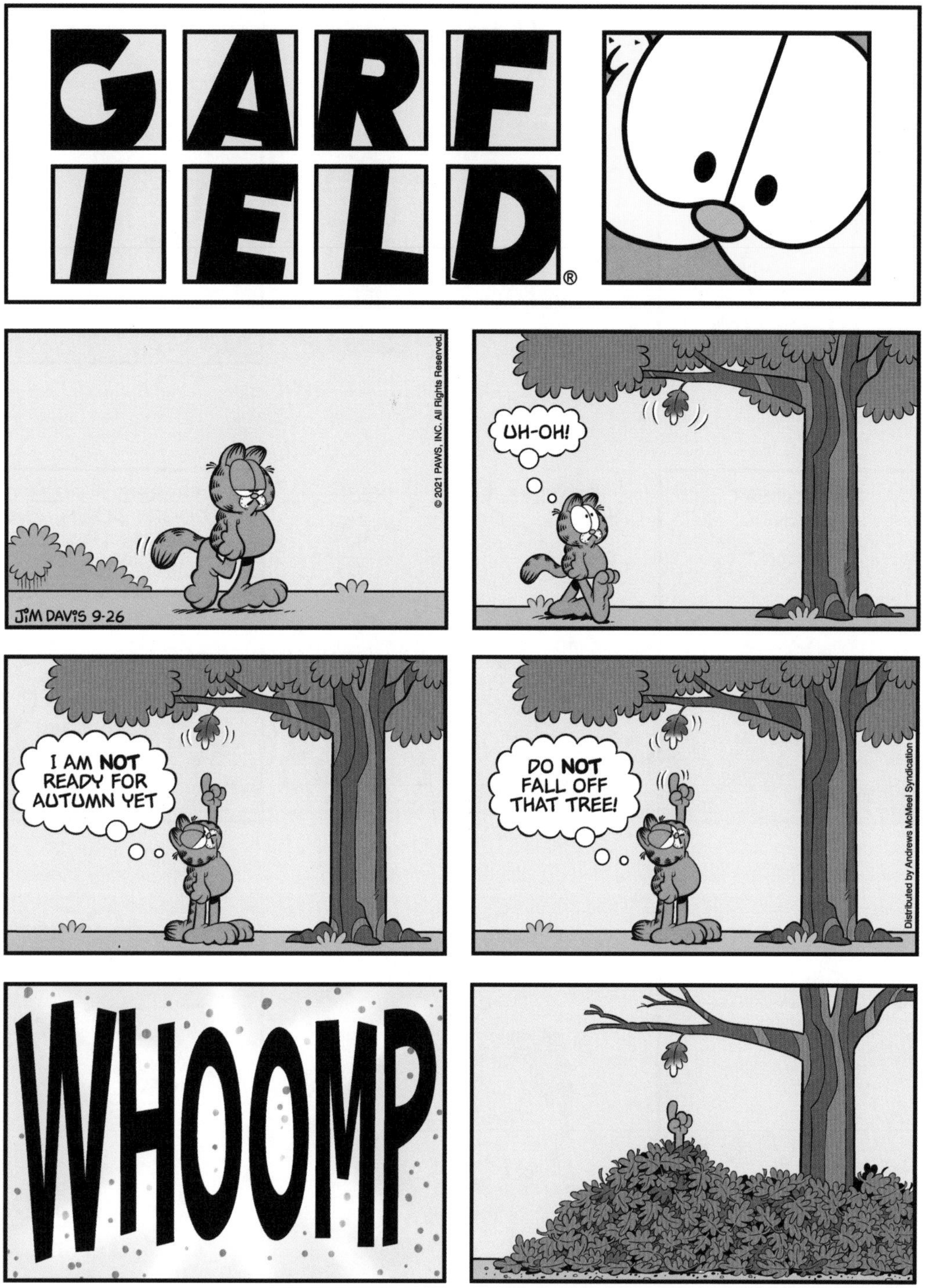
GARFIELD®
© 2021 PAWS, INC. All Rights Reserved.
JIM DAVIS 9-26
UH-OH!
I AM NOT READY FOR AUTUMN YET
DO NOT FALL OFF THAT TREE!
Distributed by Andrews McMeel Syndication
WHOOMP

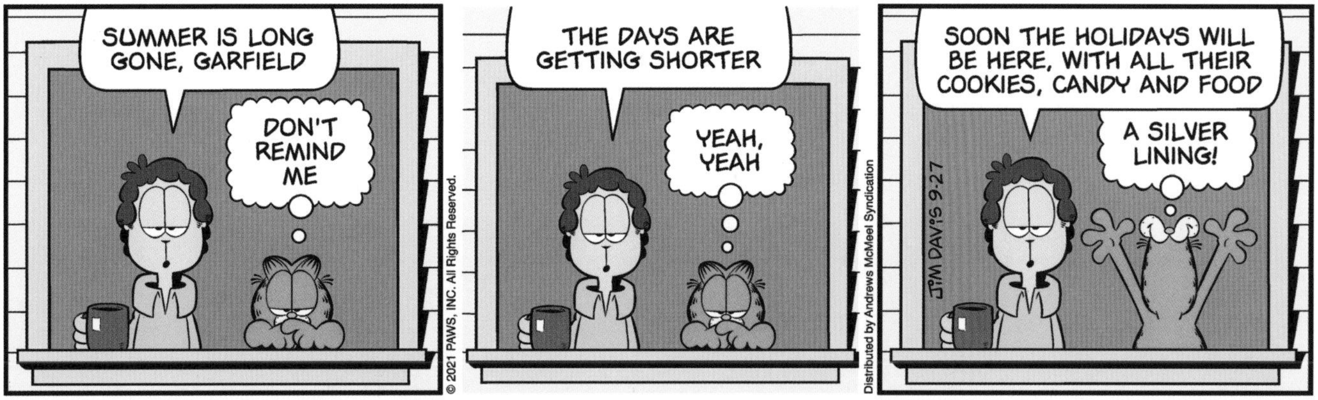
SUMMER IS LONG GONE, GARFIELD
DON'T REMIND ME
THE DAYS ARE GETTING SHORTER
YEAH, YEAH
SOON THE HOLIDAYS WILL BE HERE, WITH ALL THEIR COOKIES, CANDY AND FOOD
A SILVER LINING!
JIM DAVIS 9-27
© 2021 PAWS, INC. All Rights Reserved.
Distributed by Andrews McMeel Syndication

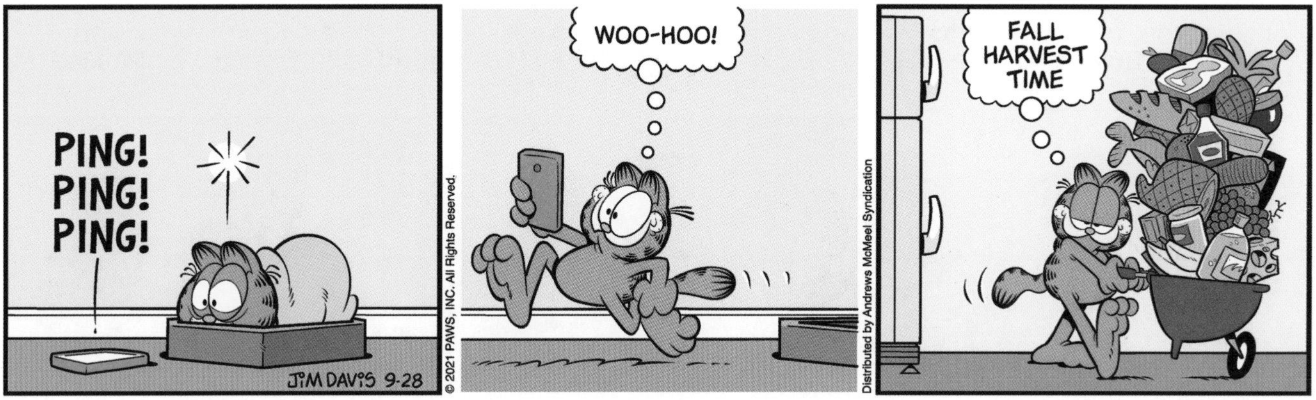
PING! PING! PING!
JIM DAVIS 9-28
WOO-HOO!
FALL HARVEST TIME
© 2021 PAWS, INC. All Rights Reserved.
Distributed by Andrews McMeel Syndication

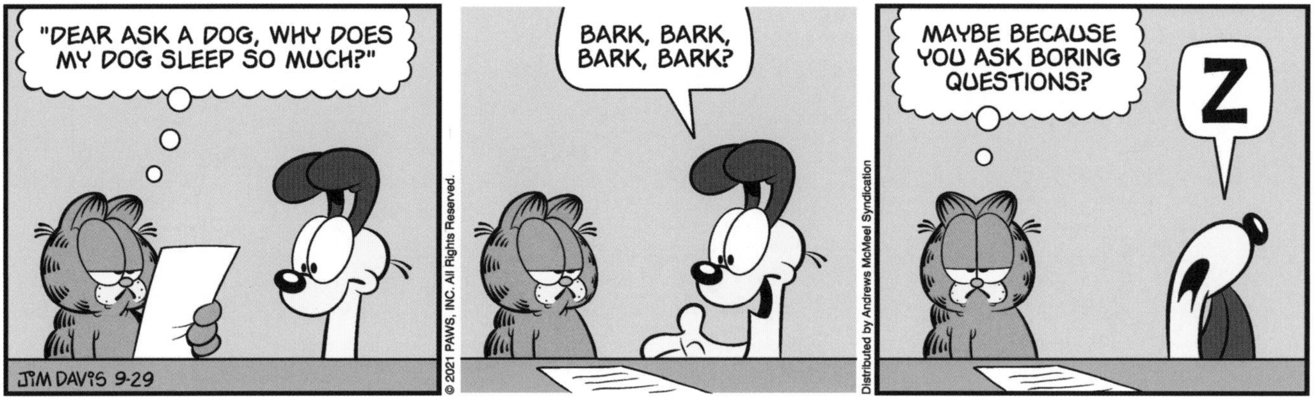
"DEAR ASK A DOG, WHY DOES MY DOG SLEEP SO MUCH?"
JIM DAVIS 9-29
BARK, BARK, BARK, BARK?
MAYBE BECAUSE YOU ASK BORING QUESTIONS?
Z
© 2021 PAWS, INC. All Rights Reserved.
Distributed by Andrews McMeel Syndication

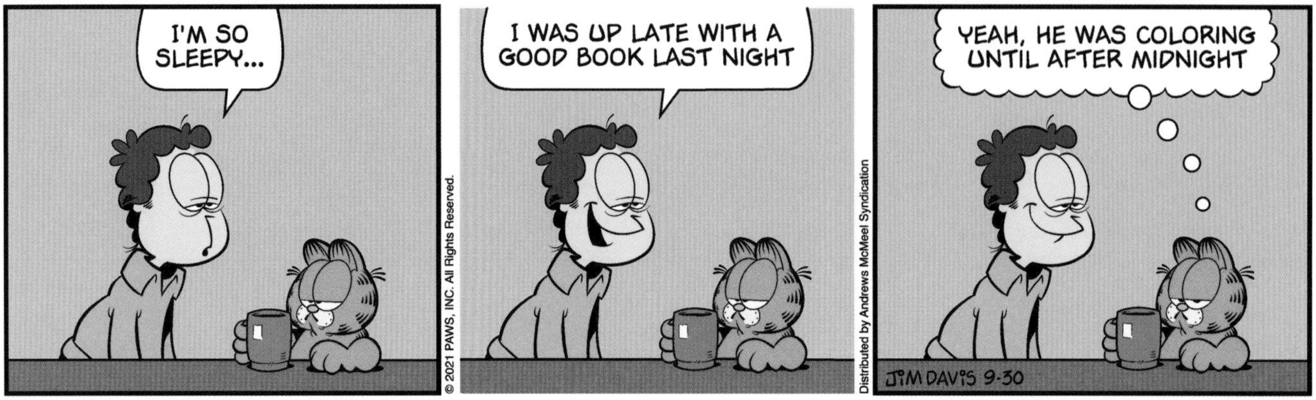
I'M SO SLEEPY...
I WAS UP LATE WITH A GOOD BOOK LAST NIGHT
YEAH, HE WAS COLORING UNTIL AFTER MIDNIGHT
JIM DAVIS 9-30
© 2021 PAWS, INC. All Rights Reserved.
Distributed by Andrews McMeel Syndication

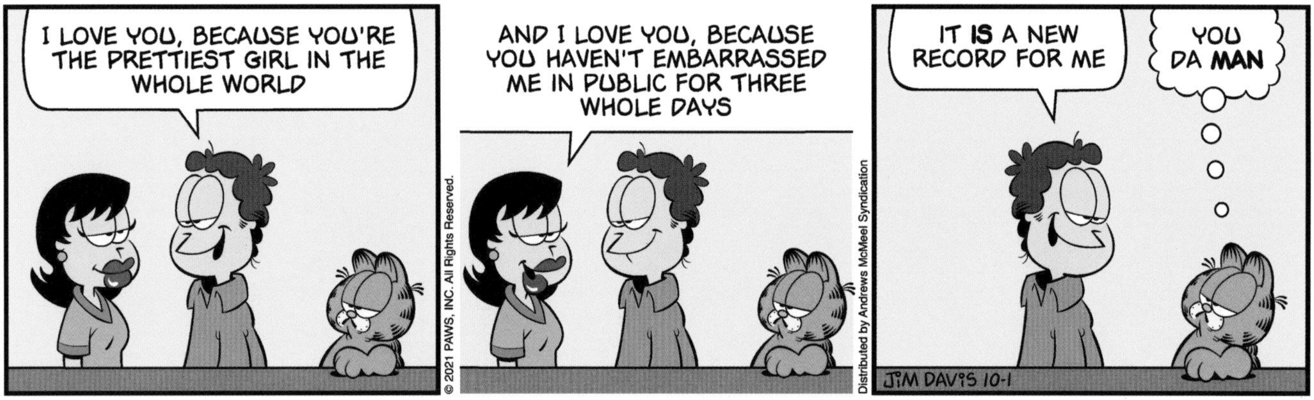
I LOVE YOU, BECAUSE YOU'RE THE PRETTIEST GIRL IN THE WHOLE WORLD
AND I LOVE YOU, BECAUSE YOU HAVEN'T EMBARRASSED ME IN PUBLIC FOR THREE WHOLE DAYS
IT **IS** A NEW RECORD FOR ME
YOU DA **MAN**
JIM DAVIS 10-1
© 2021 PAWS, INC. All Rights Reserved.
Distributed by Andrews McMeel Syndication

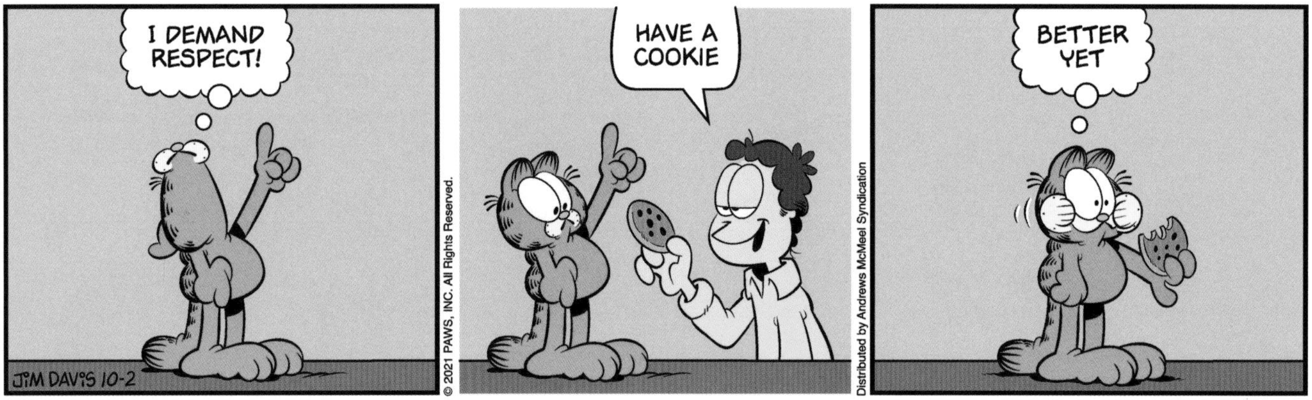
I DEMAND RESPECT!
HAVE A COOKIE
BETTER YET
JIM DAVIS 10-2
© 2021 PAWS, INC. All Rights Reserved.
Distributed by Andrews McMeel Syndication

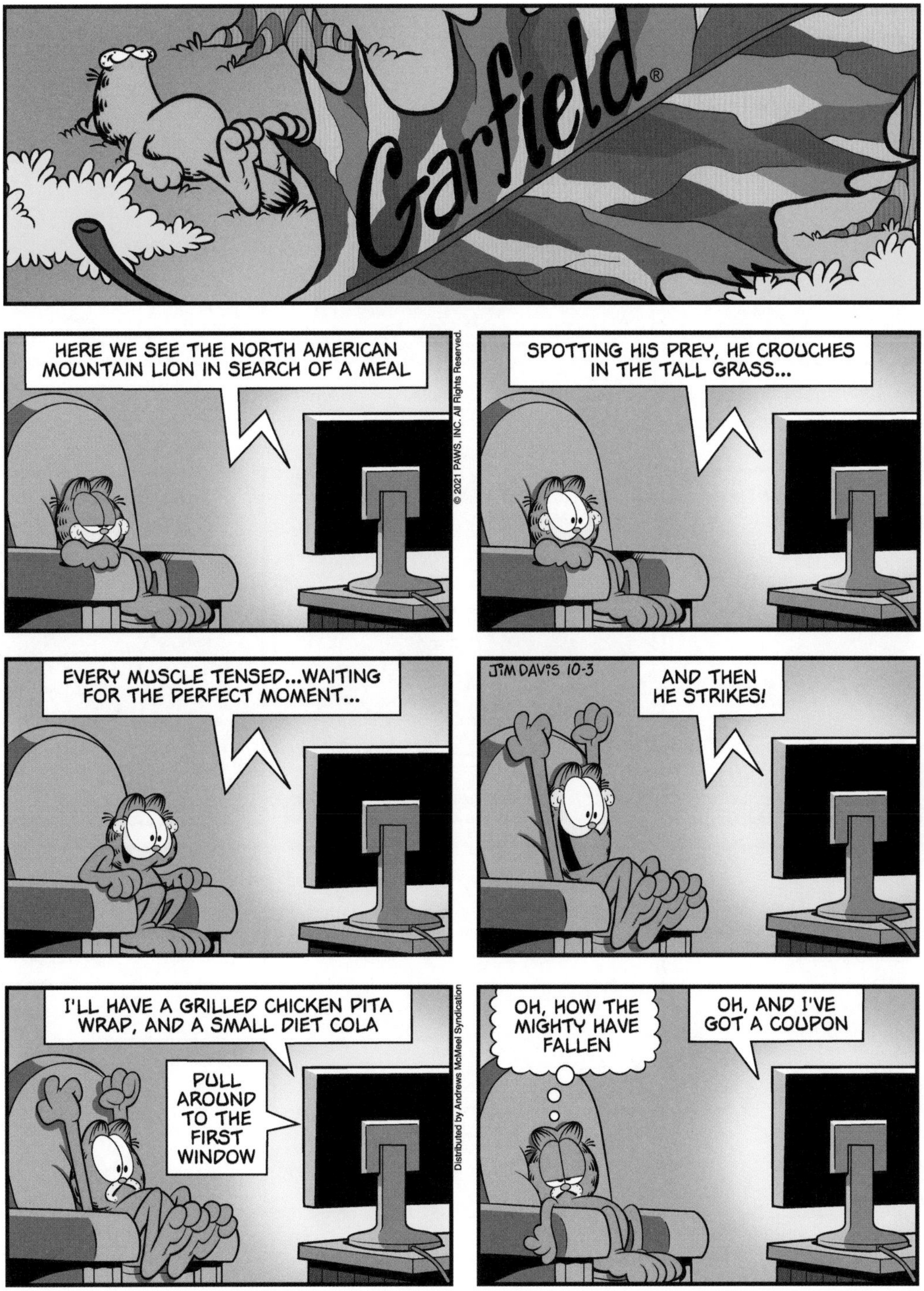
Garfield®
HERE WE SEE THE NORTH AMERICAN MOUNTAIN LION IN SEARCH OF A MEAL
SPOTTING HIS PREY, HE CROUCHES IN THE TALL GRASS...
EVERY MUSCLE TENSED...WAITING FOR THE PERFECT MOMENT...
JIM DAVIS 10-3
AND THEN HE STRIKES!
I'LL HAVE A GRILLED CHICKEN PITA WRAP, AND A SMALL DIET COLA
PULL AROUND TO THE FIRST WINDOW
OH, HOW THE MIGHTY HAVE FALLEN
OH, AND I'VE GOT A COUPON

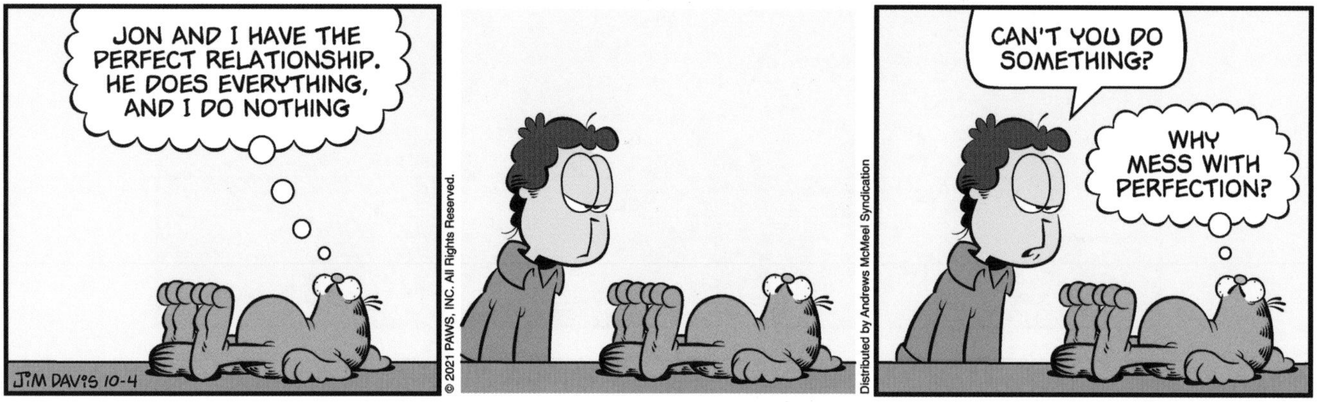
JON AND I HAVE THE PERFECT RELATIONSHIP. HE DOES EVERYTHING, AND I DO NOTHING
JIM DAVIS 10-4
CAN'T YOU DO SOMETHING?
WHY MESS WITH PERFECTION?


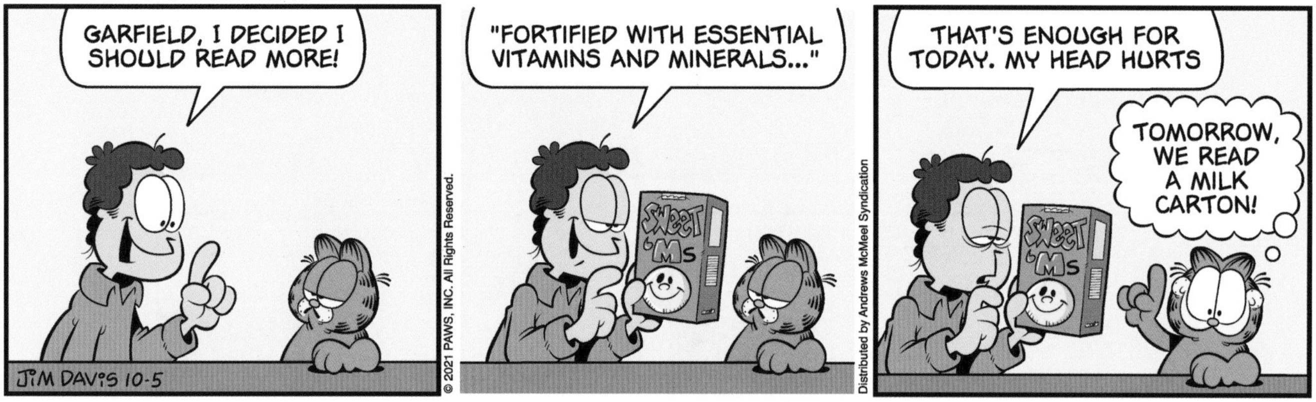
GARFIELD, I DECIDED I SHOULD READ MORE!
JIM DAVIS 10-5
"FORTIFIED WITH ESSENTIAL VITAMINS AND MINERALS..."
SWEET 'O MS
THAT'S ENOUGH FOR TODAY. MY HEAD HURTS
TOMORROW, WE READ A MILK CARTON!


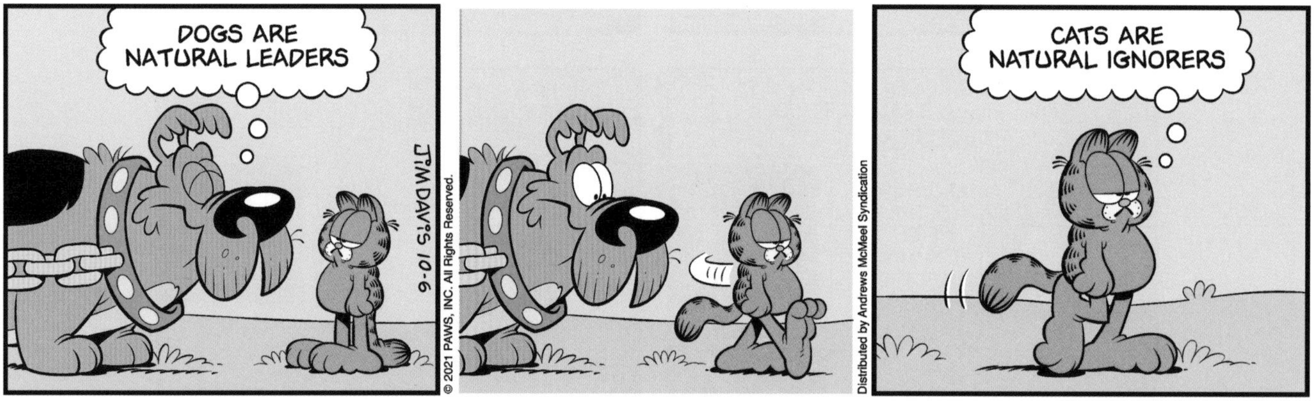
DOGS ARE NATURAL LEADERS
JIM DAVIS 10-6
CATS ARE NATURAL IGNORERS

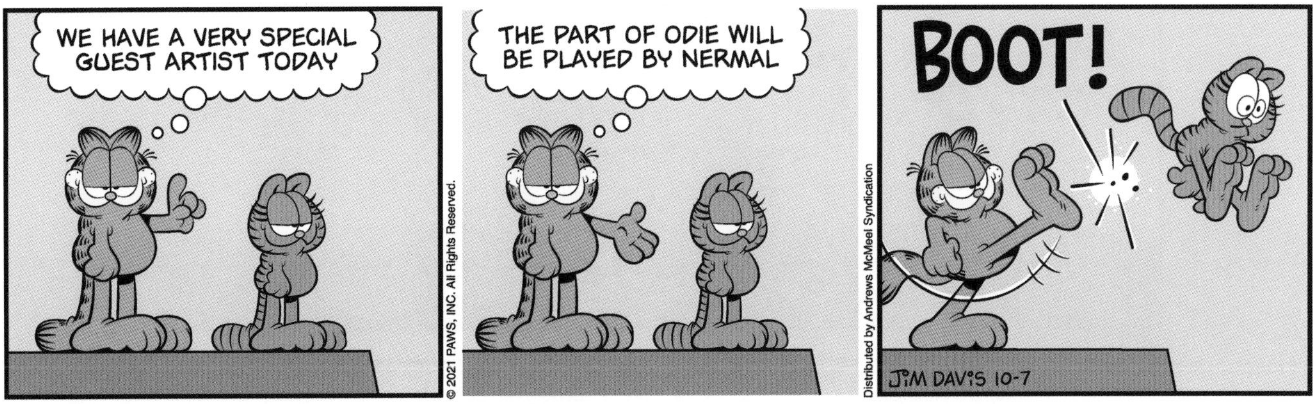
WE HAVE A VERY SPECIAL GUEST ARTIST TODAY
THE PART OF ODIE WILL BE PLAYED BY NERMAL
BOOT!
JIM DAVIS 10-7


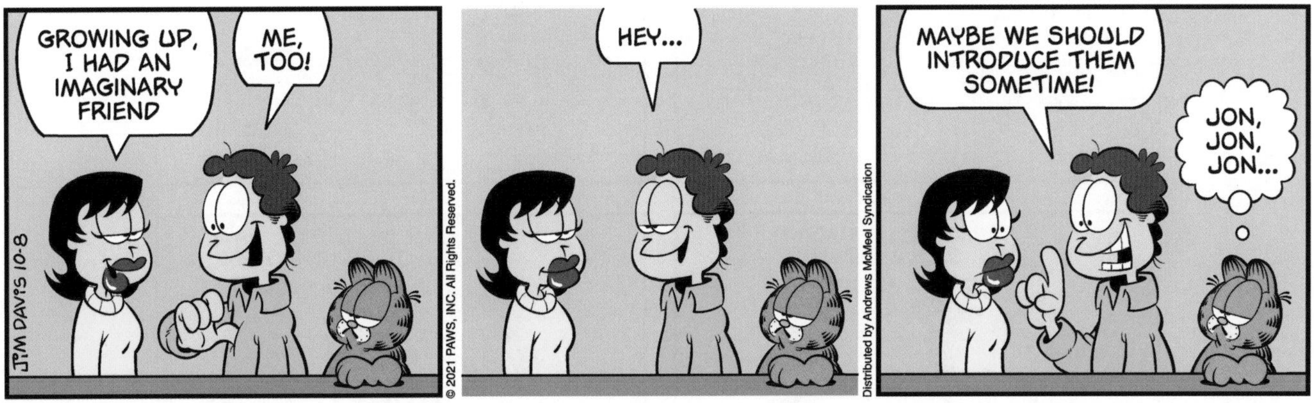
GROWING UP, I HAD AN IMAGINARY FRIEND
ME, TOO!
HEY...
MAYBE WE SHOULD INTRODUCE THEM SOMETIME!
JON, JON, JON...
JIM DAVIS 10-8


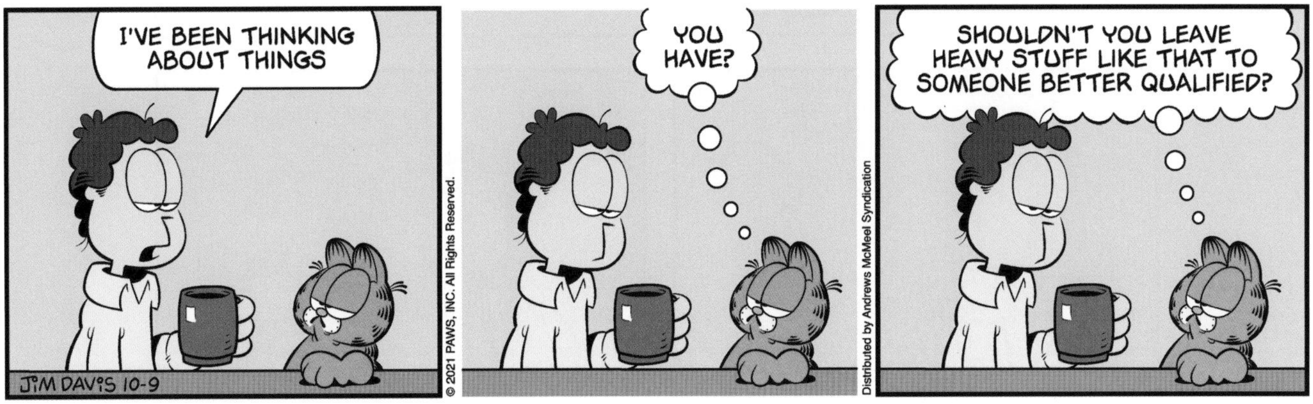
I'VE BEEN THINKING ABOUT THINGS
YOU HAVE?
SHOULDN'T YOU LEAVE HEAVY STUFF LIKE THAT TO SOMEONE BETTER QUALIFIED?
JIM DAVIS 10-9

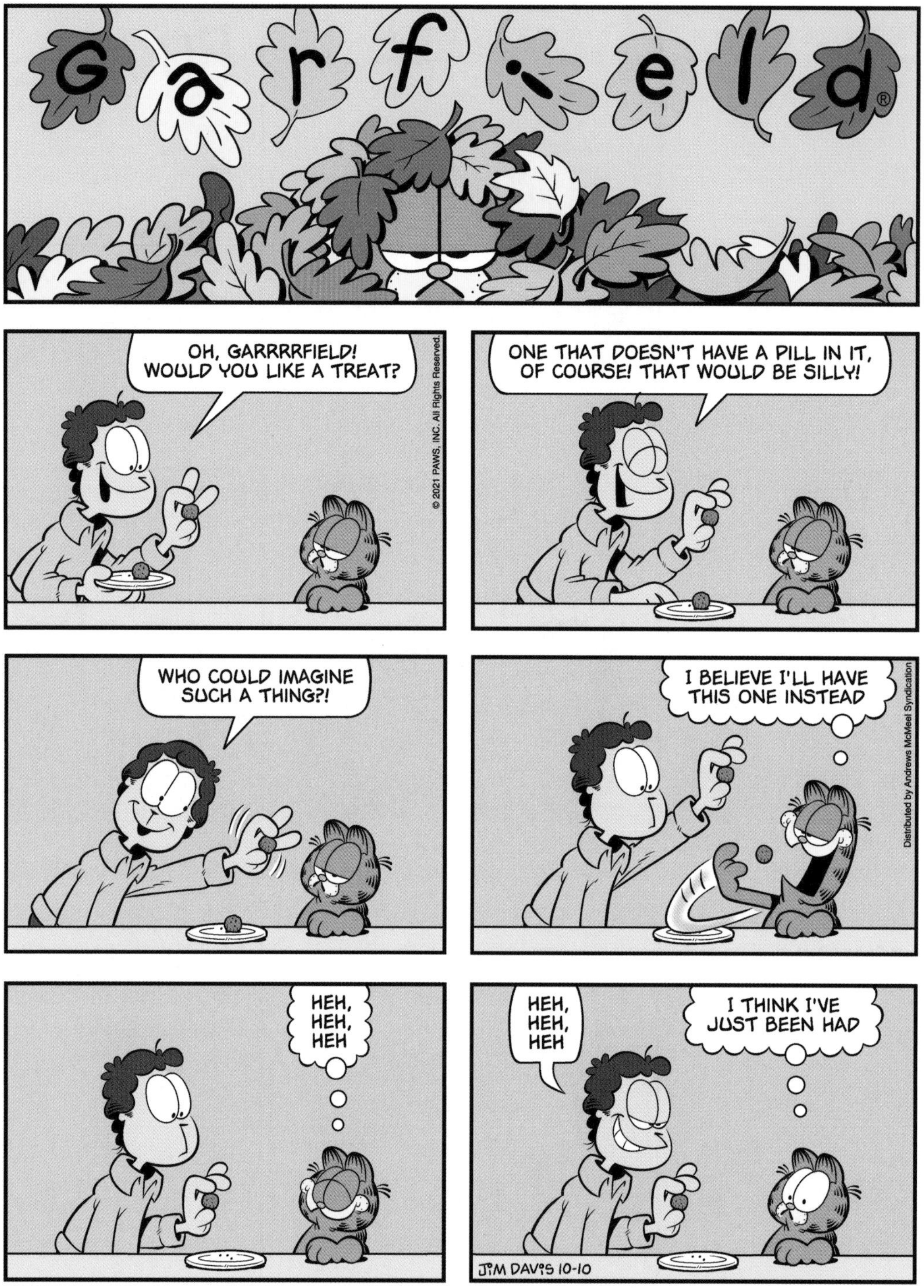
GARFIELD®
OH, GARRRRFIELD! WOULD YOU LIKE A TREAT?
© 2021 PAWS, INC. All Rights Reserved.
ONE THAT DOESN'T HAVE A PILL IN IT, OF COURSE! THAT WOULD BE SILLY!
WHO COULD IMAGINE SUCH A THING?!
I BELIEVE I'LL HAVE THIS ONE INSTEAD
Distributed by Andrews McMeel Syndication
HEH, HEH, HEH
HEH, HEH, HEH
I THINK I'VE JUST BEEN HAD
JIM DAVIS 10-10

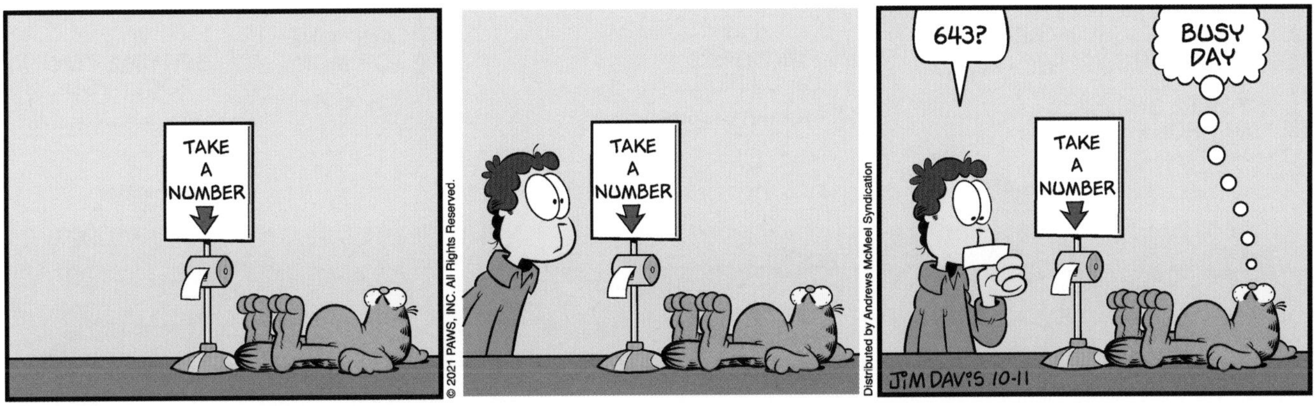
TAKE A NUMBER
7
© 2021 PAWS, INC. All Rights Reserved.
TAKE A NUMBER
7
Distributed by Andrews McMeel Syndication
643?
BUSY DAY
TAKE A NUMBER
7
JIM DAVIS 10-11

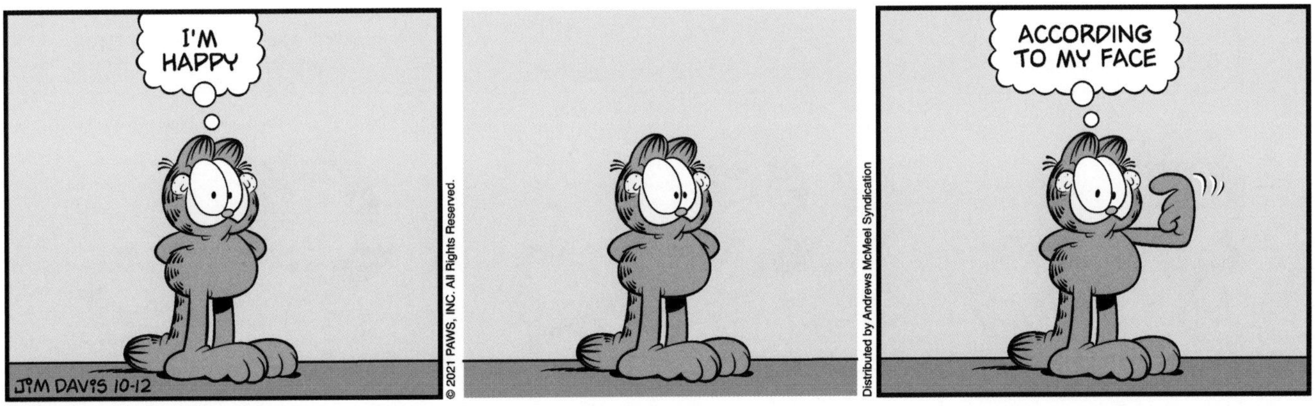
I'M HAPPY
JIM DAVIS 10-12
© 2021 PAWS, INC. All Rights Reserved.
Distributed by Andrews McMeel Syndication
ACCORDING TO MY FACE

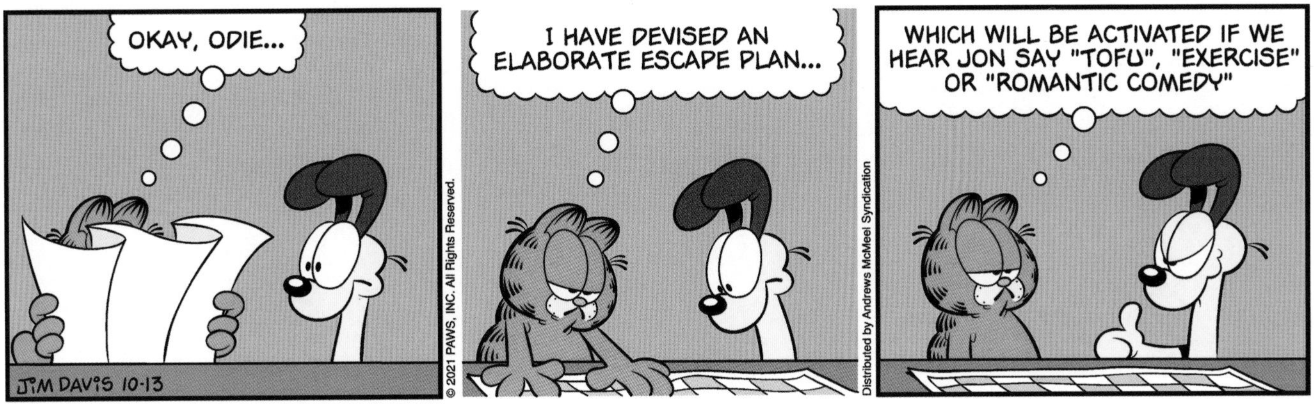
OKAY, ODIE...
JIM DAVIS 10-13
© 2021 PAWS, INC. All Rights Reserved.
I HAVE DEVISED AN ELABORATE ESCAPE PLAN...
Distributed by Andrews McMeel Syndication
WHICH WILL BE ACTIVATED IF WE HEAR JON SAY "TOFU", "EXERCISE" OR "ROMANTIC COMEDY"

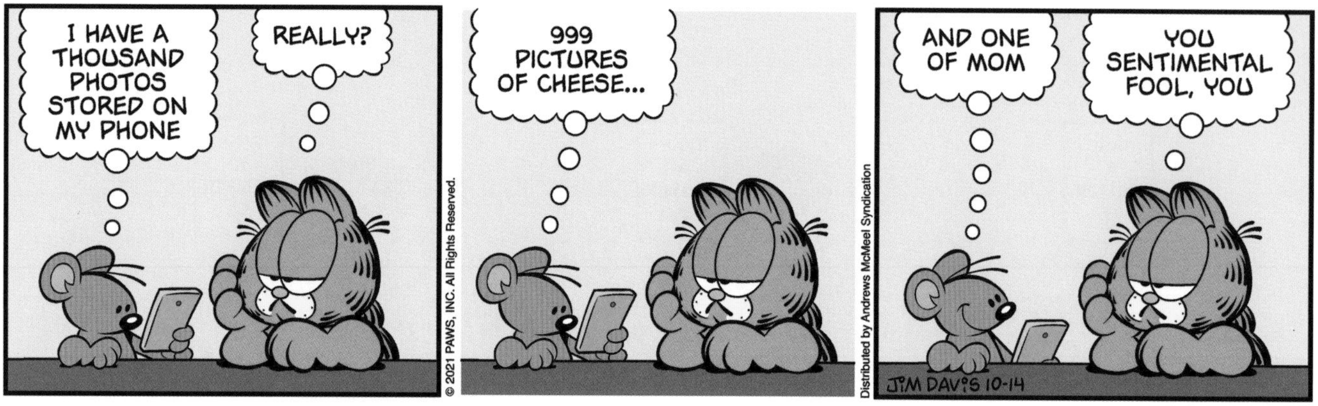
I HAVE A THOUSAND PHOTOS STORED ON MY PHONE
REALLY?
999 PICTURES OF CHEESE...
AND ONE OF MOM
YOU SENTIMENTAL FOOL, YOU
© 2021 PAWS, INC. All Rights Reserved.
Distributed by Andrews McMeel Syndication
JIM DAVIS 10-14

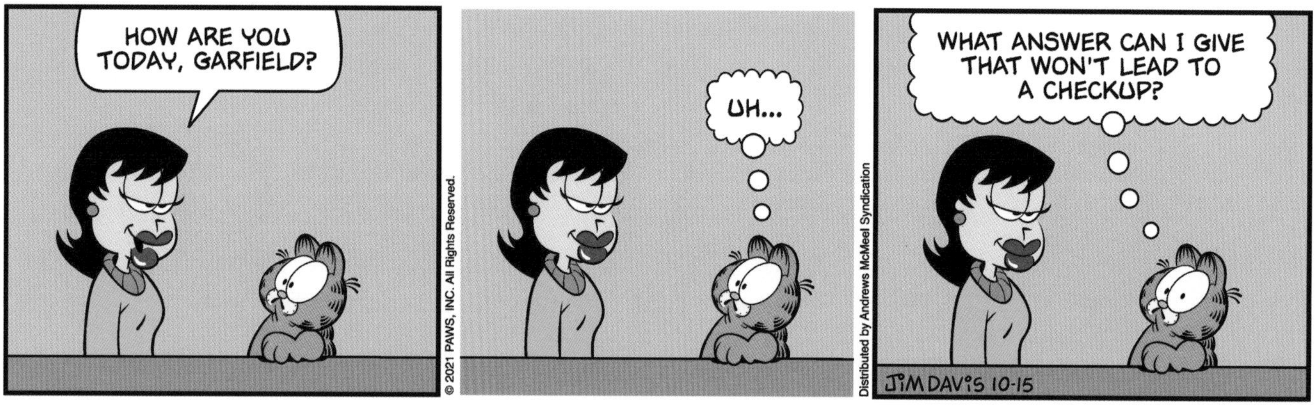
HOW ARE YOU TODAY, GARFIELD?
UH...
WHAT ANSWER CAN I GIVE THAT WON'T LEAD TO A CHECKUP?
© 2021 PAWS, INC. All Rights Reserved.
Distributed by Andrews McMeel Syndication
JIM DAVIS 10-15

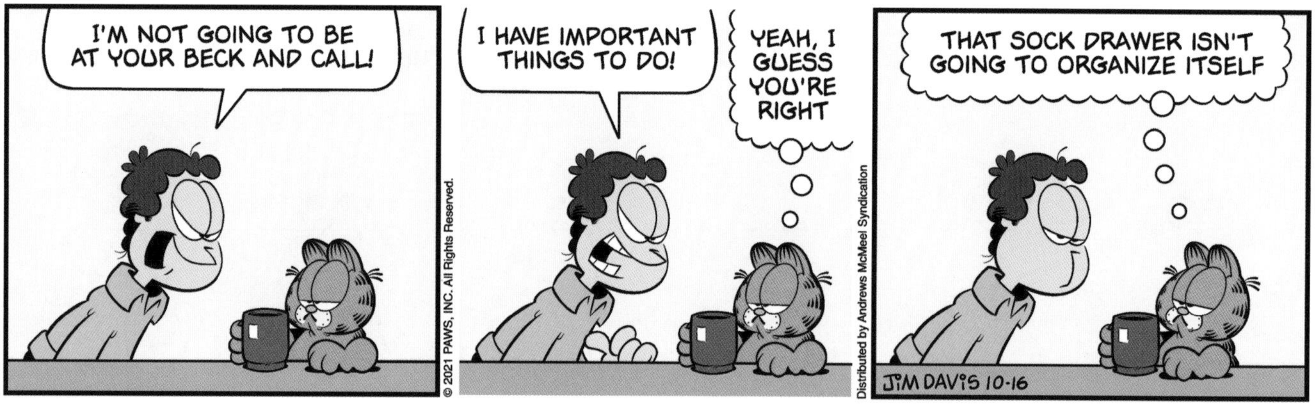
I'M NOT GOING TO BE AT YOUR BECK AND CALL!
I HAVE IMPORTANT THINGS TO DO!
YEAH, I GUESS YOU'RE RIGHT
THAT SOCK DRAWER ISN'T GOING TO ORGANIZE ITSELF
© 2021 PAWS, INC. All Rights Reserved.
Distributed by Andrews McMeel Syndication
JIM DAVIS 10-16

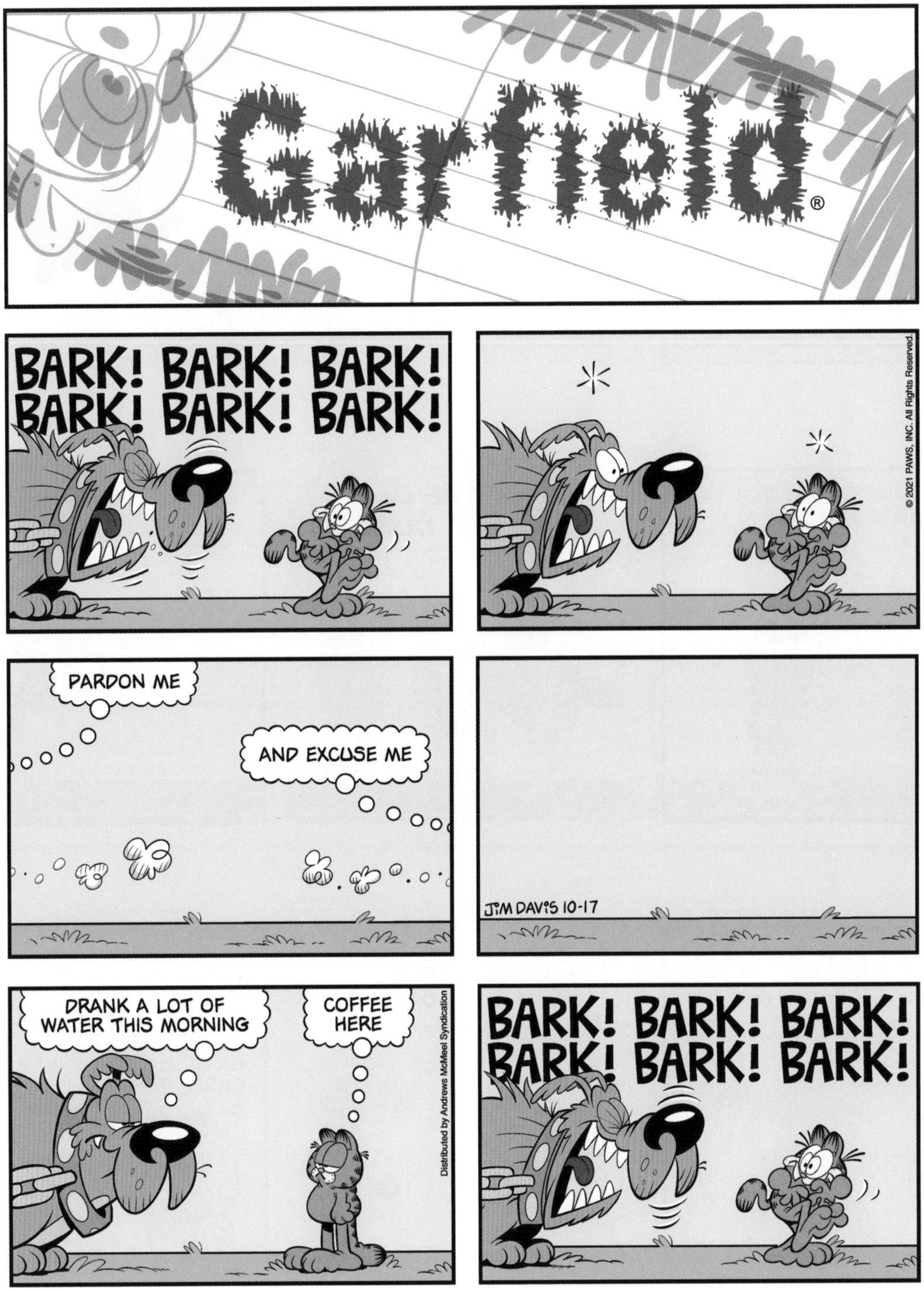
Garfield®
BARK! BARK! BARK! BARK! BARK! BARK!
© 2021 PAWS, INC. All Rights Reserved.
PARDON ME
AND EXCUSE ME
JIM DAVIS 10-17
DRANK A LOT OF WATER THIS MORNING
COFFEE HERE
Distributed by Andrews McMeel Syndication
BARK! BARK! BARK! BARK! BARK! BARK!

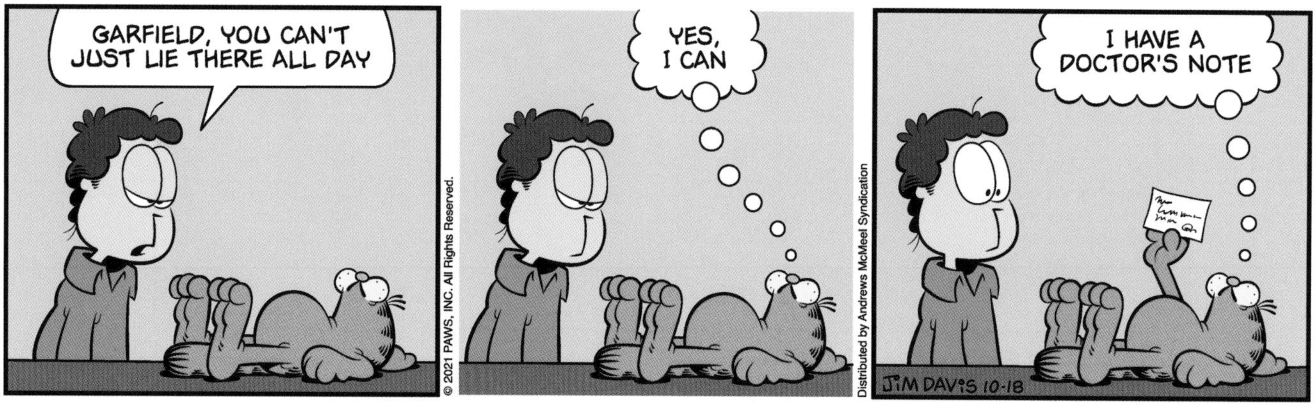
GARFIELD, YOU CAN'T JUST LIE THERE ALL DAY
YES, I CAN
I HAVE A DOCTOR'S NOTE
© 2021 PAWS, INC. All Rights Reserved.
Distributed by Andrews McMeel Syndication
JIM DAVIS 10-18

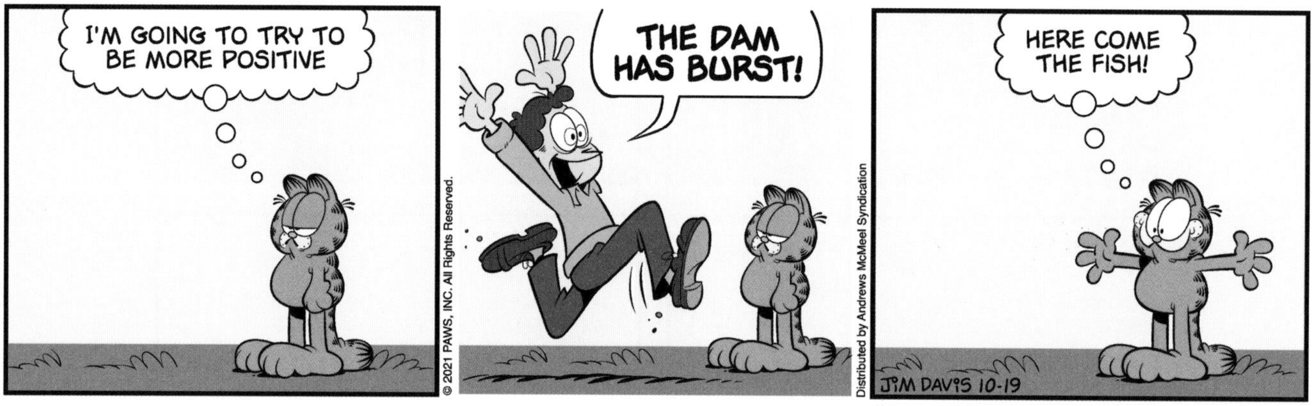
I'M GOING TO TRY TO BE MORE POSITIVE
THE DAM HAS BURST!
HERE COME THE FISH!
© 2021 PAWS, INC. All Rights Reserved.
Distributed by Andrews McMeel Syndication
JIM DAVIS 10-19

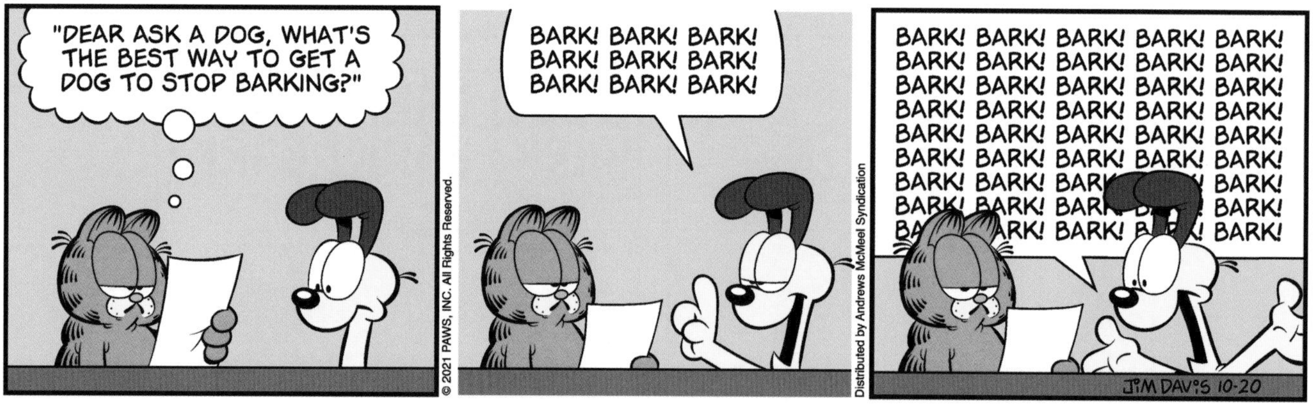
"DEAR ASK A DOG, WHAT'S THE BEST WAY TO GET A DOG TO STOP BARKING?"
BARK! BARK! BARK! BARK! BARK! BARK! BARK! BARK! BARK!
BARK! BARK! BARK! BARK! BARK!
BARK! BARK! BARK! BARK! BARK!
BARK! BARK! BARK! BARK! BARK!
BARK! BARK! BARK! BARK! BARK!
BARK! BARK! BARK! BARK! BARK!
BARK! BARK! BARK! BARK! BARK!
BARK! BARK! BARK!
BARK! BARK!
BARK! BARK!
© 2021 PAWS, INC. All Rights Reserved.
Distributed by Andrews McMeel Syndication
JIM DAVIS 10-20

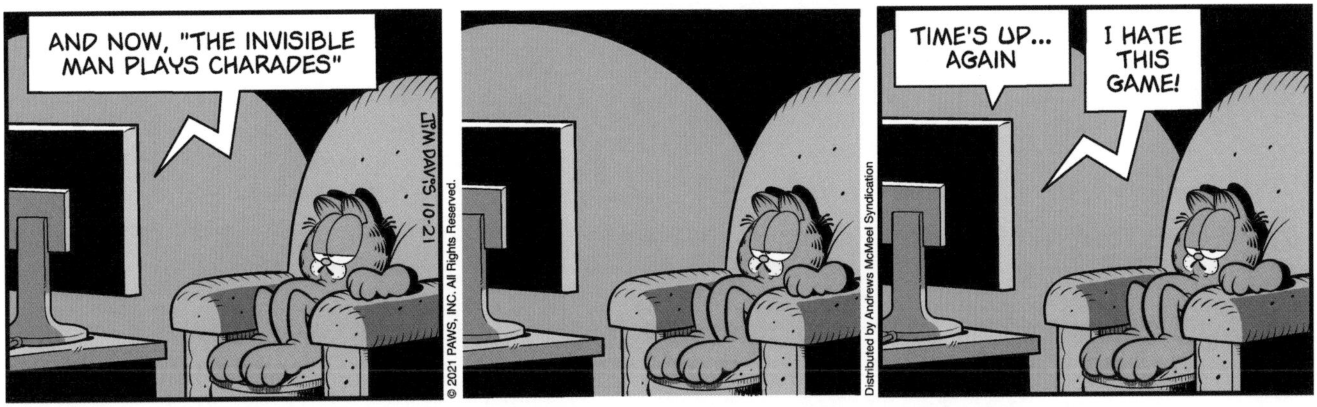
AND NOW, "THE INVISIBLE MAN PLAYS CHARADES"
JIM DAVIS 10-21
© 2021 PAWS, INC. All Rights Reserved.
Distributed by Andrews McMeel Syndication
TIME'S UP... AGAIN
I HATE THIS GAME!

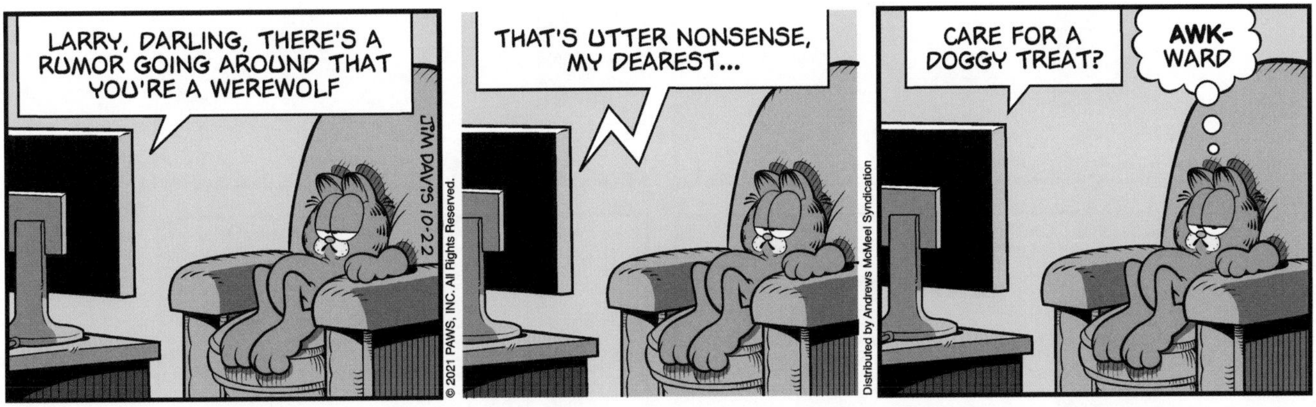
LARRY, DARLING, THERE'S A RUMOR GOING AROUND THAT YOU'RE A WEREWOLF
JIM DAVIS 10-22
© 2021 PAWS, INC. All Rights Reserved.
THAT'S UTTER NONSENSE, MY DEAREST...
Distributed by Andrews McMeel Syndication
CARE FOR A DOGGY TREAT?
AWK-WARD

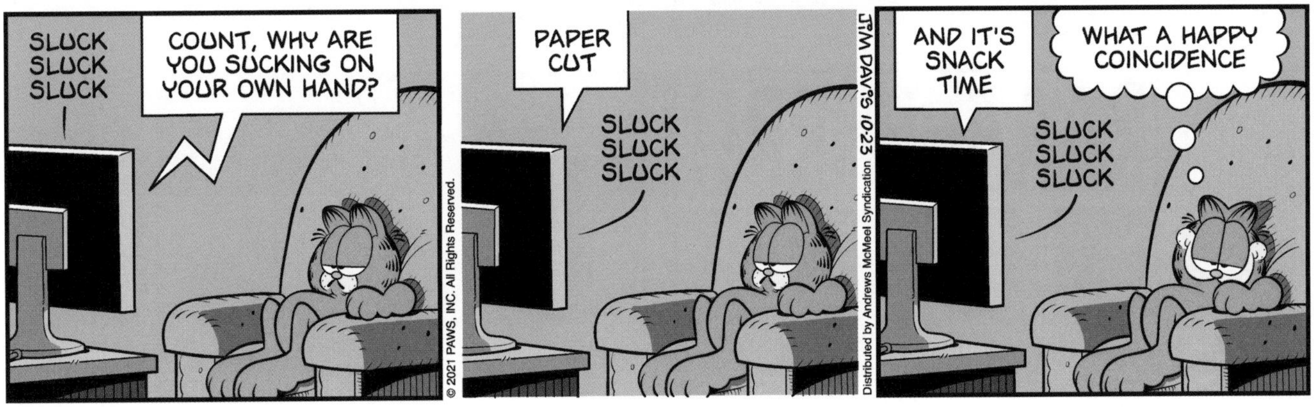
SLUCK SLUCK SLUCK
COUNT, WHY ARE YOU SUCKING ON YOUR OWN HAND?
© 2021 PAWS, INC. All Rights Reserved.
PAPER CUT
SLUCK SLUCK SLUCK
JIM DAVIS 10-23
Distributed by Andrews McMeel Syndication
AND IT'S SNACK TIME
WHAT A HAPPY COINCIDENCE
SLUCK SLUCK SLUCK

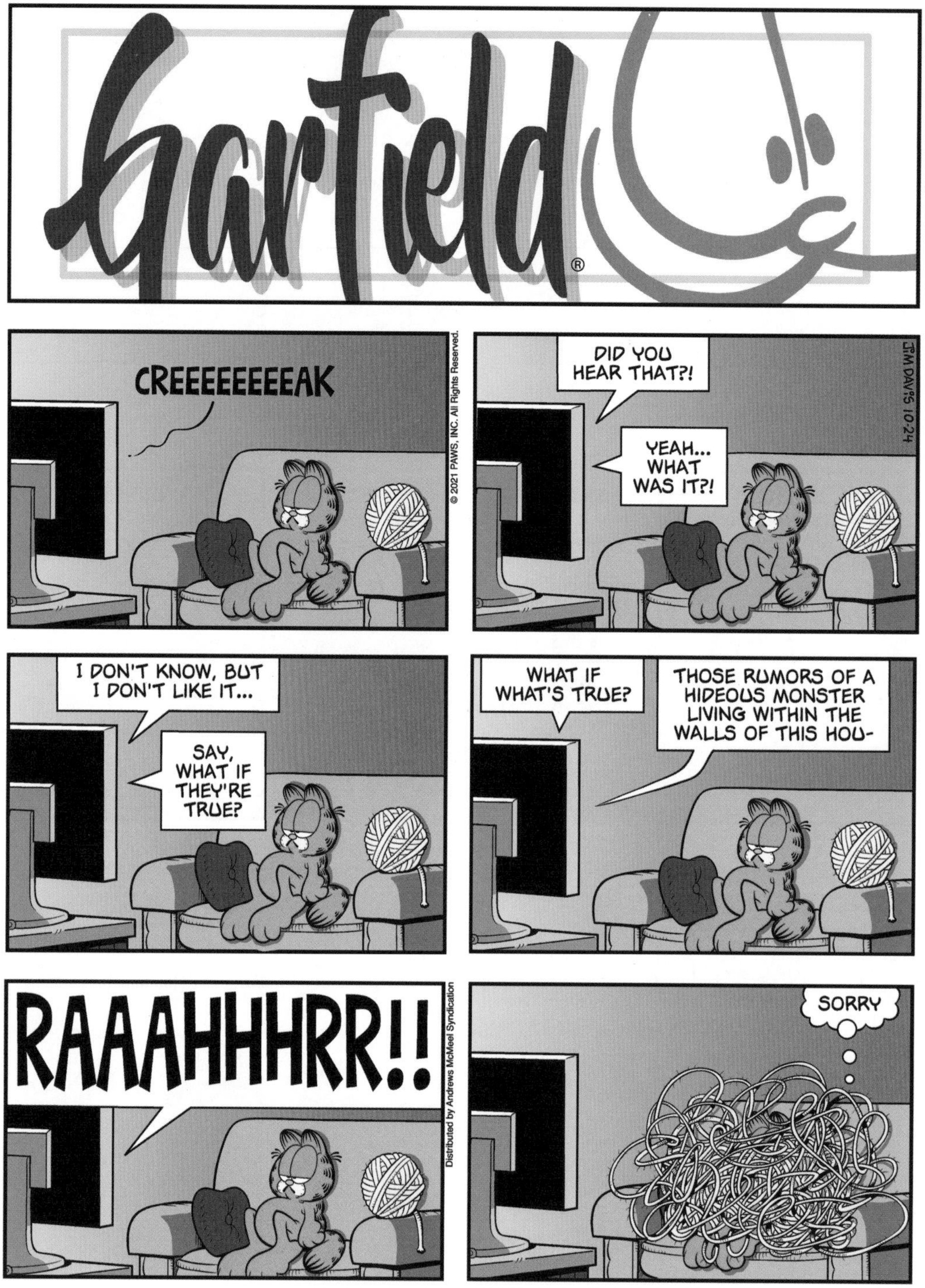
Garfield®
CREEEEEEEEAK
© 2021 PAWS, INC. All Rights Reserved.
DID YOU HEAR THAT?!
YEAH... WHAT WAS IT?!
JIM DAVIS 10-24
I DON'T KNOW, BUT I DON'T LIKE IT...
SAY, WHAT IF THEY'RE TRUE?
WHAT IF WHAT'S TRUE?
THOSE RUMORS OF A HIDEOUS MONSTER LIVING WITHIN THE WALLS OF THIS HOU-
RAAAHHHRR!!
Distributed by Andrews McMeel Syndication
SORRY

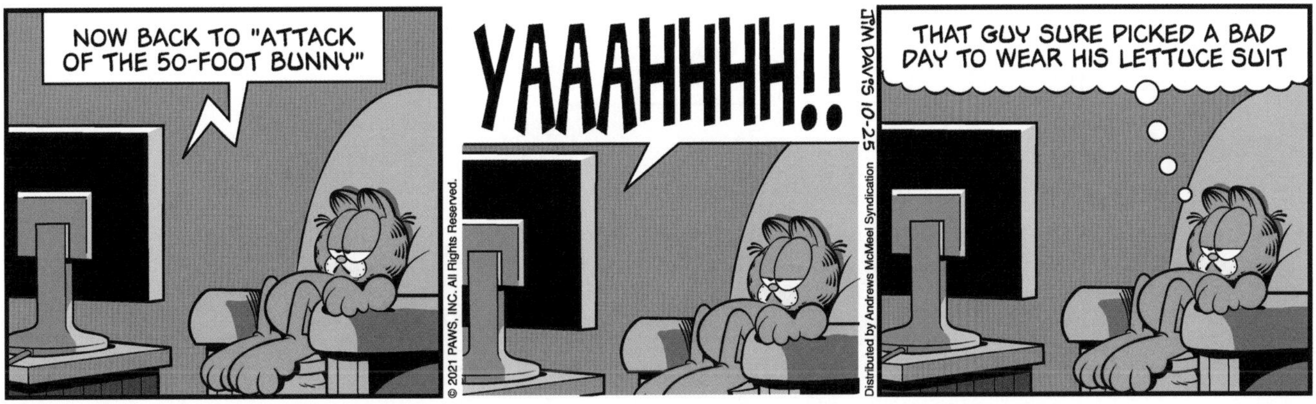
NOW BACK TO "ATTACK OF THE 50-FOOT BUNNY"
YAAAHHHH!!
THAT GUY SURE PICKED A BAD DAY TO WEAR HIS LETTUCE SUIT
JIM DAVIS 10-25
© 2021 PAWS, INC. All Rights Reserved.
Distributed by Andrews McMeel Syndication

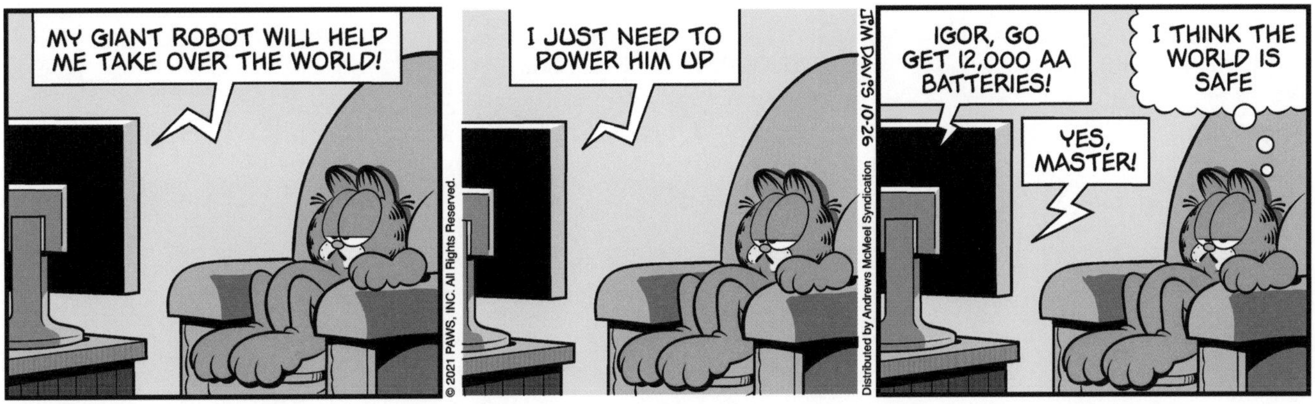
MY GIANT ROBOT WILL HELP ME TAKE OVER THE WORLD!
I JUST NEED TO POWER HIM UP
IGOR, GO GET 12,000 AA BATTERIES!
YES, MASTER!
I THINK THE WORLD IS SAFE
JIM DAVIS 10-26
© 2021 PAWS, INC. All Rights Reserved.
Distributed by Andrews McMeel Syndication

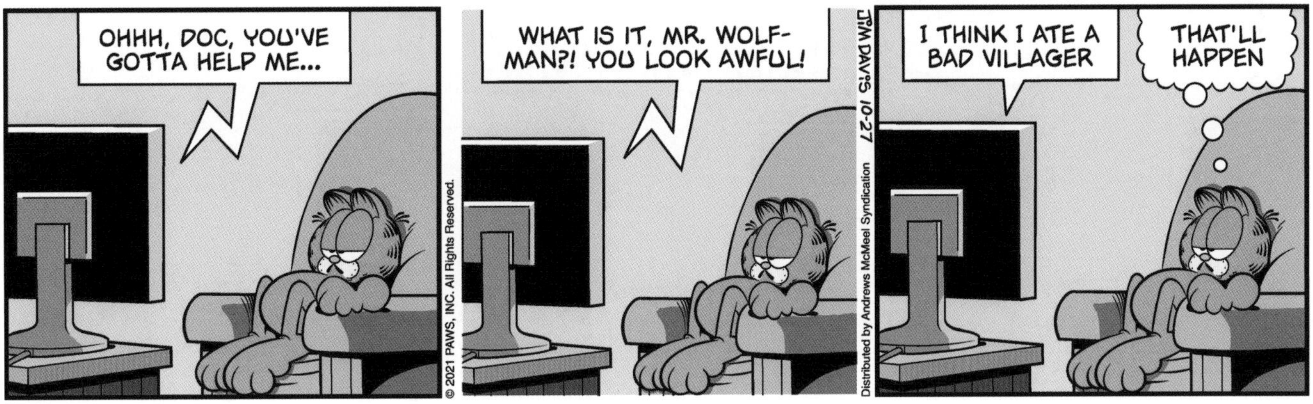
OHHH, DOC, YOU'VE GOTTA HELP ME...
WHAT IS IT, MR. WOLF-MAN?! YOU LOOK AWFUL!
I THINK I ATE A BAD VILLAGER
THAT'LL HAPPEN
JIM DAVIS 10-27
© 2021 PAWS, INC. All Rights Reserved.
Distributed by Andrews McMeel Syndication

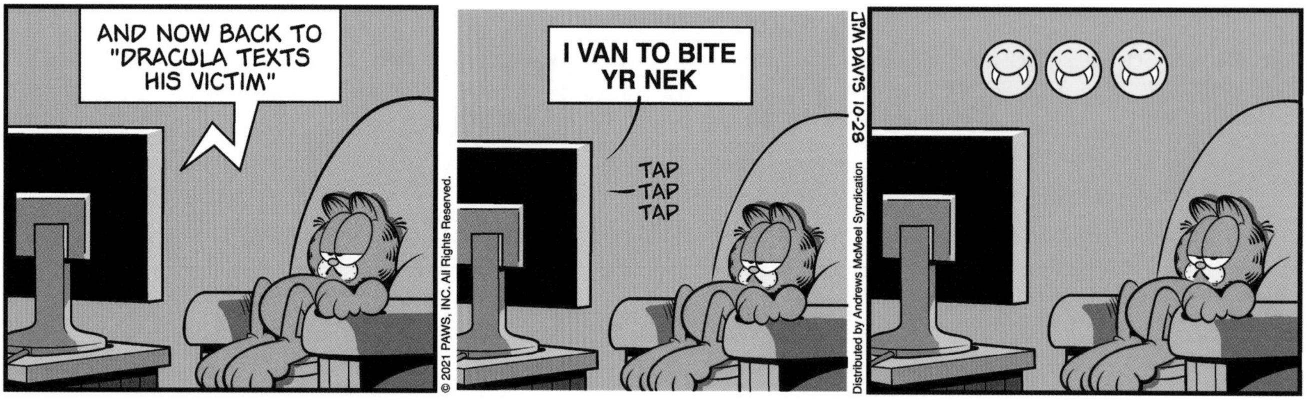
AND NOW BACK TO "DRACULA TEXTS HIS VICTIM"
© 2021 PAWS, INC. All Rights Reserved.
I VAN TO BITE YR NEK
TAP TAP TAP
JIM DAVIS 10-28
Distributed by Andrews McMeel Syndication

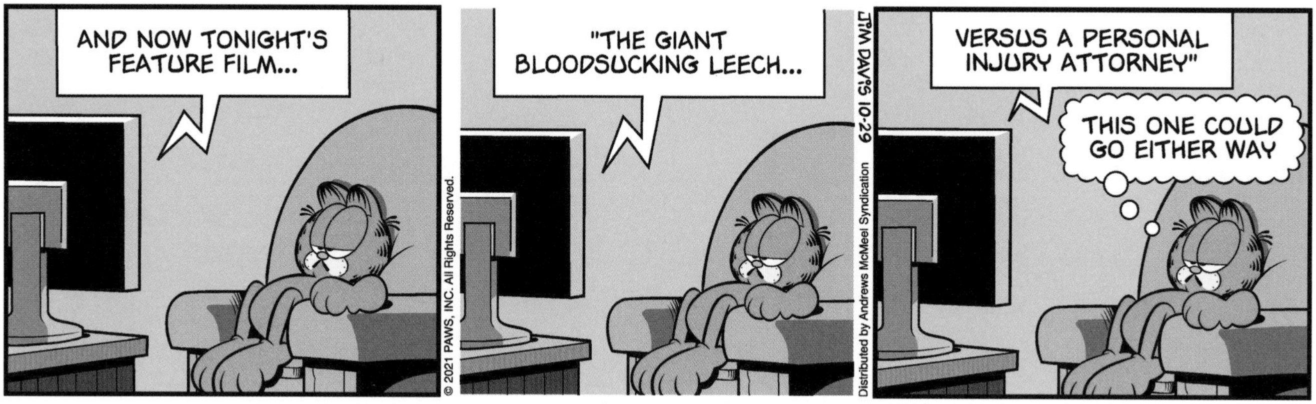
AND NOW TONIGHT'S FEATURE FILM...
© 2021 PAWS, INC. All Rights Reserved.
"THE GIANT BLOODSUCKING LEECH...
JIM DAVIS 10-29
Distributed by Andrews McMeel Syndication
VERSUS A PERSONAL INJURY ATTORNEY"
THIS ONE COULD GO EITHER WAY

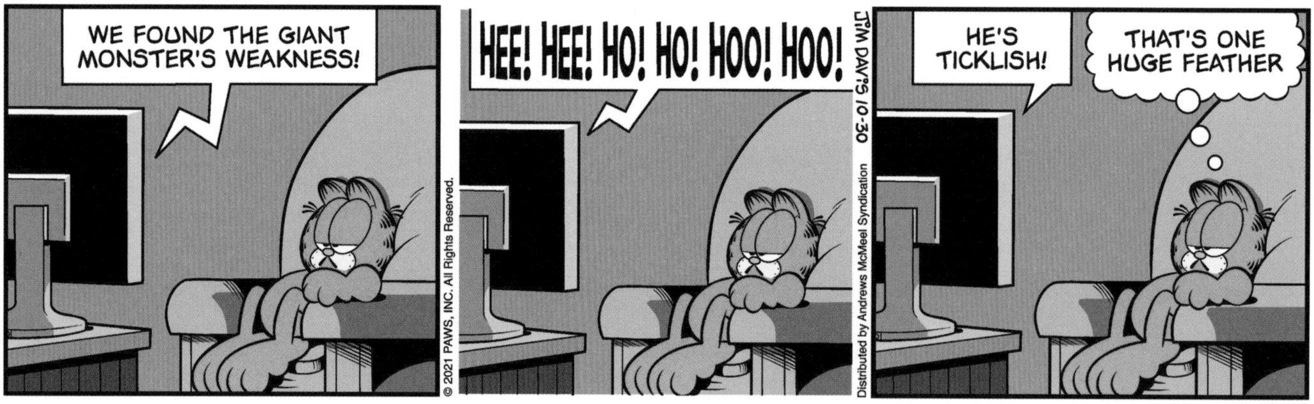
WE FOUND THE GIANT MONSTER'S WEAKNESS!
© 2021 PAWS, INC. All Rights Reserved.
HEE! HEE! HO! HO! HOO! HOO!
JIM DAVIS 10-30
Distributed by Andrews McMeel Syndication
HE'S TICKLISH!
THAT'S ONE HUGE FEATHER

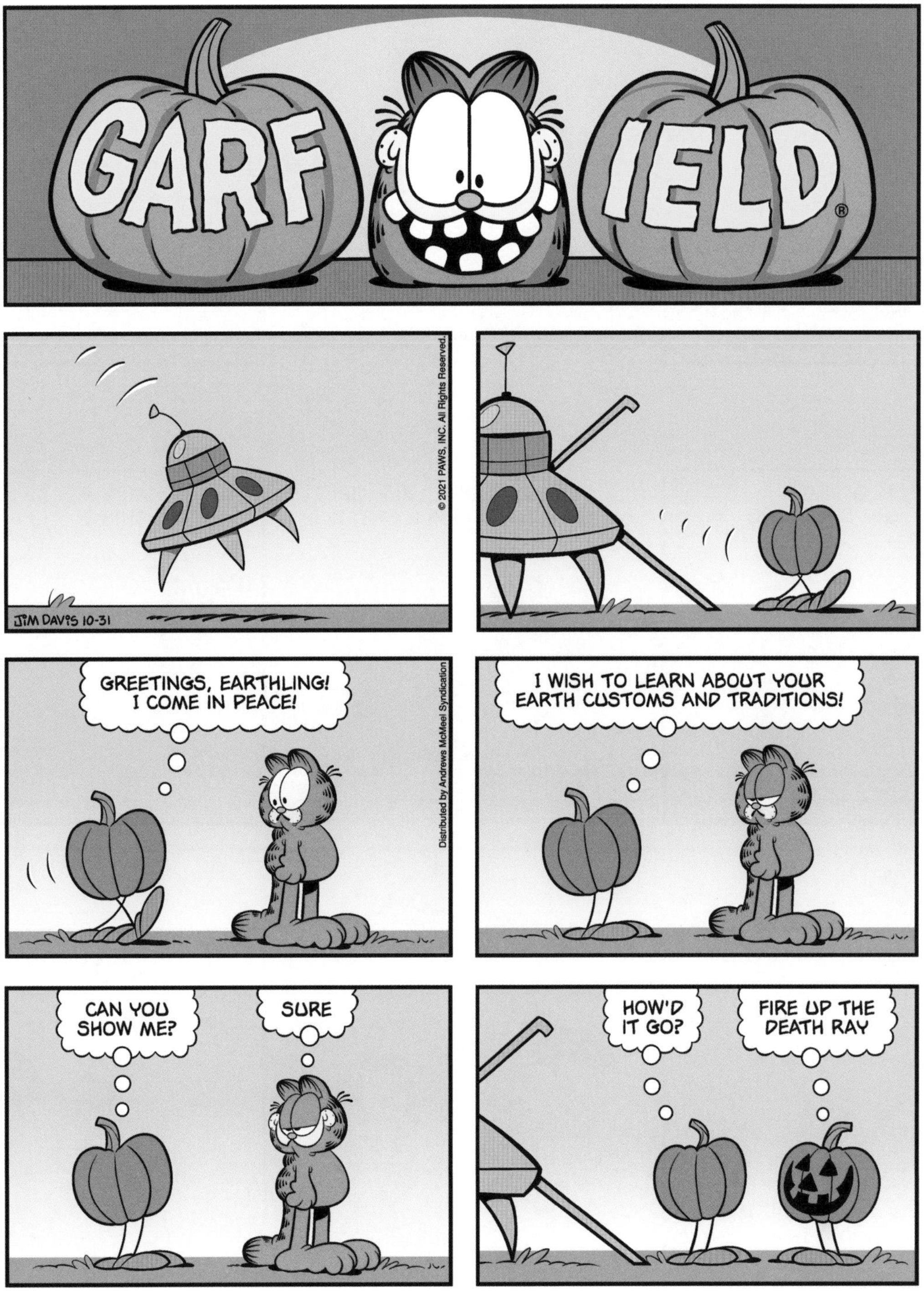
GARFIELD®
JIM DAVIS 10-31
© 2021 PAWS, INC. All Rights Reserved.
Distributed by Andrews McMeel Syndication
GREETINGS, EARTHLING! I COME IN PEACE!
I WISH TO LEARN ABOUT YOUR EARTH CUSTOMS AND TRADITIONS!
CAN YOU SHOW ME?
SURE
HOW'D IT GO?
FIRE UP THE DEATH RAY

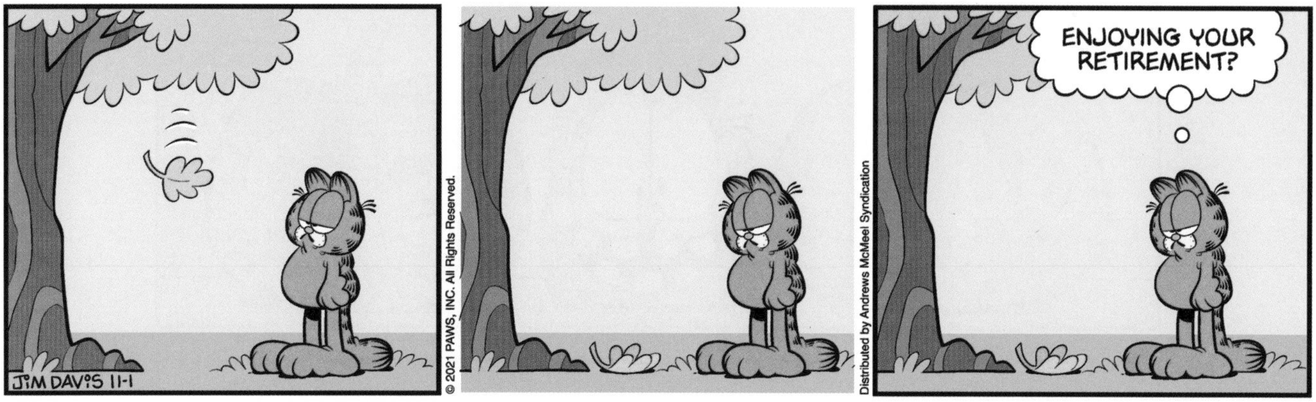
ENJOYING YOUR RETIREMENT?
JIM DAVIS 11-1
© 2021 PAWS, INC. All Rights Reserved.
Distributed by Andrews McMeel Syndication

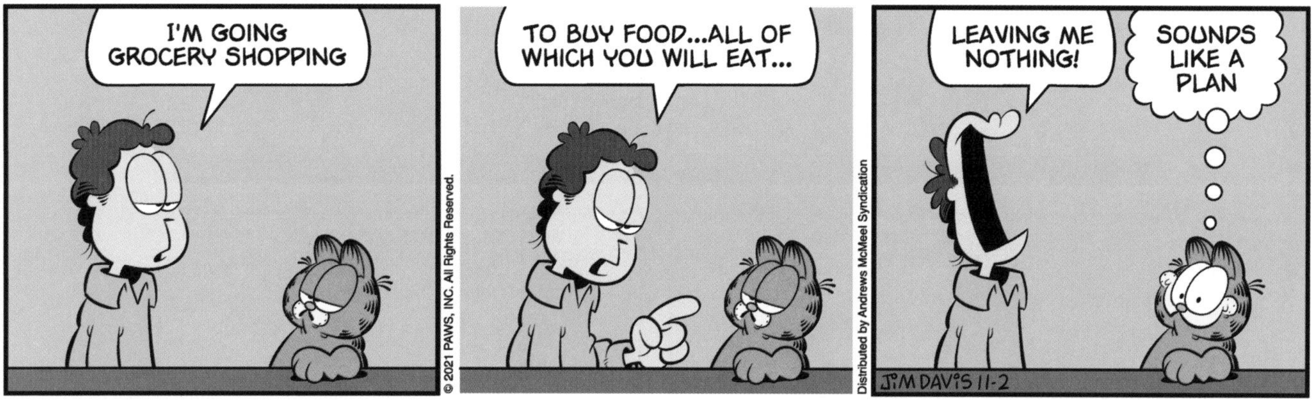
I'M GOING GROCERY SHOPPING
TO BUY FOOD...ALL OF WHICH YOU WILL EAT...
LEAVING ME NOTHING!
SOUNDS LIKE A PLAN
JIM DAVIS 11-2
© 2021 PAWS, INC. All Rights Reserved.
Distributed by Andrews McMeel Syndication

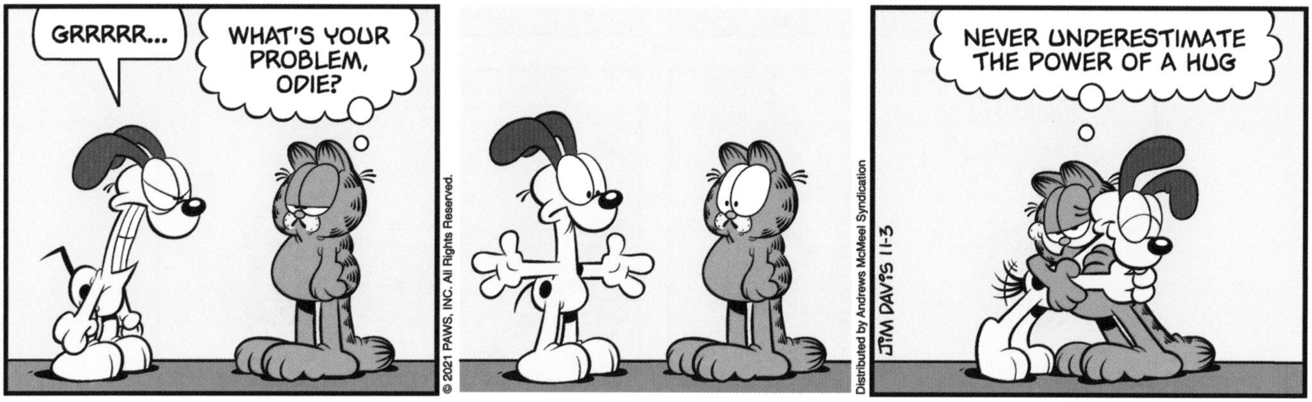
GRRRRR...
WHAT'S YOUR PROBLEM, ODIE?
NEVER UNDERESTIMATE THE POWER OF A HUG
JIM DAVIS 11-3
© 2021 PAWS, INC. All Rights Reserved.
Distributed by Andrews McMeel Syndication

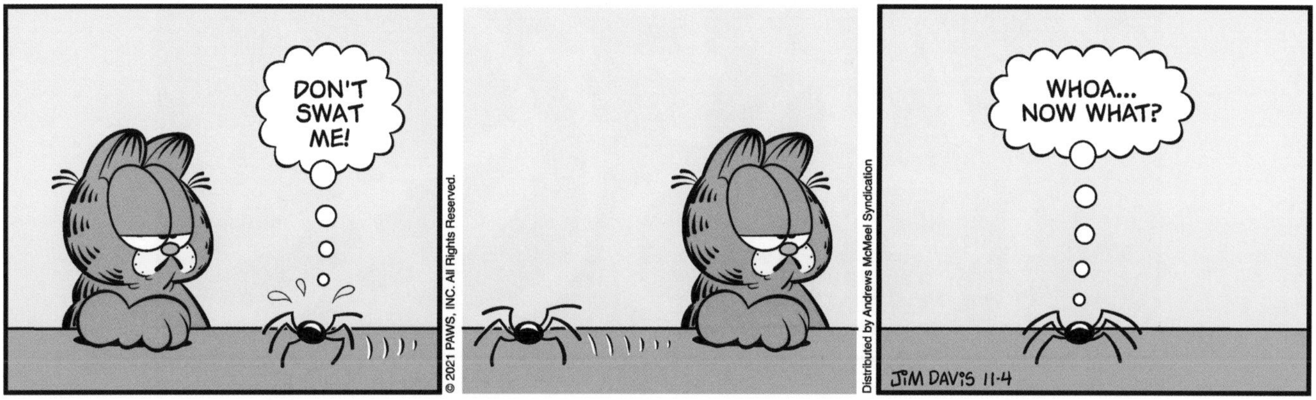
DON'T SWAT ME!
© 2021 PAWS, INC. All Rights Reserved.
Distributed by Andrews McMeel Syndication
WHOA... NOW WHAT?
JIM DAVIS 11-4

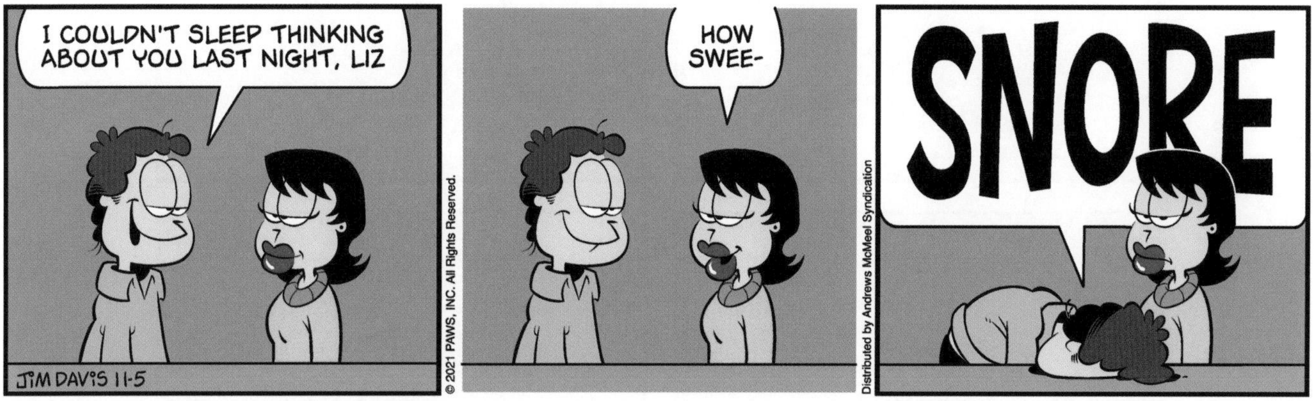
I COULDN'T SLEEP THINKING ABOUT YOU LAST NIGHT, LIZ
JIM DAVIS 11-5
© 2021 PAWS, INC. All Rights Reserved.
HOW SWEE-
Distributed by Andrews McMeel Syndication
SNORE

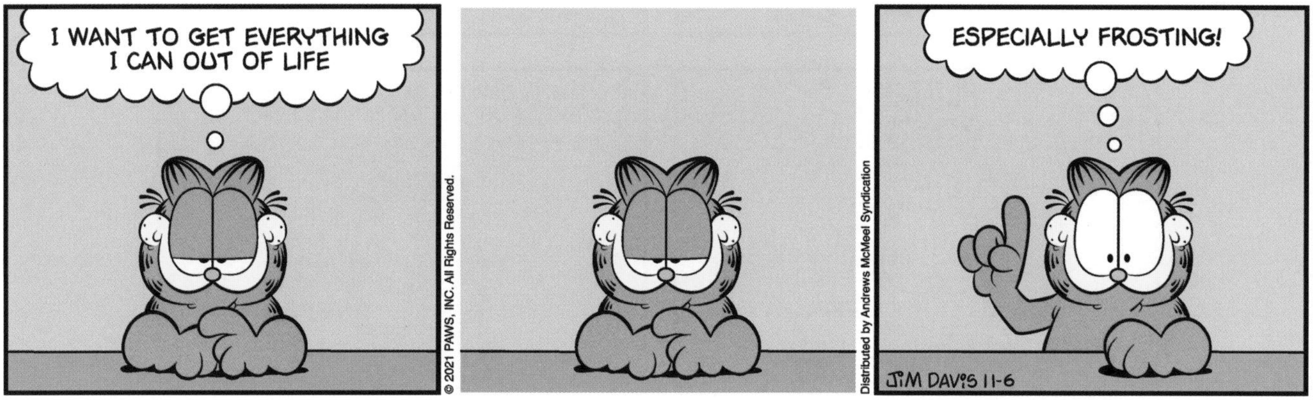
I WANT TO GET EVERYTHING I CAN OUT OF LIFE
© 2021 PAWS, INC. All Rights Reserved.
Distributed by Andrews McMeel Syndication
ESPECIALLY FROSTING!
JIM DAVIS 11-6

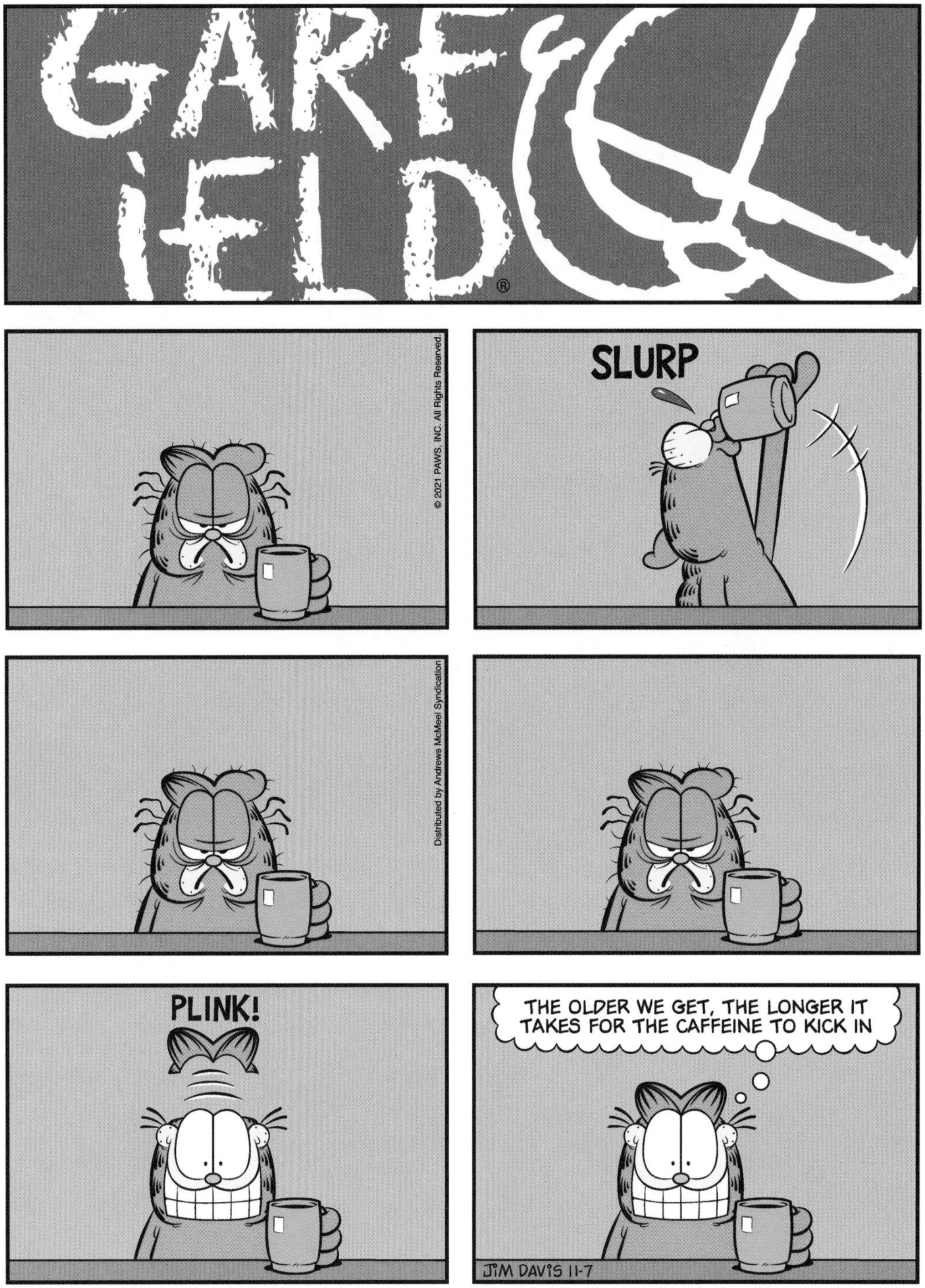
GARFIELD®
© 2021 PAWS, INC. All Rights Reserved.
SLURP
Distributed by Andrews McMeel Syndication
PLINK!
THE OLDER WE GET, THE LONGER IT TAKES FOR THE CAFFEINE TO KICK IN
JIM DAVIS 11-7

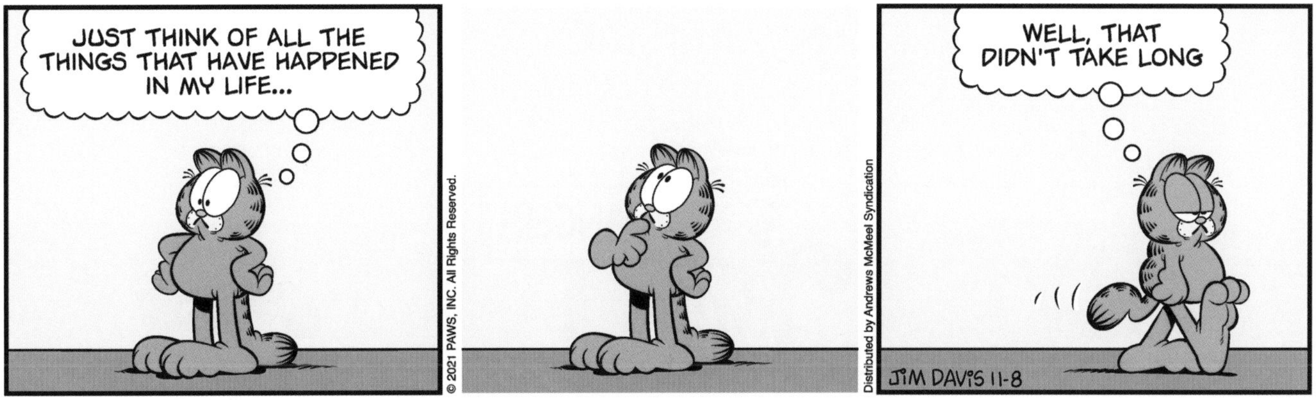
JUST THINK OF ALL THE THINGS THAT HAVE HAPPENED IN MY LIFE...
WELL, THAT DIDN'T TAKE LONG
JIM DAVIS 11-8
© 2021 PAWS, INC. All Rights Reserved.
Distributed by Andrews McMeel Syndication

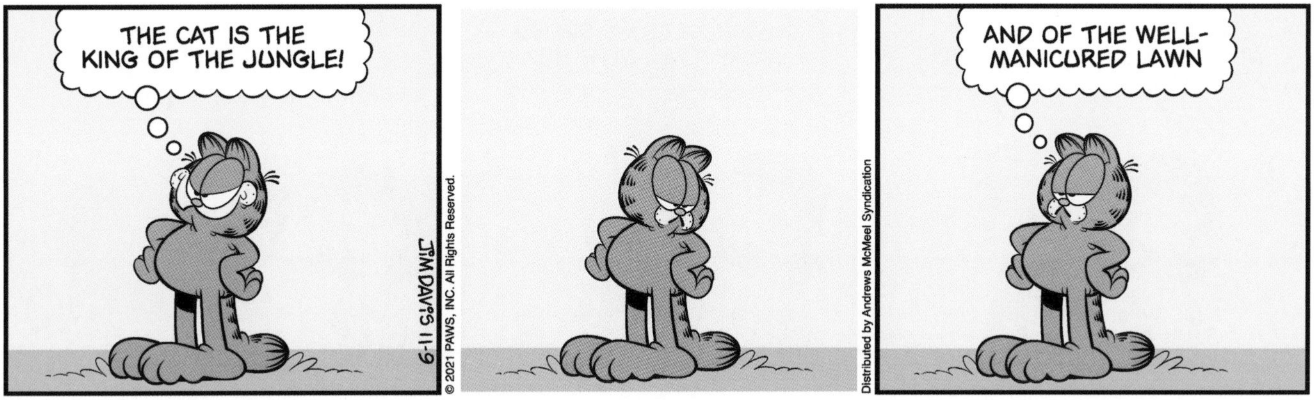
THE CAT IS THE KING OF THE JUNGLE!
JIM DAVIS 11-9
AND OF THE WELL-MANICURED LAWN
© 2021 PAWS, INC. All Rights Reserved.
Distributed by Andrews McMeel Syndication

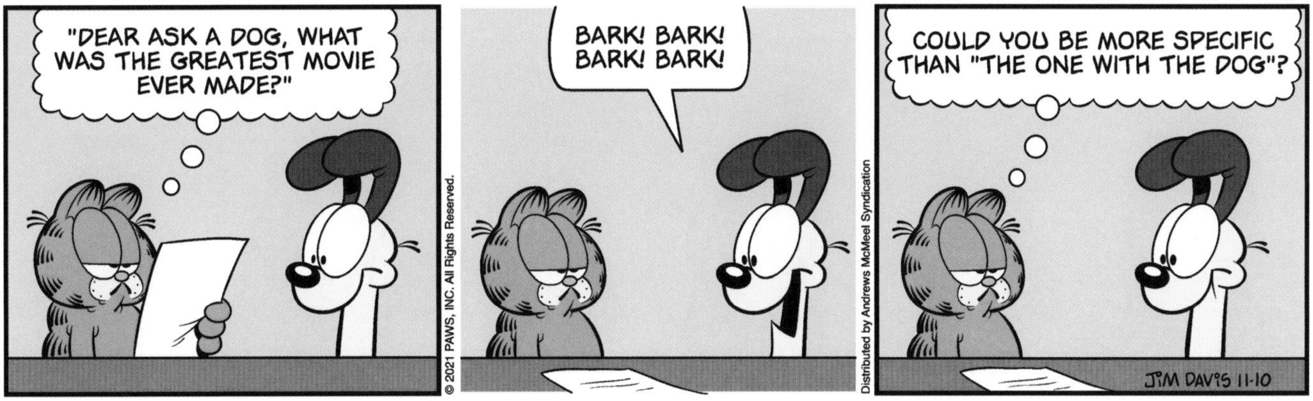
"DEAR ASK A DOG, WHAT WAS THE GREATEST MOVIE EVER MADE?"
BARK! BARK! BARK! BARK!
COULD YOU BE MORE SPECIFIC THAN "THE ONE WITH THE DOG"?
JIM DAVIS 11-10
© 2021 PAWS, INC. All Rights Reserved.
Distributed by Andrews McMeel Syndication

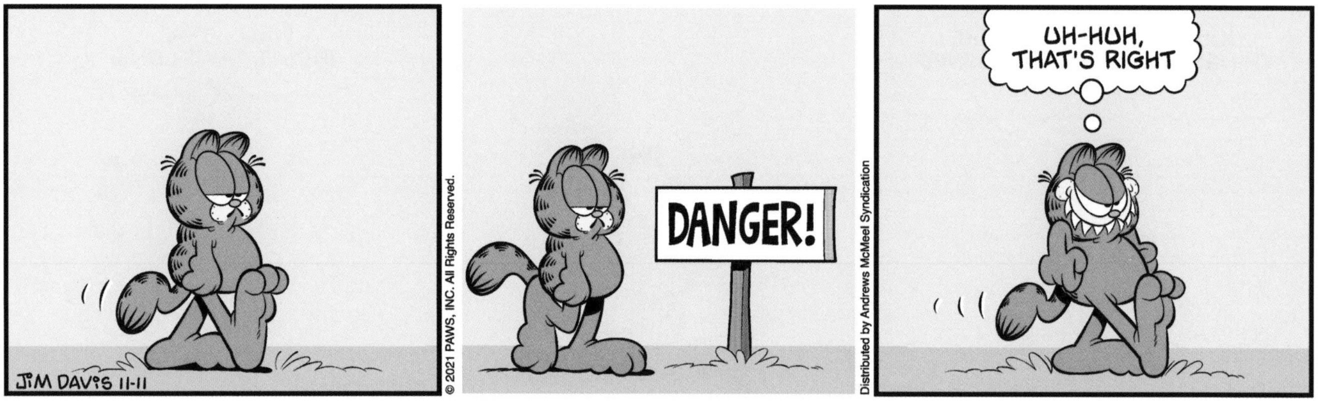
JIM DAVIS 11-11
© 2021 PAWS, INC. All Rights Reserved.
DANGER!
Distributed by Andrews McMeel Syndication
UH-HUH, THAT'S RIGHT

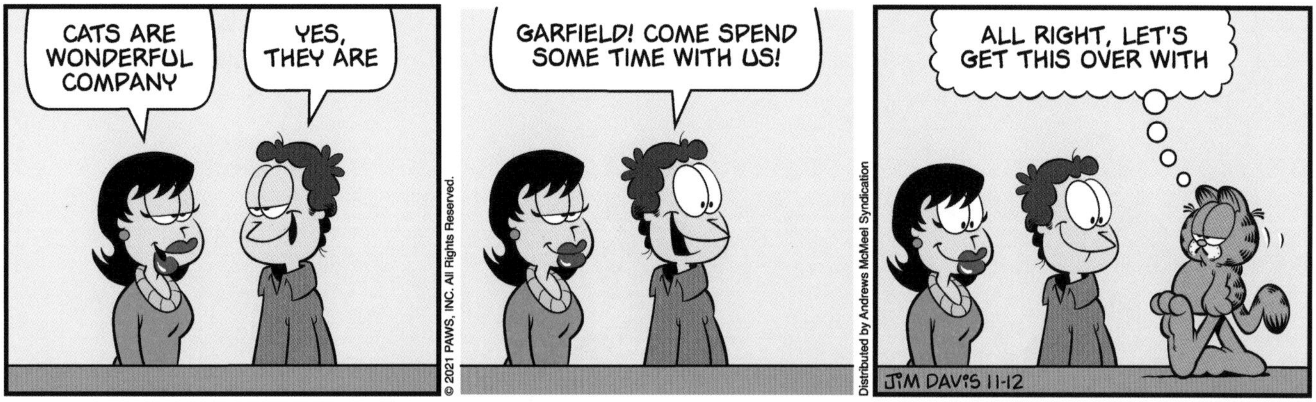
CATS ARE WONDERFUL COMPANY
YES, THEY ARE
© 2021 PAWS, INC. All Rights Reserved.
GARFIELD! COME SPEND SOME TIME WITH US!
Distributed by Andrews McMeel Syndication
ALL RIGHT, LET'S GET THIS OVER WITH
JIM DAVIS 11-12

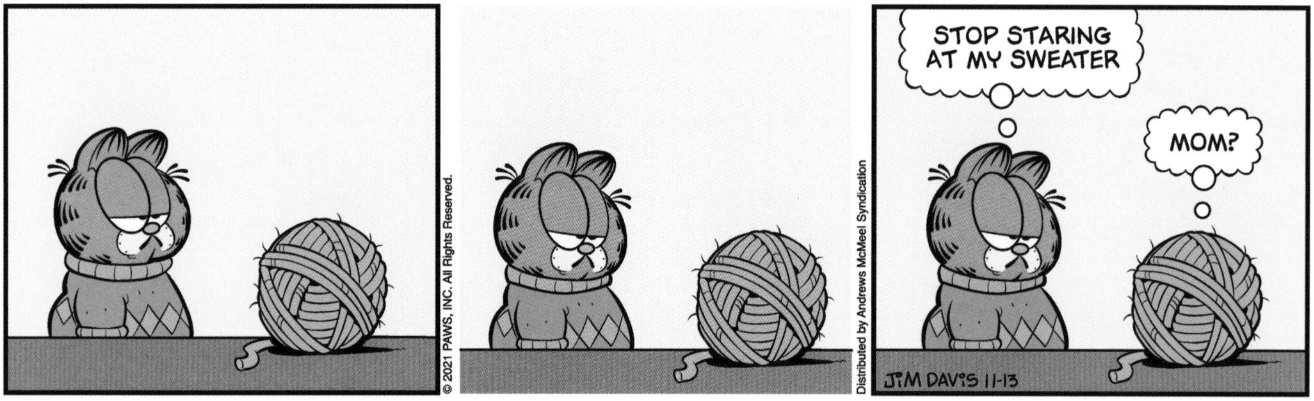
© 2021 PAWS, INC. All Rights Reserved.
Distributed by Andrews McMeel Syndication
STOP STARING AT MY SWEATER
MOM?
JIM DAVIS 11-13

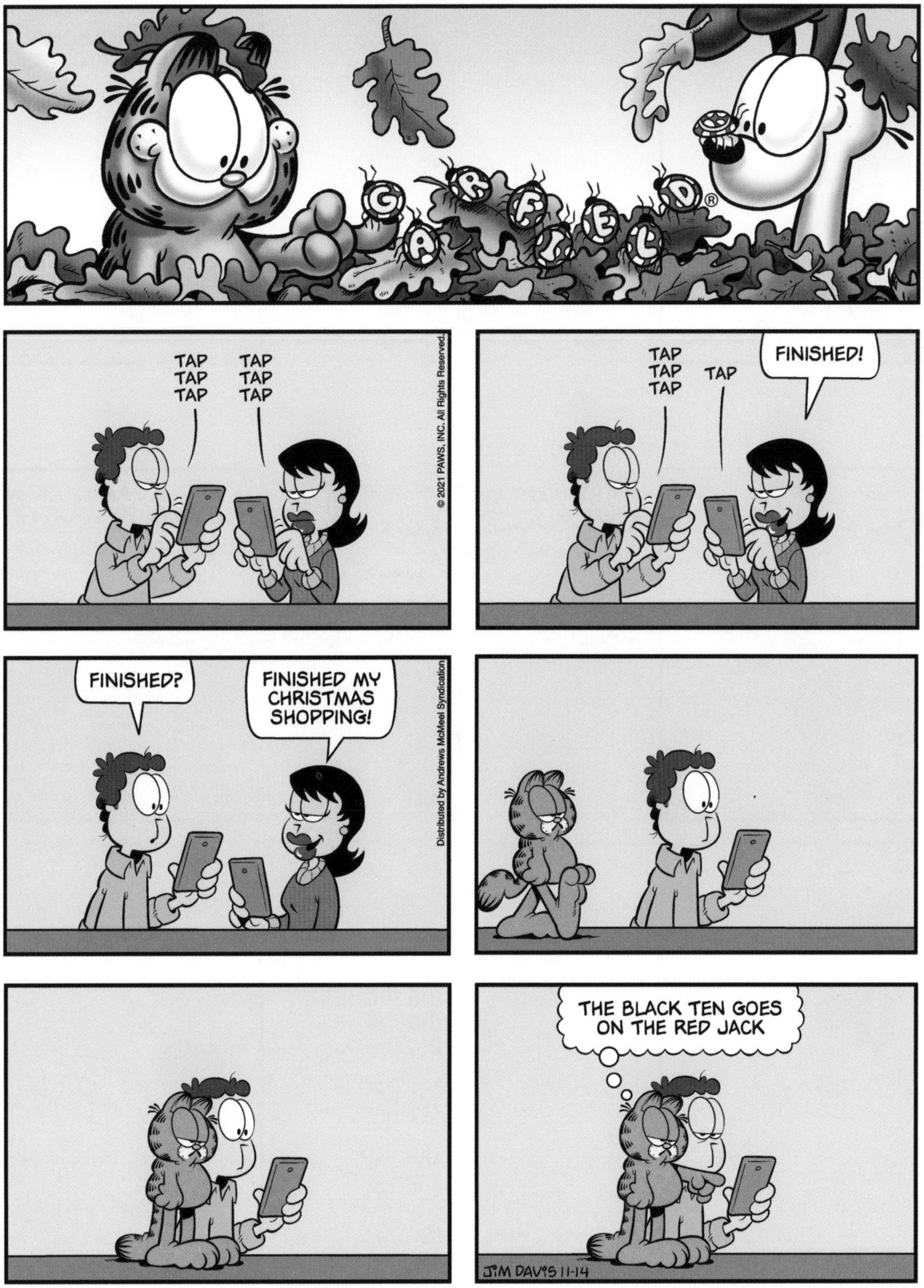
GARFIELD®
TAP TAP TAP
TAP TAP TAP
© 2021 PAWS, INC. All Rights Reserved.
TAP TAP TAP
TAP
FINISHED!
FINISHED?
FINISHED MY CHRISTMAS SHOPPING!
Distributed by Andrews McMeel Syndication
THE BLACK TEN GOES ON THE RED JACK
JIM DAVIS 11-14

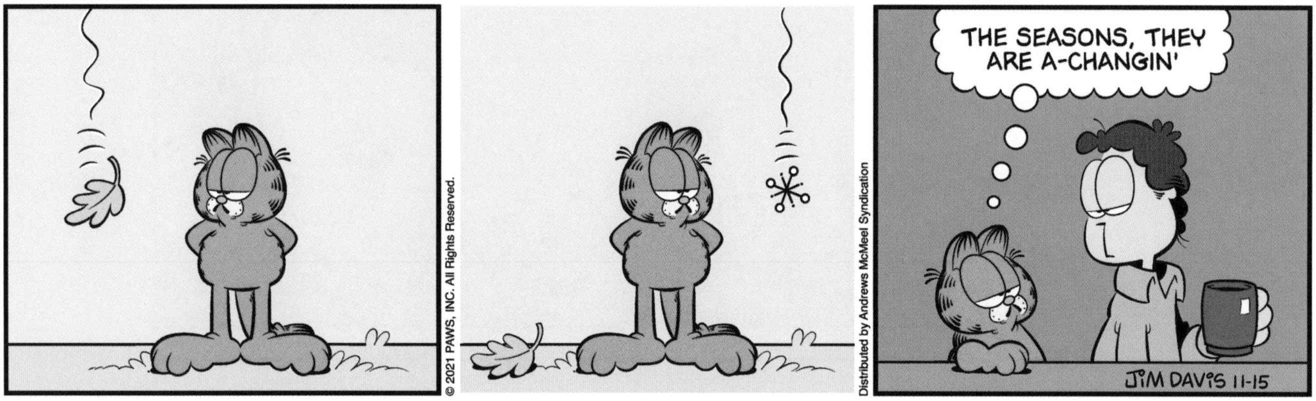

© 2021 PAWS, INC. All Rights Reserved.
Distributed by Andrews McMeel Syndication
THE SEASONS, THEY ARE A-CHANGIN'
JIM DAVIS 11-15


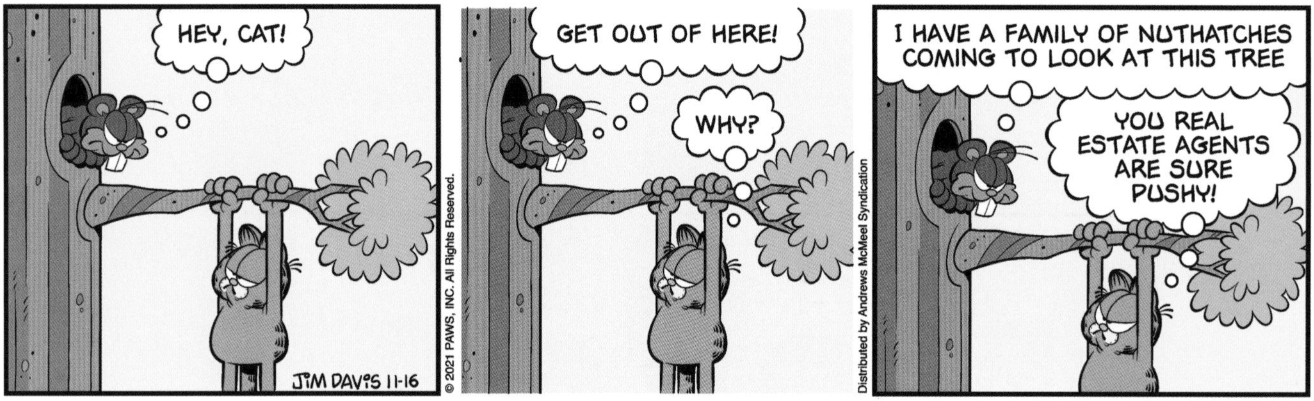

HEY, CAT!
JIM DAVIS 11-16
© 2021 PAWS, INC. All Rights Reserved.
GET OUT OF HERE!
WHY?
Distributed by Andrews McMeel Syndication
I HAVE A FAMILY OF NUTHATCHES COMING TO LOOK AT THIS TREE
YOU REAL ESTATE AGENTS ARE SURE PUSHY!


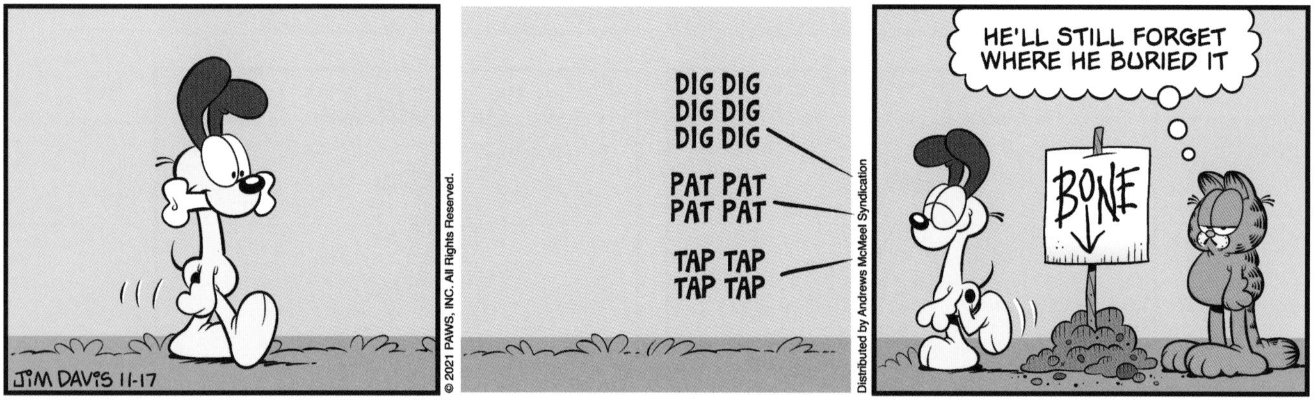

JIM DAVIS 11-17
© 2021 PAWS, INC. All Rights Reserved.
DIG DIG
DIG DIG
DIG DIG
PAT PAT
PAT PAT
TAP TAP
TAP TAP
Distributed by Andrews McMeel Syndication
HE'LL STILL FORGET WHERE HE BURIED IT
BONE

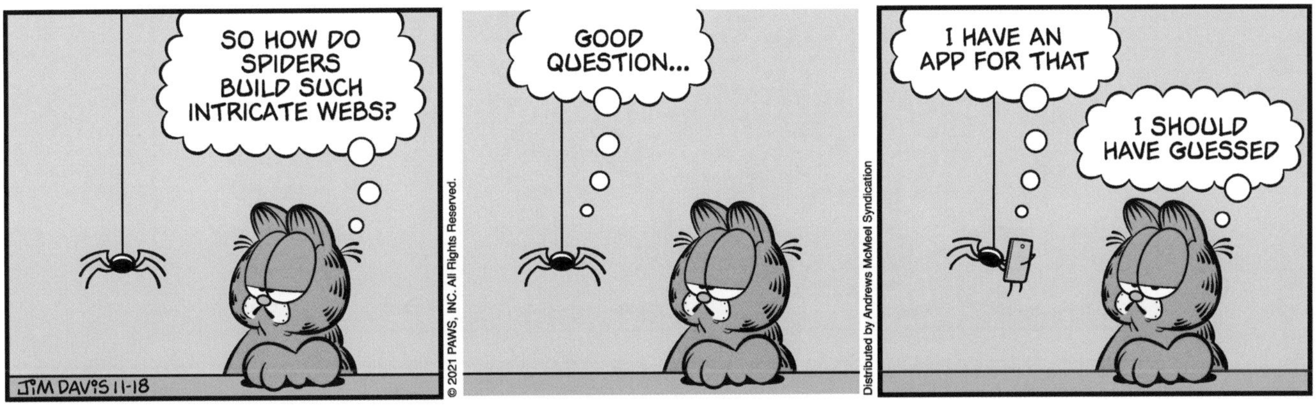
SO HOW DO SPIDERS BUILD SUCH INTRICATE WEBS?
GOOD QUESTION...
I HAVE AN APP FOR THAT
I SHOULD HAVE GUESSED
JIM DAVIS 11-18
© 2021 PAWS, INC. All Rights Reserved.
Distributed by Andrews McMeel Syndication

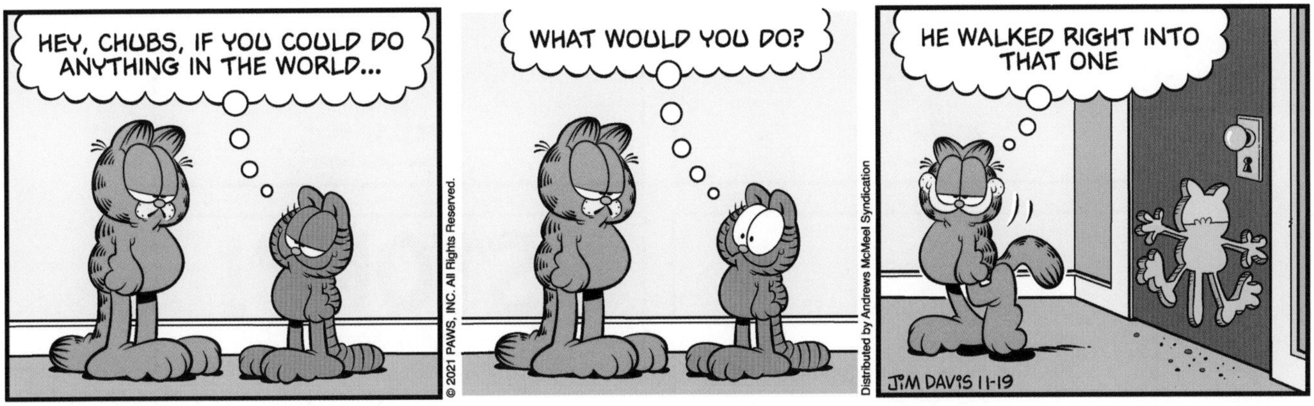
HEY, CHUBS, IF YOU COULD DO ANYTHING IN THE WORLD...
WHAT WOULD YOU DO?
HE WALKED RIGHT INTO THAT ONE
JIM DAVIS 11-19
© 2021 PAWS, INC. All Rights Reserved.
Distributed by Andrews McMeel Syndication

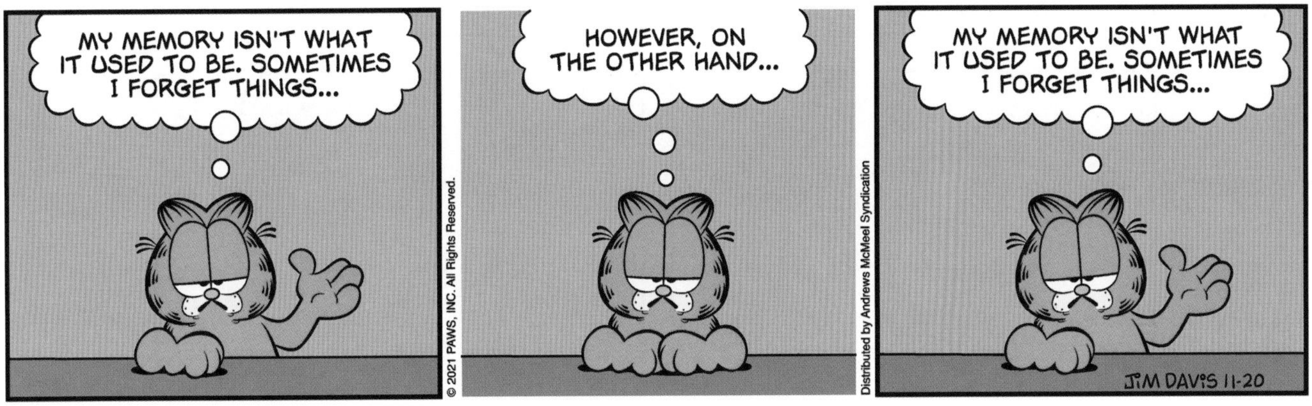
MY MEMORY ISN'T WHAT IT USED TO BE. SOMETIMES I FORGET THINGS...
HOWEVER, ON THE OTHER HAND...
MY MEMORY ISN'T WHAT IT USED TO BE. SOMETIMES I FORGET THINGS...
JIM DAVIS 11-20
© 2021 PAWS, INC. All Rights Reserved.
Distributed by Andrews McMeel Syndication

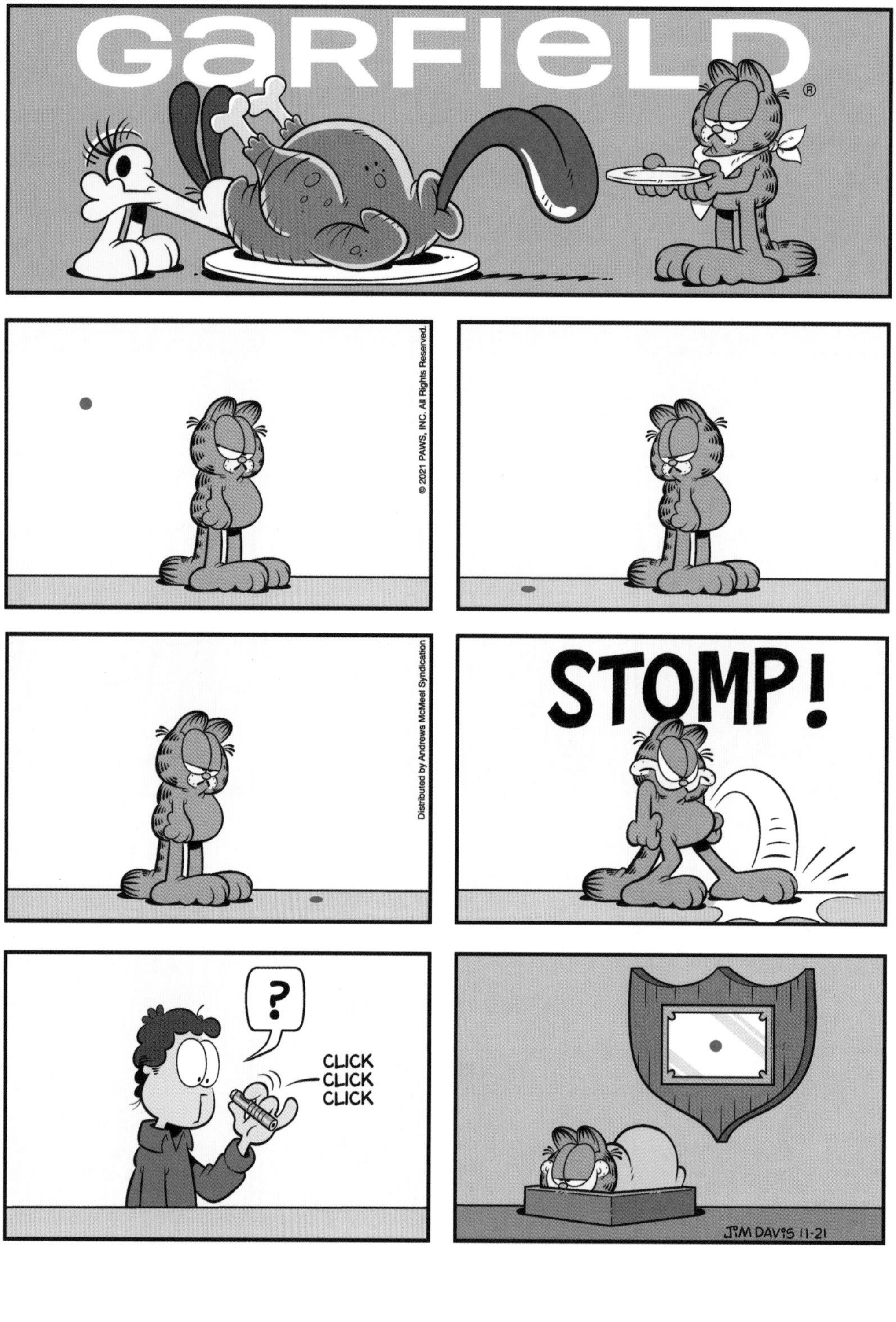
GARFIELD
© 2021 PAWS, INC. All Rights Reserved.
Distributed by Andrews McMeel Syndication
STOMP!
?
CLICK
CLICK
CLICK
JIM DAVIS 11-21

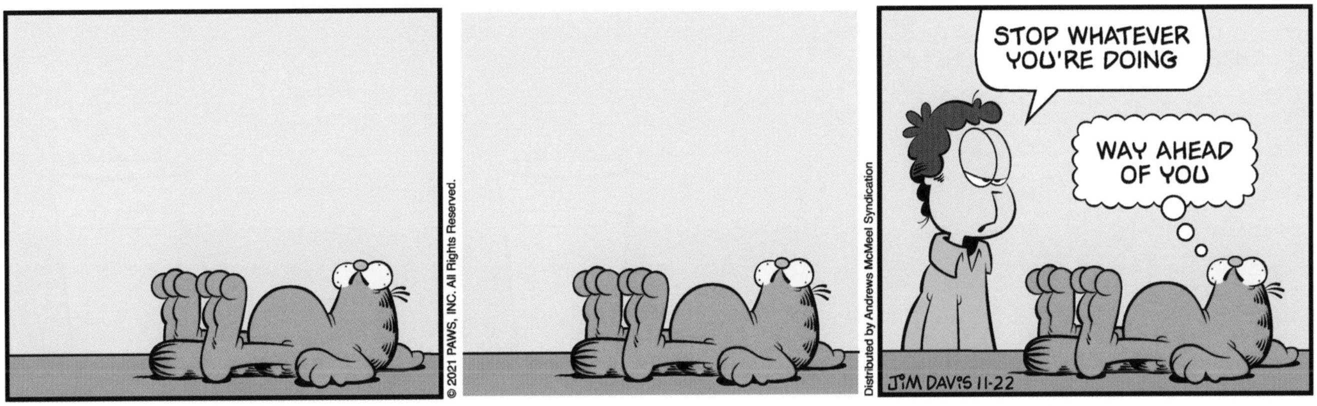
© 2021 PAWS, INC. All Rights Reserved.
Distributed by Andrews McMeel Syndication
STOP WHATEVER YOU'RE DOING
WAY AHEAD OF YOU
JIM DAVIS 11-22

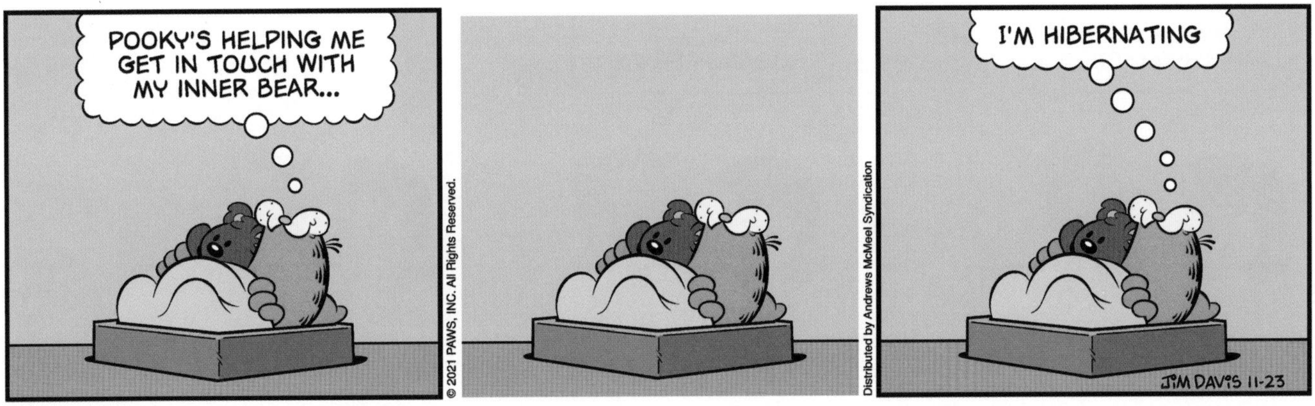
POOKY'S HELPING ME GET IN TOUCH WITH MY INNER BEAR...
© 2021 PAWS, INC. All Rights Reserved.
Distributed by Andrews McMeel Syndication
I'M HIBERNATING
JIM DAVIS 11-23

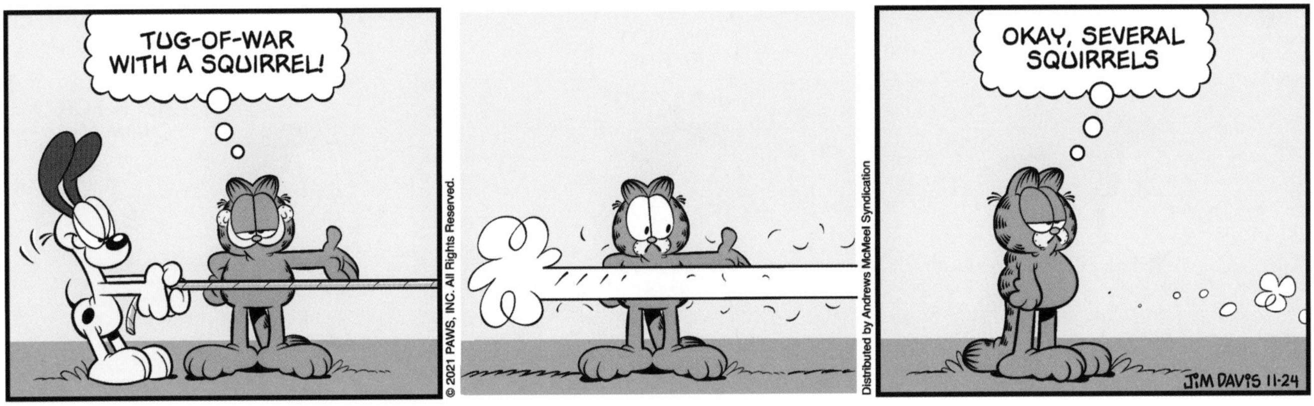
TUG-OF-WAR WITH A SQUIRREL!
© 2021 PAWS, INC. All Rights Reserved.
Distributed by Andrews McMeel Syndication
OKAY, SEVERAL SQUIRRELS
JIM DAVIS 11-24

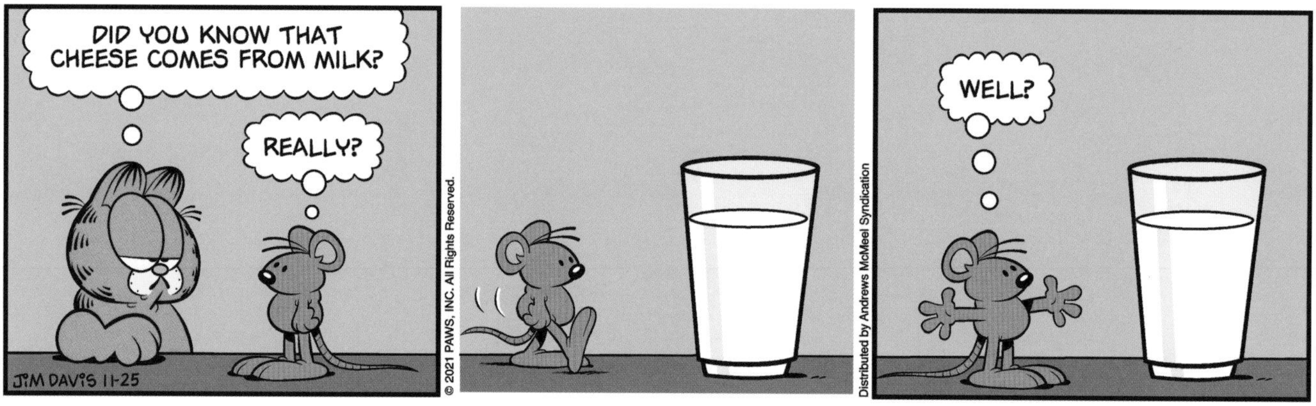
DID YOU KNOW THAT CHEESE COMES FROM MILK?
REALLY?
JIM DAVIS 11-25
© 2021 PAWS, INC. All Rights Reserved.
Distributed by Andrews McMeel Syndication
WELL?

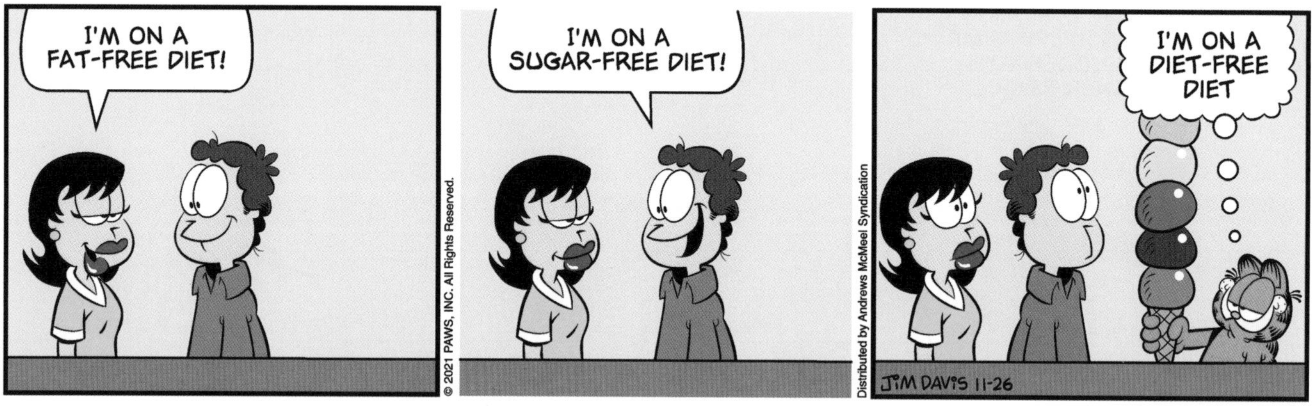
I'M ON A FAT-FREE DIET!
© 2021 PAWS, INC. All Rights Reserved.
I'M ON A SUGAR-FREE DIET!
Distributed by Andrews McMeel Syndication
I'M ON A DIET-FREE DIET
JIM DAVIS 11-26

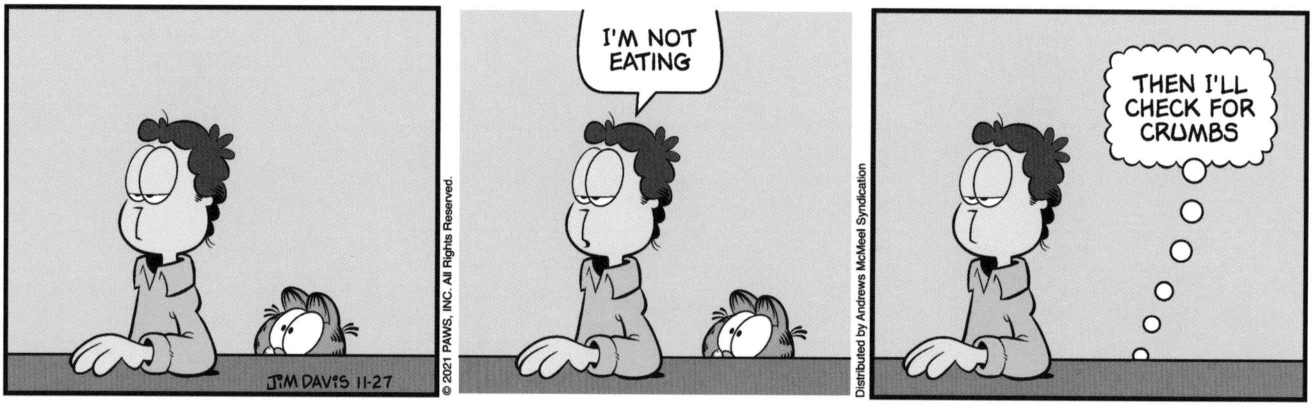
JIM DAVIS 11-27
© 2021 PAWS, INC. All Rights Reserved.
I'M NOT EATING
Distributed by Andrews McMeel Syndication
THEN I'LL CHECK FOR CRUMBS

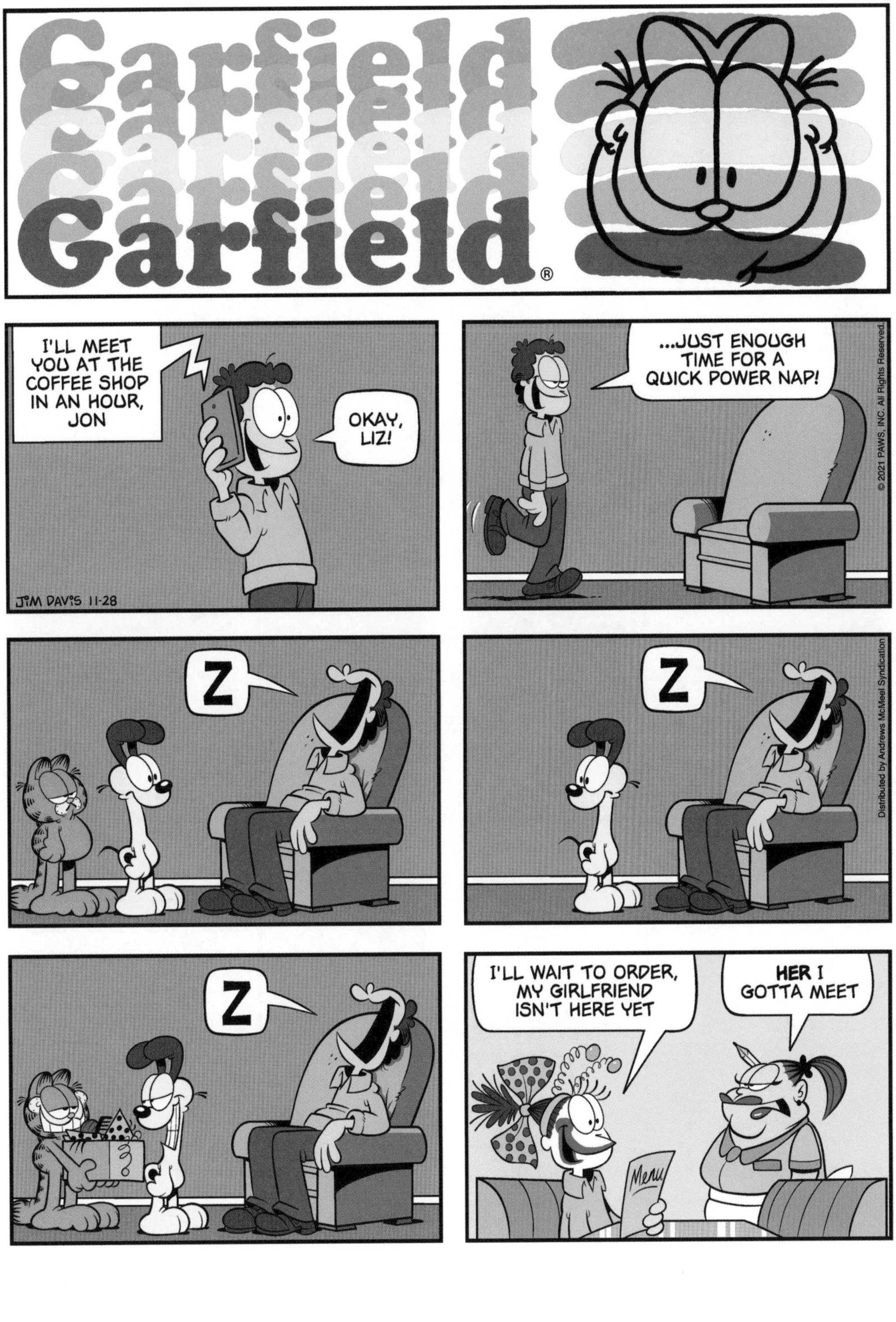
Garfield
I'LL MEET YOU AT THE COFFEE SHOP IN AN HOUR, JON
OKAY, LIZ!
JIM DAVIS 11-28
...JUST ENOUGH TIME FOR A QUICK POWER NAP!
© 2021 PAWS, INC. All Rights Reserved.
Z
Z
Distributed by Andrews McMeel Syndication
Z
I'LL WAIT TO ORDER, MY GIRLFRIEND ISN'T HERE YET
HER I GOTTA MEET
Menu

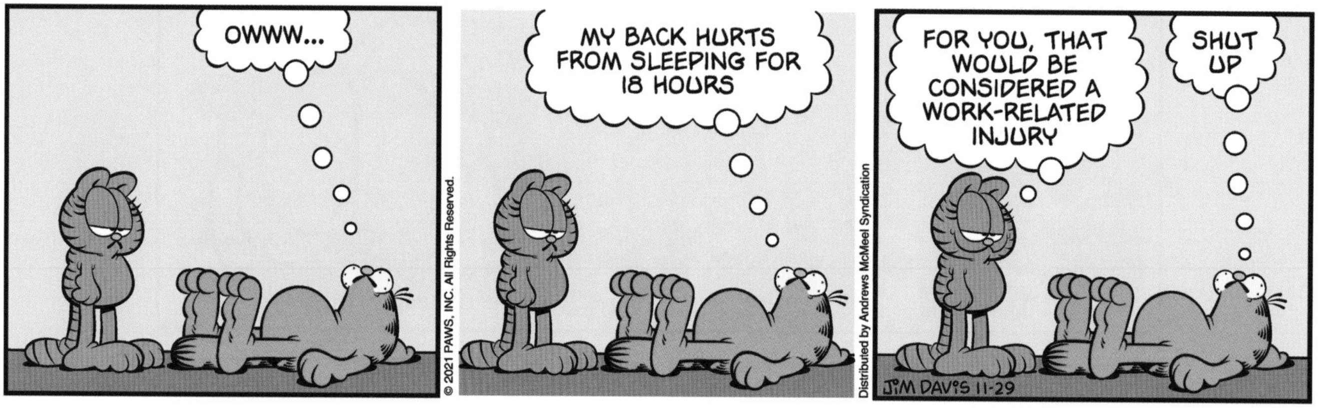
OWWW...
MY BACK HURTS FROM SLEEPING FOR 18 HOURS
FOR YOU, THAT WOULD BE CONSIDERED A WORK-RELATED INJURY
SHUT UP
JIM DAVIS 11-29


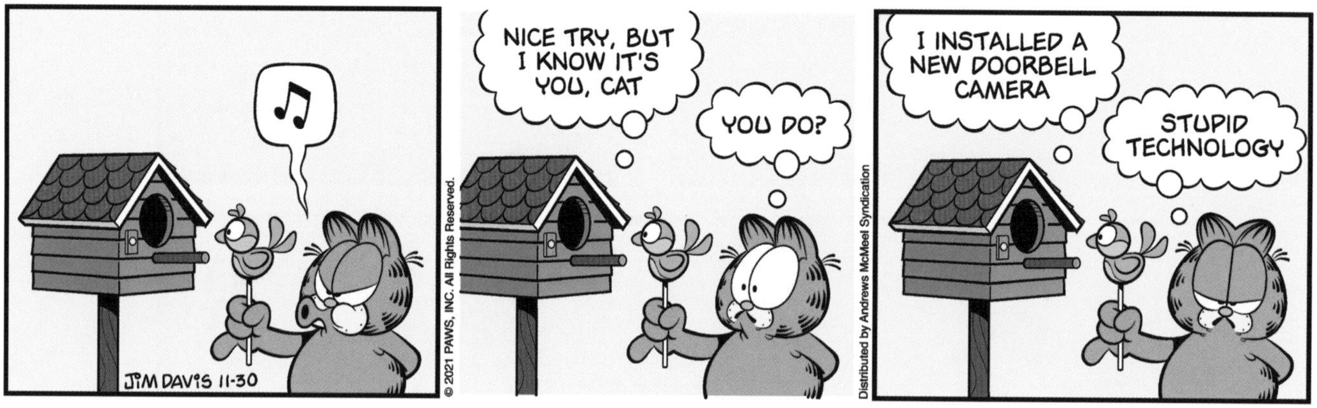
♫
JIM DAVIS 11-30
NICE TRY, BUT I KNOW IT'S YOU, CAT
YOU DO?
I INSTALLED A NEW DOORBELL CAMERA
STUPID TECHNOLOGY


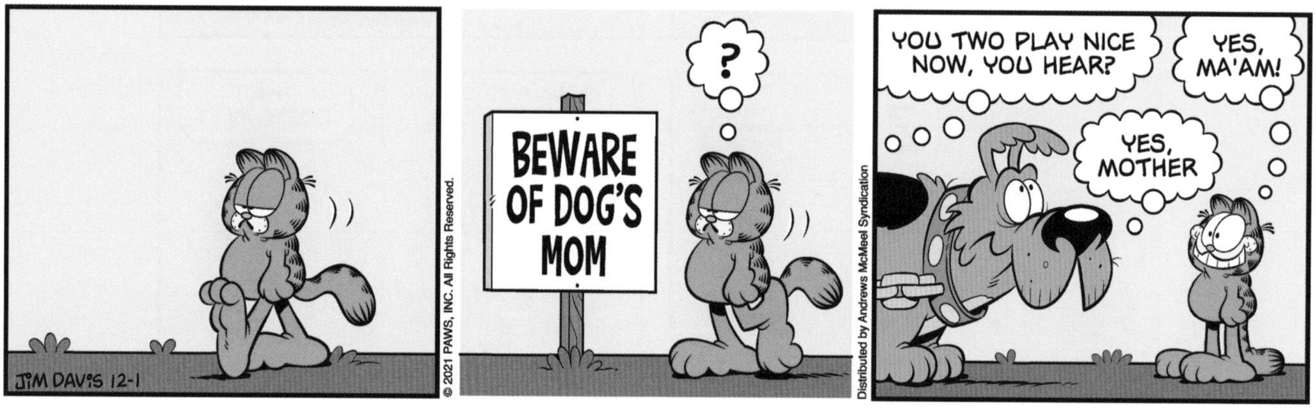
JIM DAVIS 12-1
BEWARE OF DOG'S MOM
?
YOU TWO PLAY NICE NOW, YOU HEAR?
YES, MA'AM!
YES, MOTHER

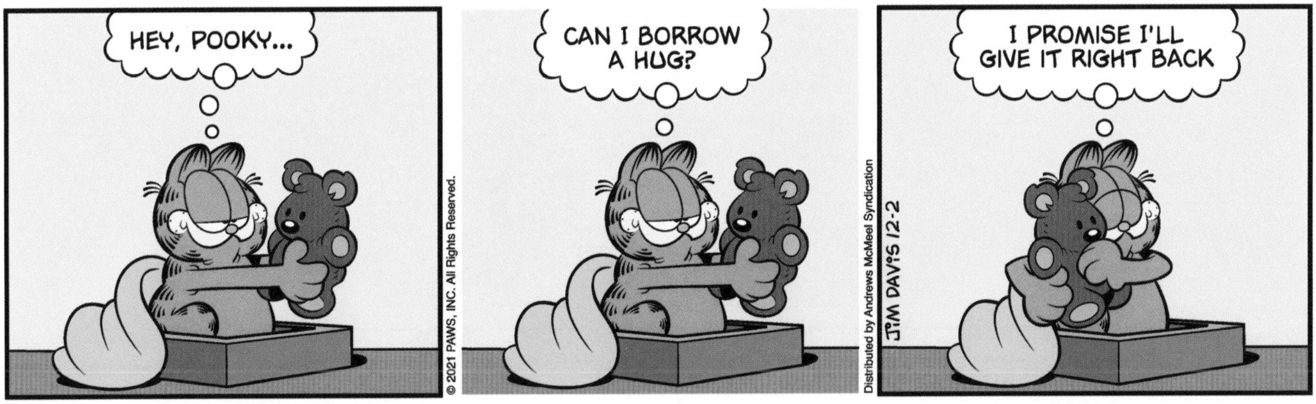
HEY, POOKY...
CAN I BORROW A HUG?
I PROMISE I'LL GIVE IT RIGHT BACK
JIM DAVIS 12-2
© 2021 PAWS, INC. All Rights Reserved.
Distributed by Andrews McMeel Syndication

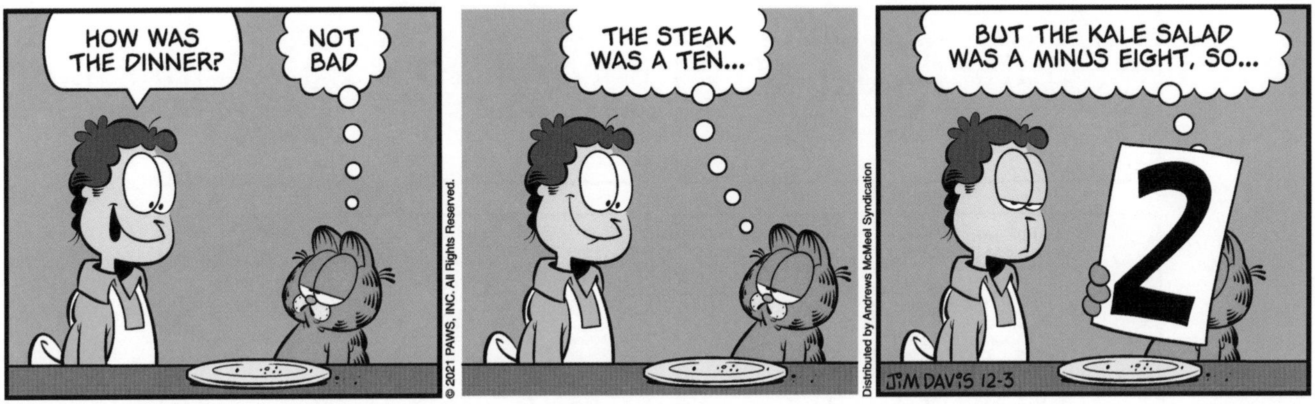
HOW WAS THE DINNER?
NOT BAD
THE STEAK WAS A TEN...
BUT THE KALE SALAD WAS A MINUS EIGHT, SO...
2
JIM DAVIS 12-3
© 2021 PAWS, INC. All Rights Reserved.
Distributed by Andrews McMeel Syndication

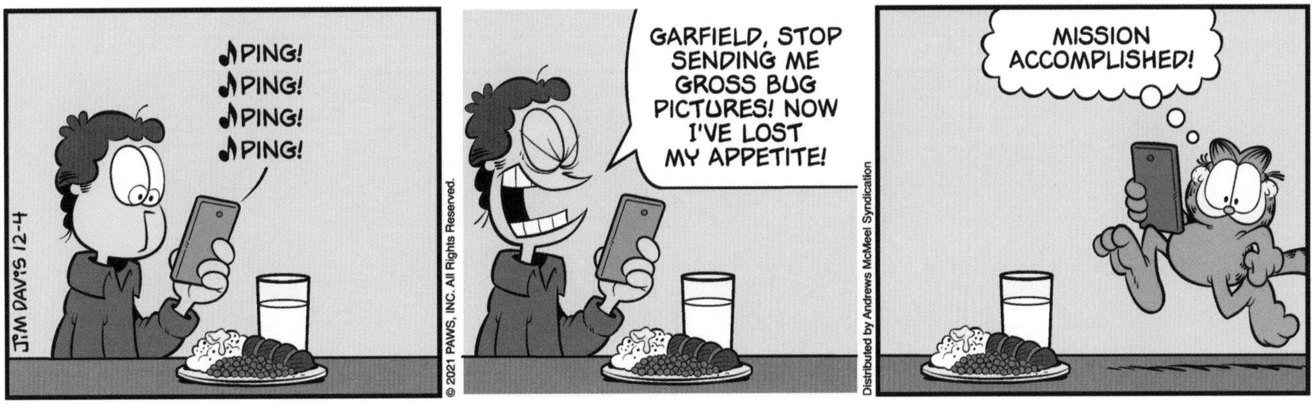
PING!
PING!
PING!
PING!
JIM DAVIS 12-4
GARFIELD, STOP SENDING ME GROSS BUG PICTURES! NOW I'VE LOST MY APPETITE!
MISSION ACCOMPLISHED!
© 2021 PAWS, INC. All Rights Reserved.
Distributed by Andrews McMeel Syndication

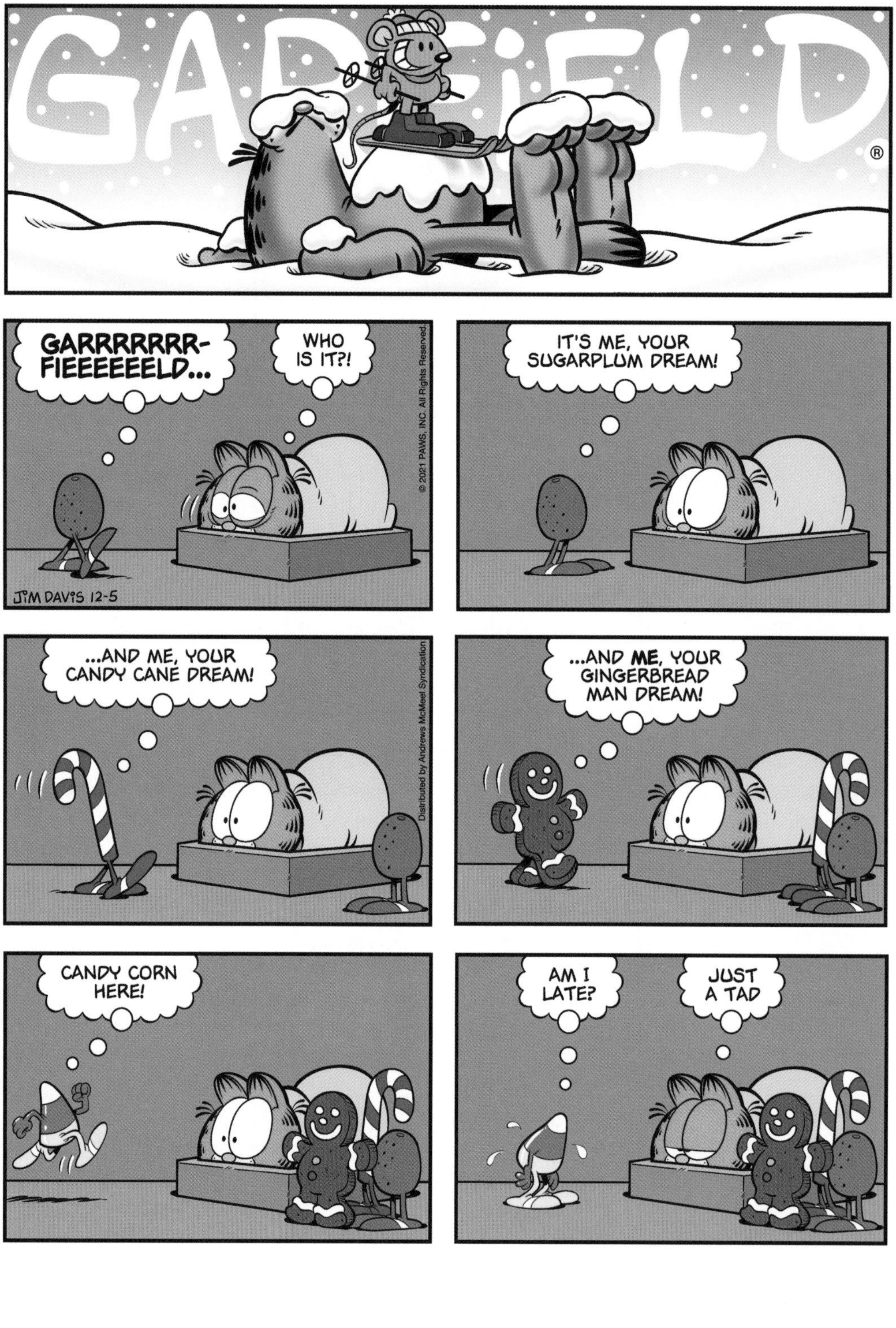
GARFIELD®
GARRRRRRR-FIEEEEEELD...
WHO IS IT?!
© 2021 PAWS, INC. All Rights Reserved.
JIM DAVIS 12-5
IT'S ME, YOUR SUGARPLUM DREAM!
...AND ME, YOUR CANDY CANE DREAM!
Distributed by Andrews McMeel Syndication
...AND **ME**, YOUR GINGERBREAD MAN DREAM!
CANDY CORN HERE!
AM I LATE?
JUST A TAD

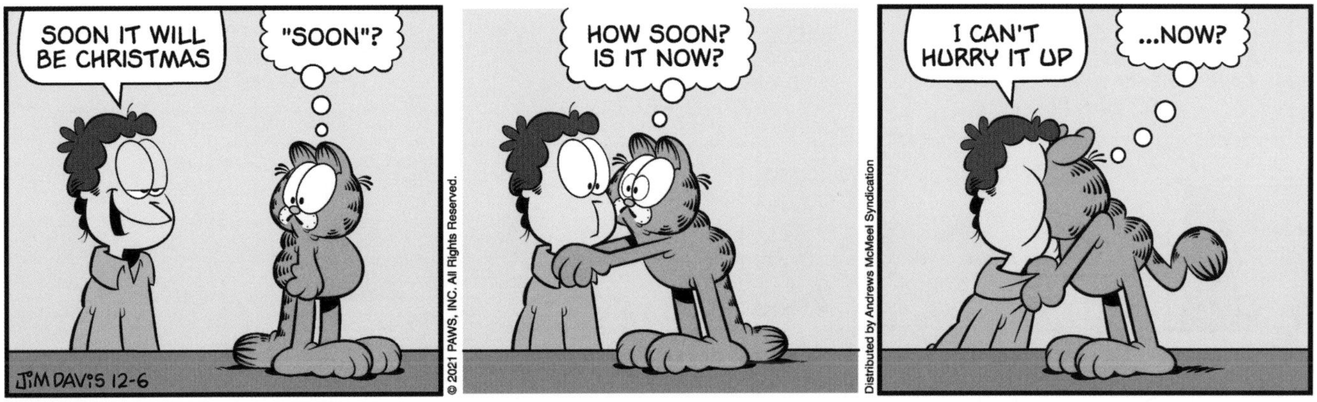
SOON IT WILL BE CHRISTMAS
"SOON"?
JIM DAVIS 12-6
© 2021 PAWS, INC. All Rights Reserved.
HOW SOON? IS IT NOW?
Distributed by Andrews McMeel Syndication
I CAN'T HURRY IT UP
...NOW?

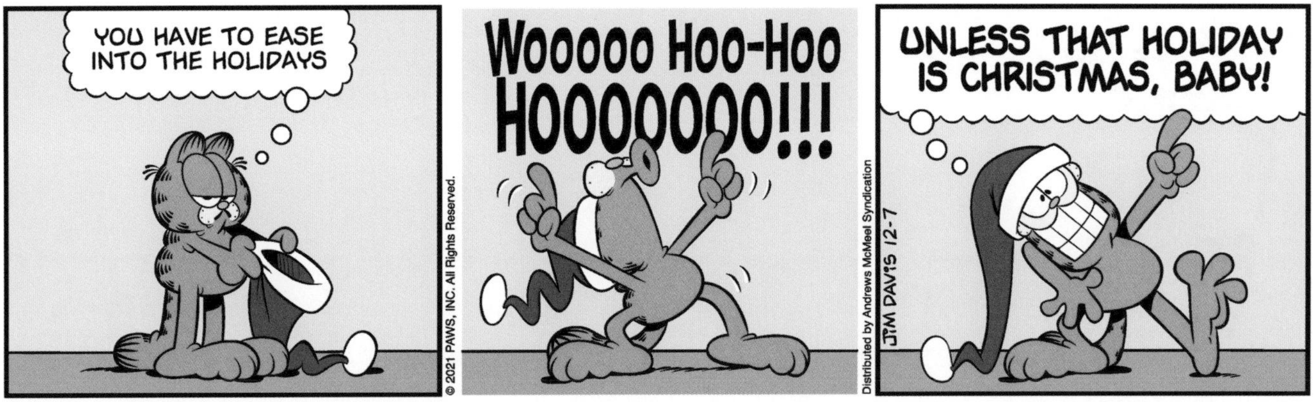
YOU HAVE TO EASE INTO THE HOLIDAYS
© 2021 PAWS, INC. All Rights Reserved.
WOOOOO HOO-HOO HOOOOOOO!!!
Distributed by Andrews McMeel Syndication
JIM DAVIS 12-7
UNLESS THAT HOLIDAY IS CHRISTMAS, BABY!

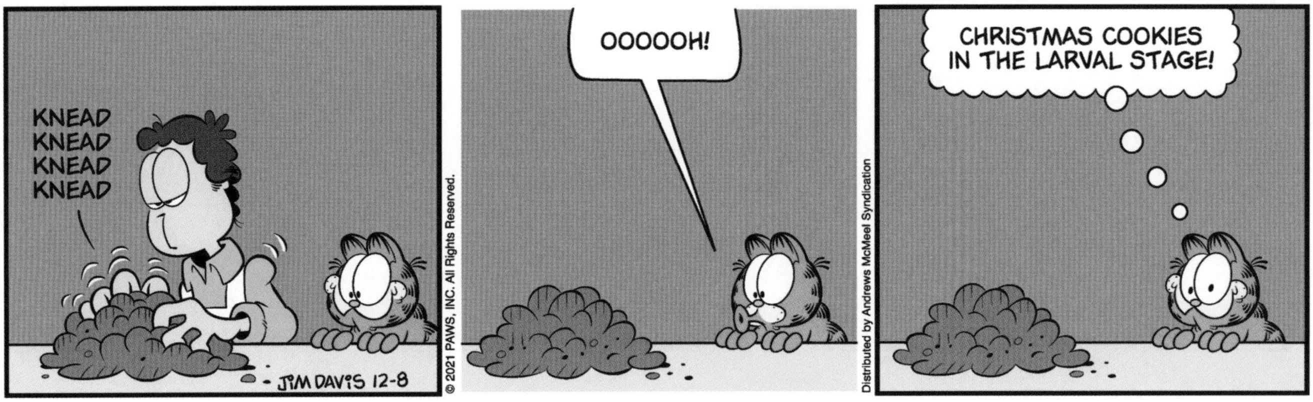
KNEAD KNEAD KNEAD KNEAD
JIM DAVIS 12-8
© 2021 PAWS, INC. All Rights Reserved.
OOOOOH!
Distributed by Andrews McMeel Syndication
CHRISTMAS COOKIES IN THE LARVAL STAGE!

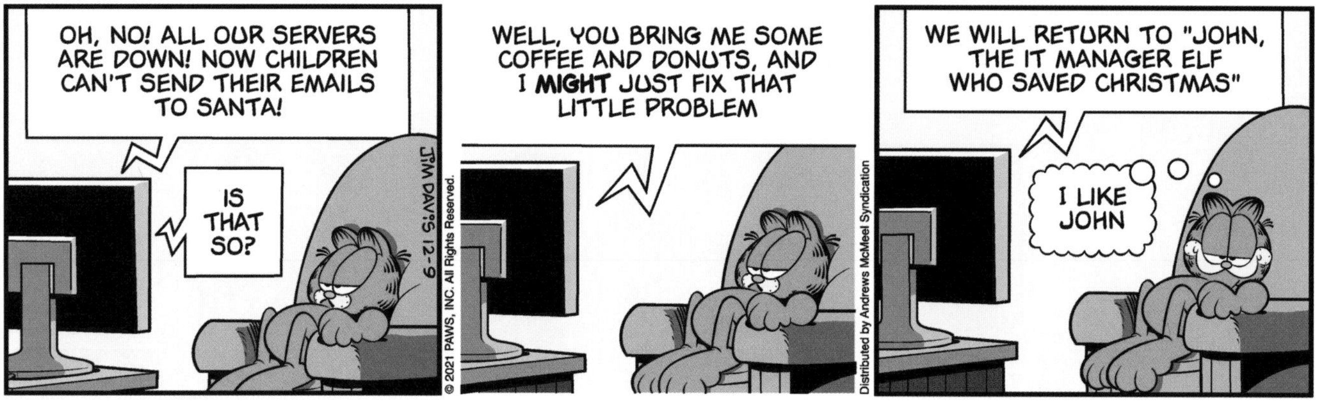
OH, NO! ALL OUR SERVERS ARE DOWN! NOW CHILDREN CAN'T SEND THEIR EMAILS TO SANTA!
IS THAT SO?
JIM DAVIS 12-9
© 2021 PAWS, INC. All Rights Reserved.
WELL, YOU BRING ME SOME COFFEE AND DONUTS, AND I MIGHT JUST FIX THAT LITTLE PROBLEM
Distributed by Andrews McMeel Syndication
WE WILL RETURN TO "JOHN, THE IT MANAGER ELF WHO SAVED CHRISTMAS"
I LIKE JOHN

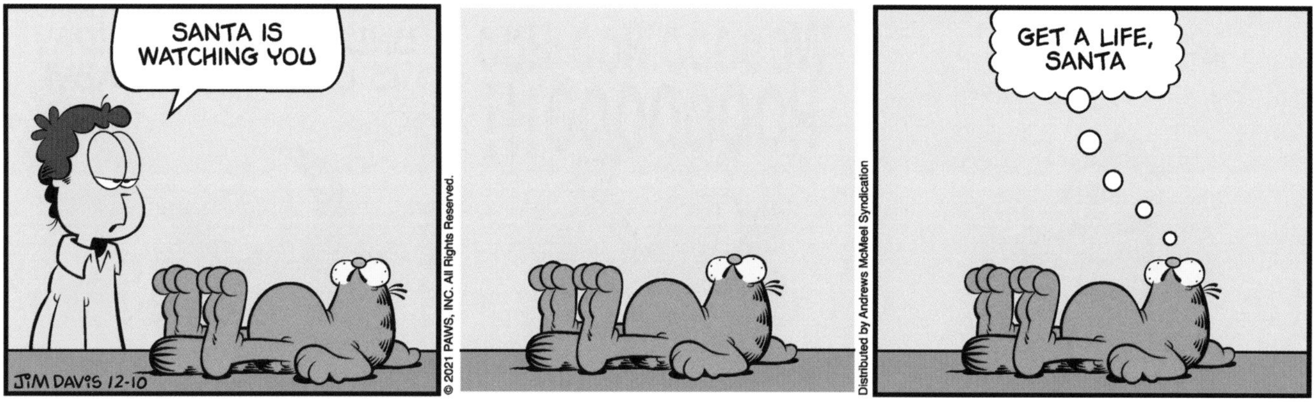
SANTA IS WATCHING YOU
JIM DAVIS 12-10
© 2021 PAWS, INC. All Rights Reserved.
Distributed by Andrews McMeel Syndication
GET A LIFE, SANTA

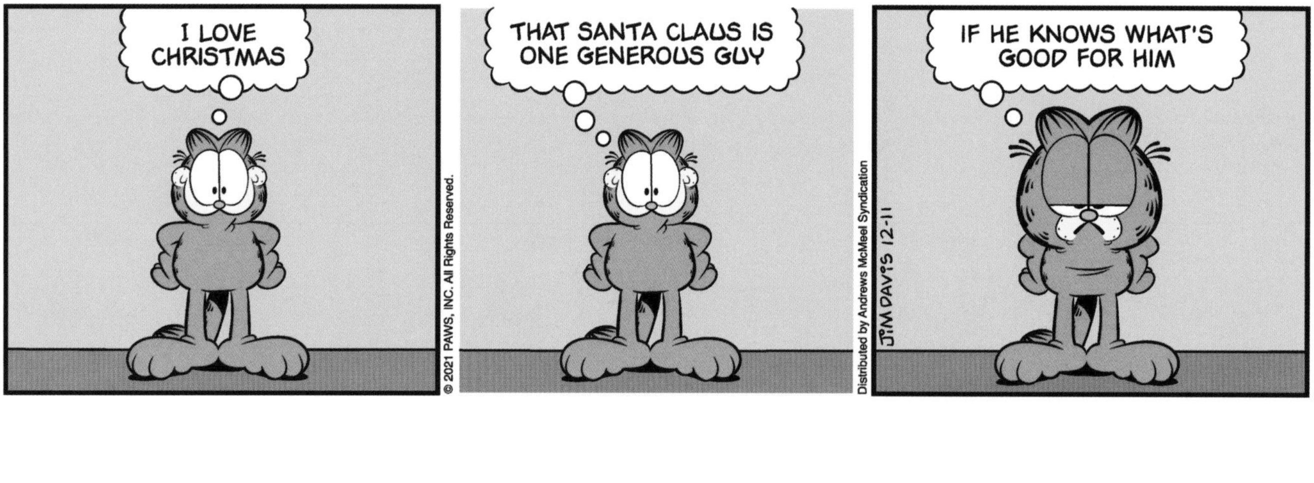
I LOVE CHRISTMAS
© 2021 PAWS, INC. All Rights Reserved.
THAT SANTA CLAUS IS ONE GENEROUS GUY
Distributed by Andrews McMeel Syndication
JIM DAVIS 12-11
IF HE KNOWS WHAT'S GOOD FOR HIM

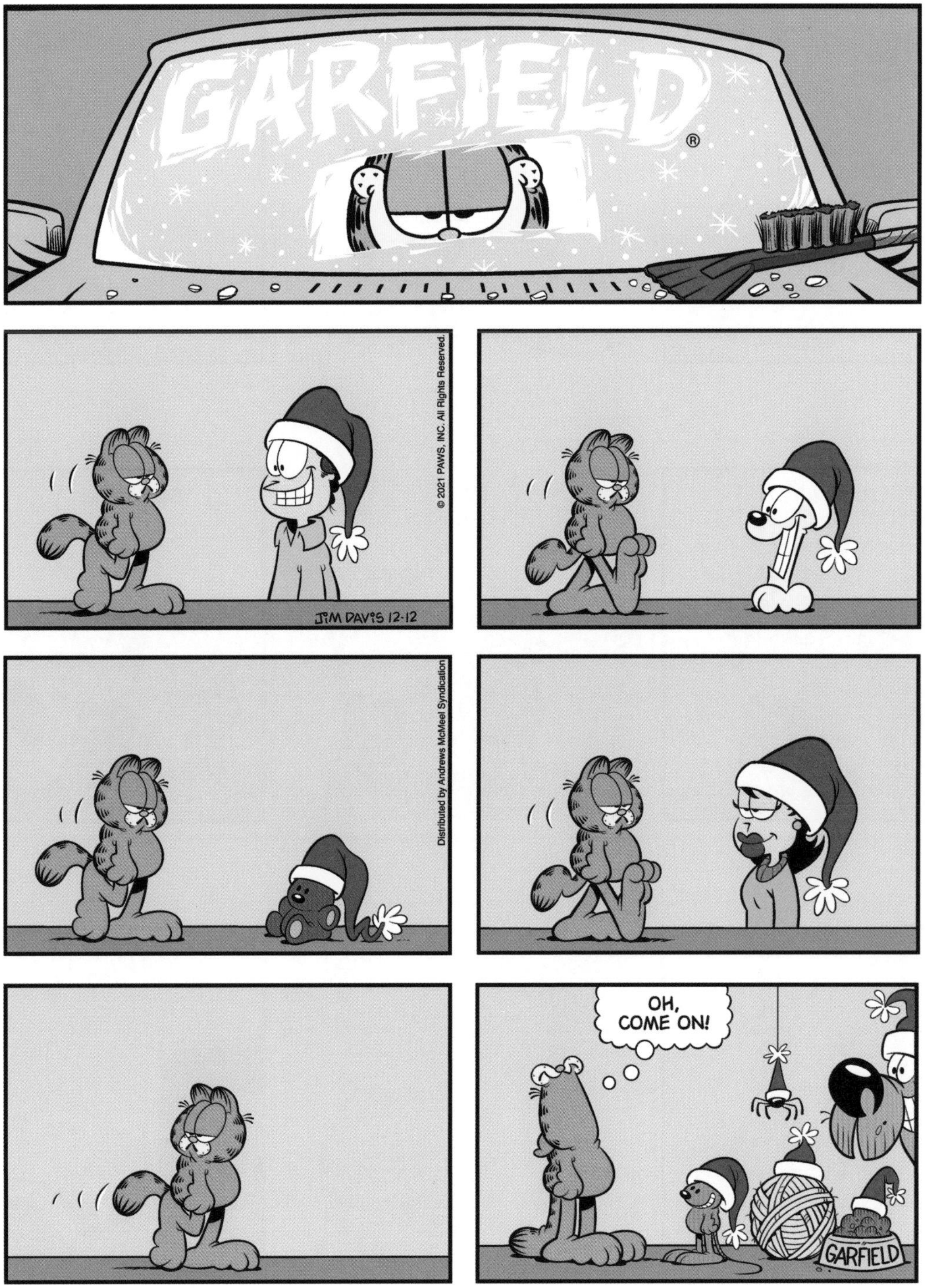
GARFIELD®
© 2021 PAWS, INC. All Rights Reserved.
JIM DAVIS 12-12
Distributed by Andrews McMeel Syndication
OH, COME ON!
GARFIELD

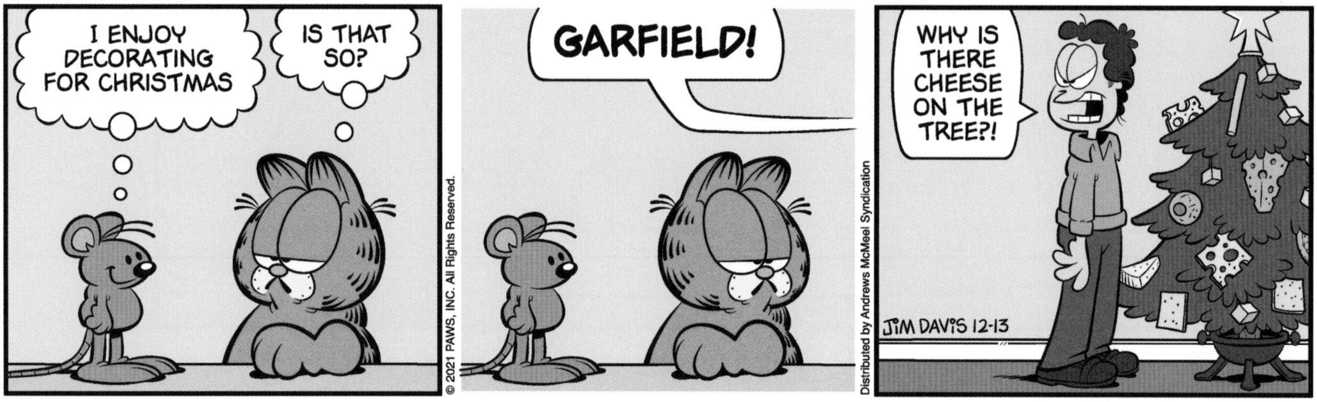
I ENJOY DECORATING FOR CHRISTMAS
IS THAT SO?
GARFIELD!
WHY IS THERE CHEESE ON THE TREE?!
JIM DAVIS 12-13


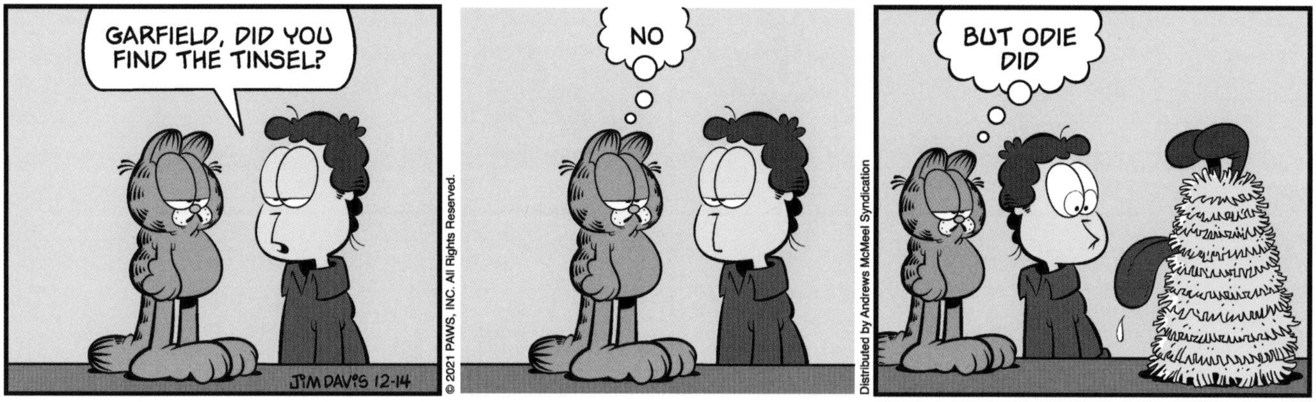
GARFIELD, DID YOU FIND THE TINSEL?
JIM DAVIS 12-14
NO
BUT ODIE DID


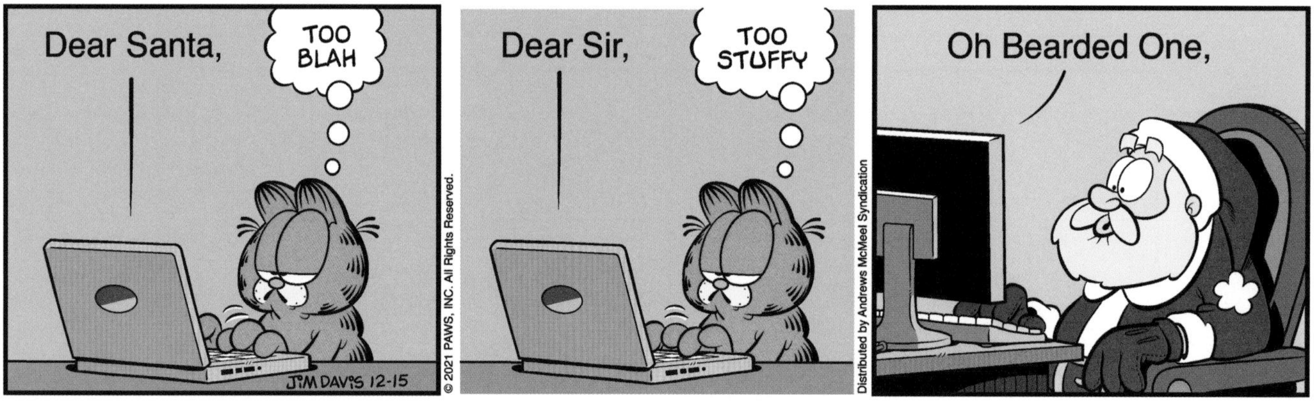
Dear Santa,
TOO BLAH
JIM DAVIS 12-15
Dear Sir,
TOO STUFFY
Oh Bearded One,

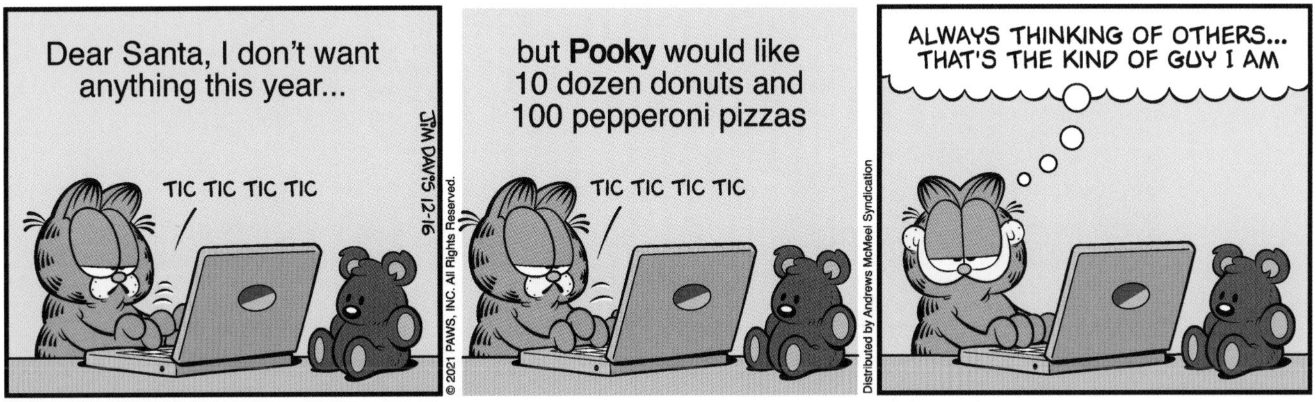
Dear Santa, I don't want anything this year...
TIC TIC TIC TIC
JIM DAVIS 12-16
© 2021 PAWS, INC. All Rights Reserved.
but **Pooky** would like 10 dozen donuts and 100 pepperoni pizzas
TIC TIC TIC TIC
Distributed by Andrews McMeel Syndication
ALWAYS THINKING OF OTHERS... THAT'S THE KIND OF GUY I AM

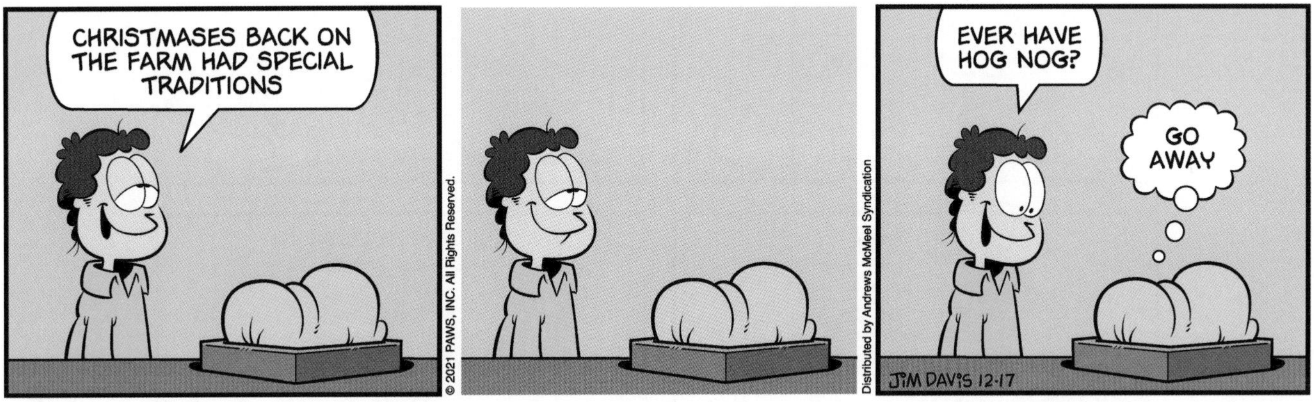
CHRISTMASES BACK ON THE FARM HAD SPECIAL TRADITIONS
© 2021 PAWS, INC. All Rights Reserved.
Distributed by Andrews McMeel Syndication
EVER HAVE HOG NOG?
GO AWAY
JIM DAVIS 12-17

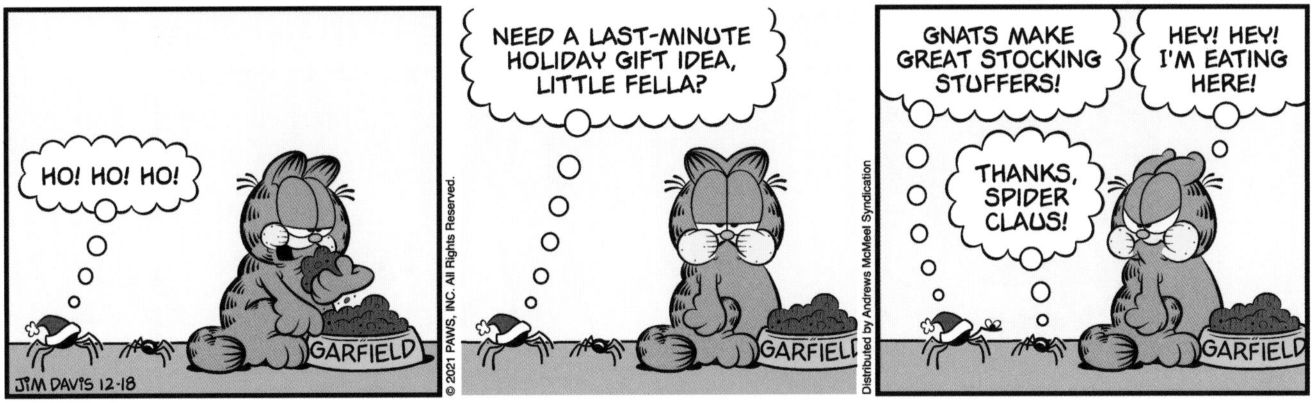
HO! HO! HO!
GARFIELD
JIM DAVIS 12-18
© 2021 PAWS, INC. All Rights Reserved.
NEED A LAST-MINUTE HOLIDAY GIFT IDEA, LITTLE FELLA?
Distributed by Andrews McMeel Syndication
GNATS MAKE GREAT STOCKING STUFFERS!
HEY! HEY! I'M EATING HERE!
THANKS, SPIDER CLAUS!
GARFIELD

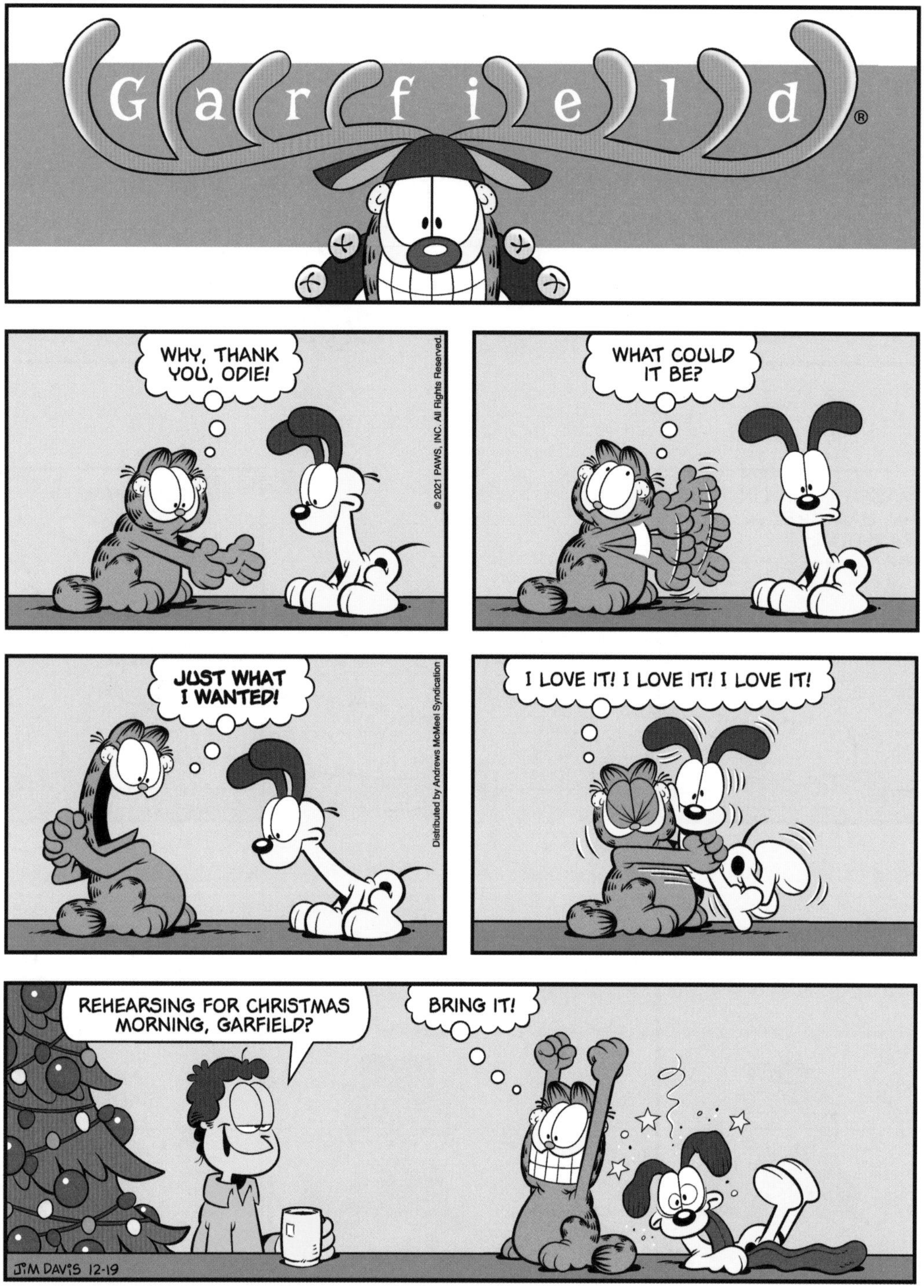
Garfield®
WHY, THANK YOU, ODIE!
© 2021 PAWS, INC. All Rights Reserved.
WHAT COULD IT BE?
JUST WHAT I WANTED!
Distributed by Andrews McMeel Syndication
I LOVE IT! I LOVE IT! I LOVE IT!
REHEARSING FOR CHRISTMAS MORNING, GARFIELD?
BRING IT!
JIM DAVIS 12-19

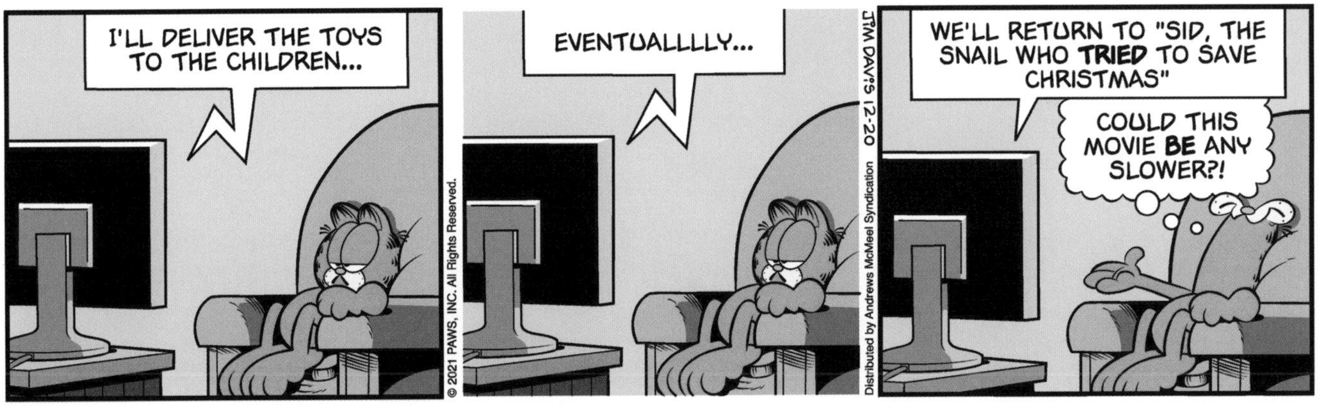
I'LL DELIVER THE TOYS TO THE CHILDREN...
© 2021 PAWS, INC. All Rights Reserved.
EVENTUALLLLY...
JIM DAVIS 12-20
Distributed by Andrews McMeel Syndication
WE'LL RETURN TO "SID, THE SNAIL WHO TRIED TO SAVE CHRISTMAS"
COULD THIS MOVIE BE ANY SLOWER?!

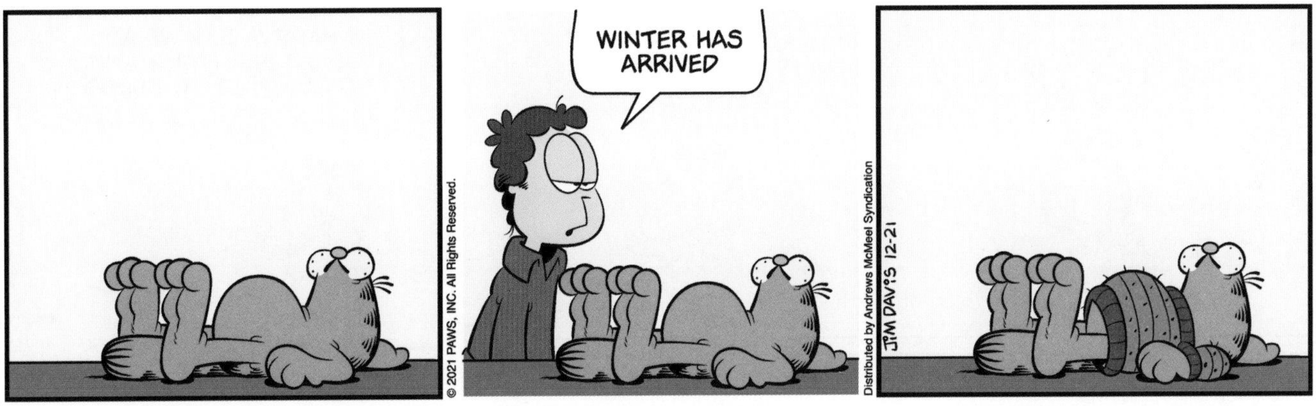
© 2021 PAWS, INC. All Rights Reserved.
WINTER HAS ARRIVED
Distributed by Andrews McMeel Syndication
JIM DAVIS 12-21

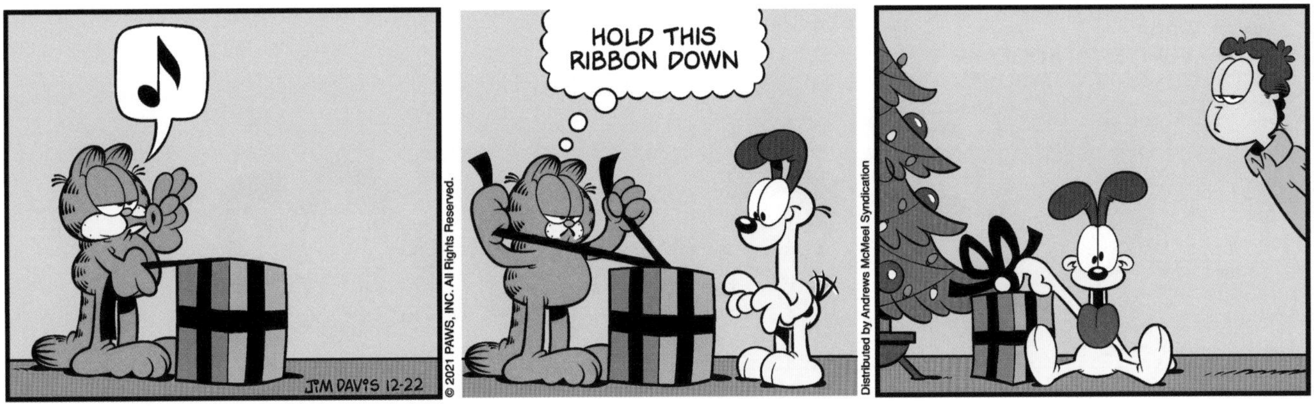
♪
JIM DAVIS 12-22
© 2021 PAWS, INC. All Rights Reserved.
HOLD THIS RIBBON DOWN
Distributed by Andrews McMeel Syndication

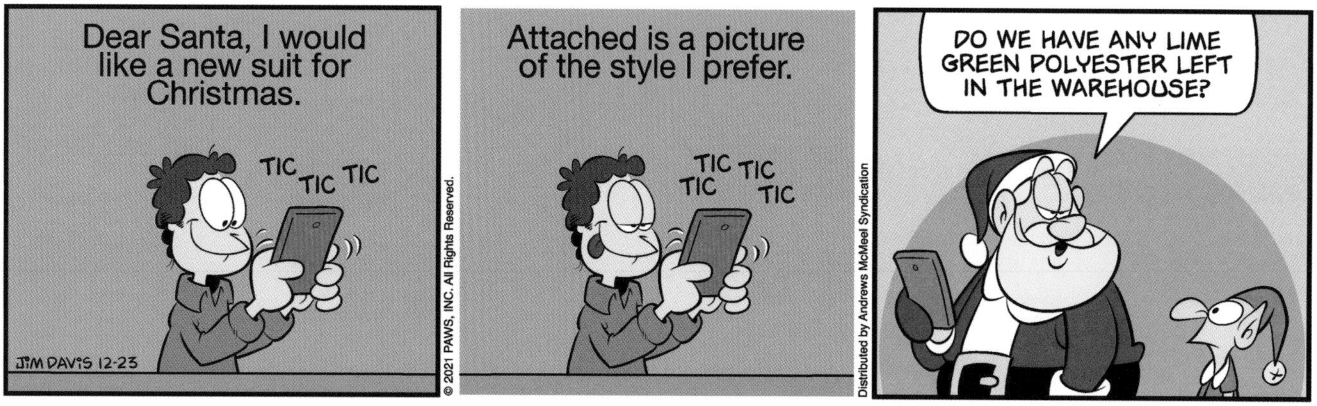
Dear Santa, I would like a new suit for Christmas.
TIC TIC TIC
JIM DAVIS 12-23
Attached is a picture of the style I prefer.
TIC TIC TIC TIC
© 2021 PAWS, INC. All Rights Reserved.
DO WE HAVE ANY LIME GREEN POLYESTER LEFT IN THE WAREHOUSE?
Distributed by Andrews McMeel Syndication

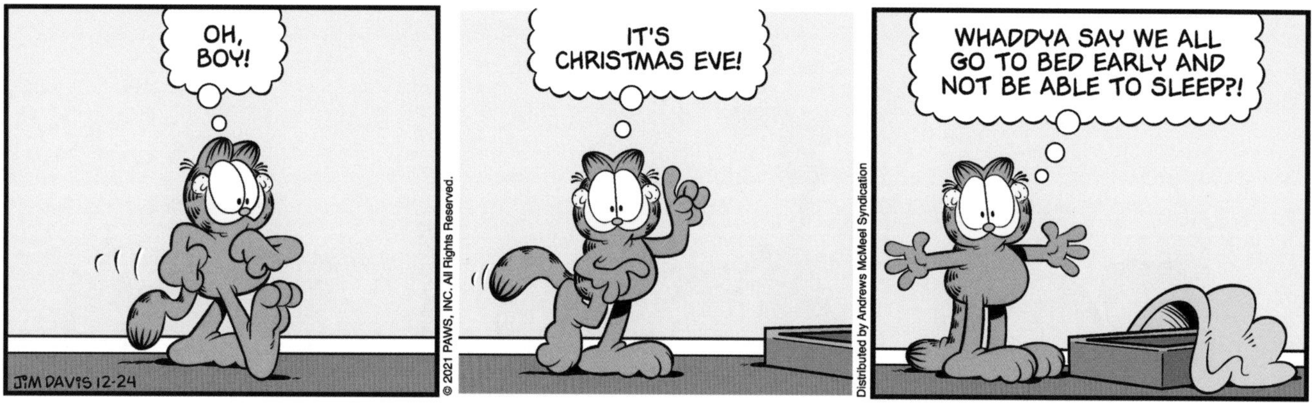
OH, BOY!
JIM DAVIS 12-24
IT'S CHRISTMAS EVE!
© 2021 PAWS, INC. All Rights Reserved.
WHADDYA SAY WE ALL GO TO BED EARLY AND NOT BE ABLE TO SLEEP?!
Distributed by Andrews McMeel Syndication

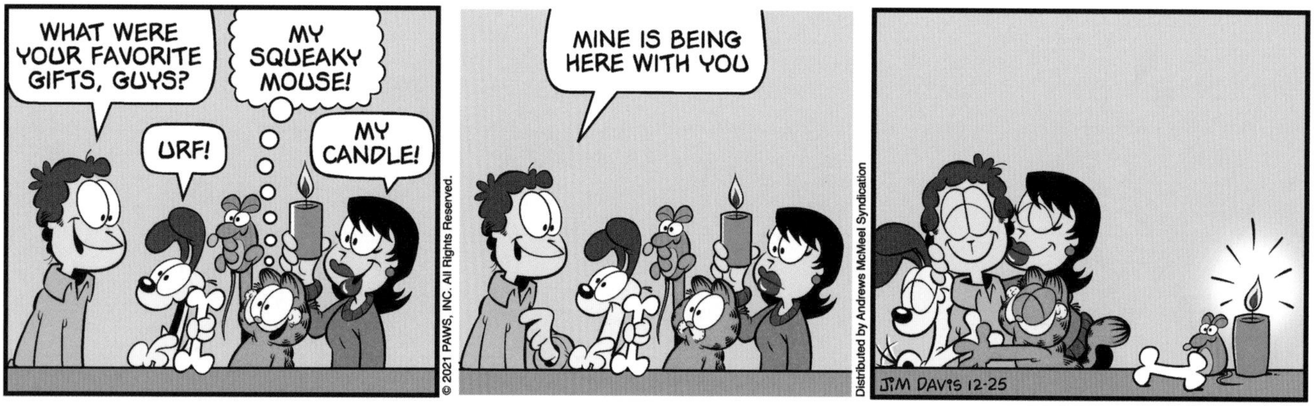
WHAT WERE YOUR FAVORITE GIFTS, GUYS?
MY SQUEAKY MOUSE!
URF!
MY CANDLE!
© 2021 PAWS, INC. All Rights Reserved.
MINE IS BEING HERE WITH YOU
Distributed by Andrews McMeel Syndication
JIM DAVIS 12-25

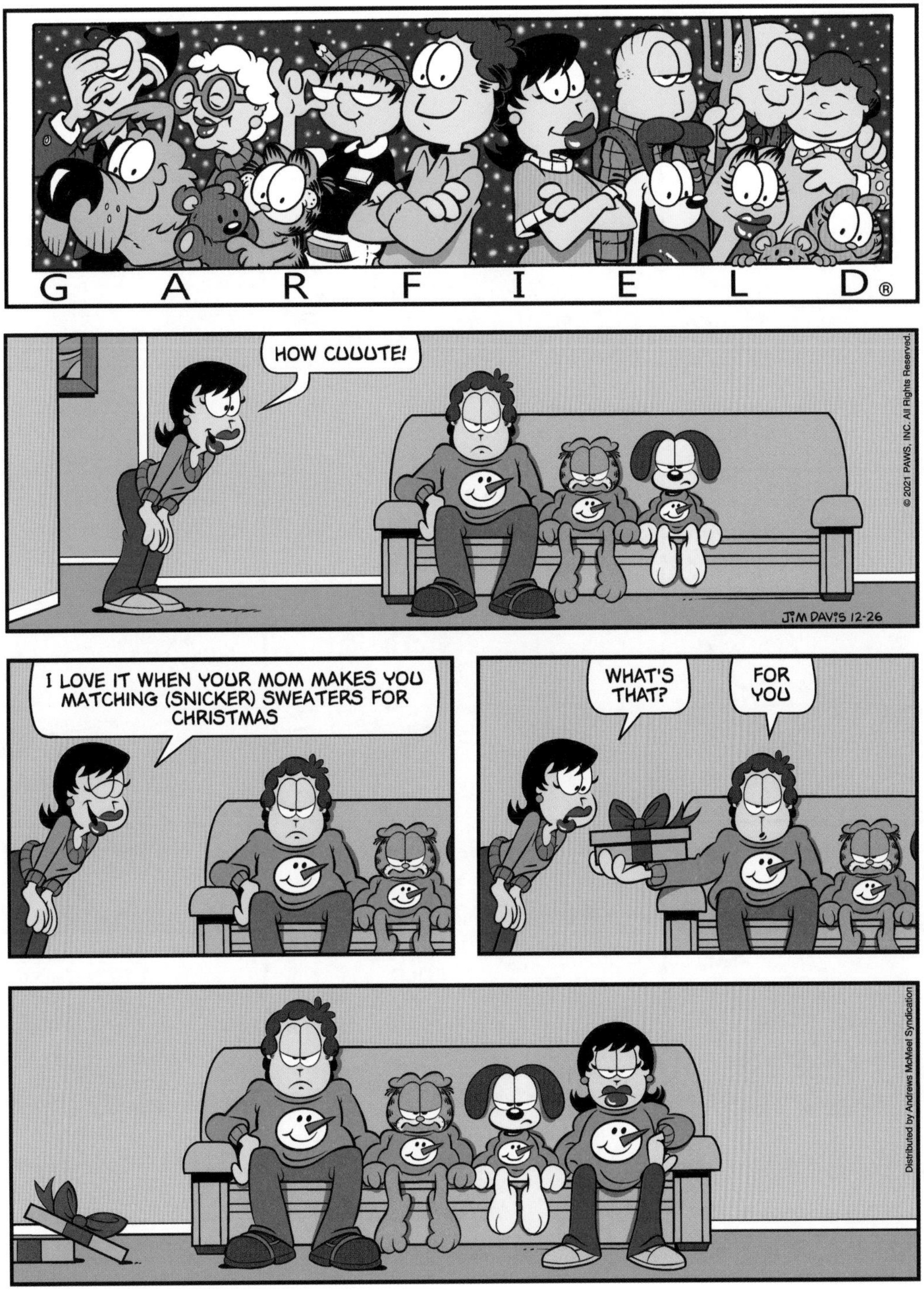

GARFIELD®
HOW CUUUTE!
© 2021 PAWS, INC. All Rights Reserved.
JIM DAVIS 12-26
I LOVE IT WHEN YOUR MOM MAKES YOU MATCHING (SNICKER) SWEATERS FOR CHRISTMAS
WHAT'S THAT?
FOR YOU
Distributed by Andrews McMeel Syndication

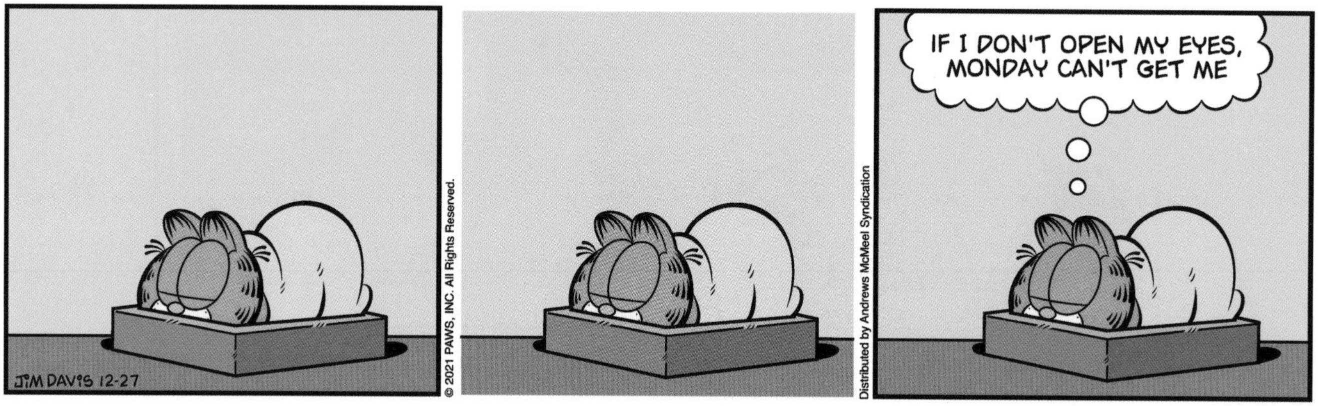
JIM DAVIS 12-27
© 2021 PAWS, INC. All Rights Reserved.
Distributed by Andrews McMeel Syndication
IF I DON'T OPEN MY EYES, MONDAY CAN'T GET ME

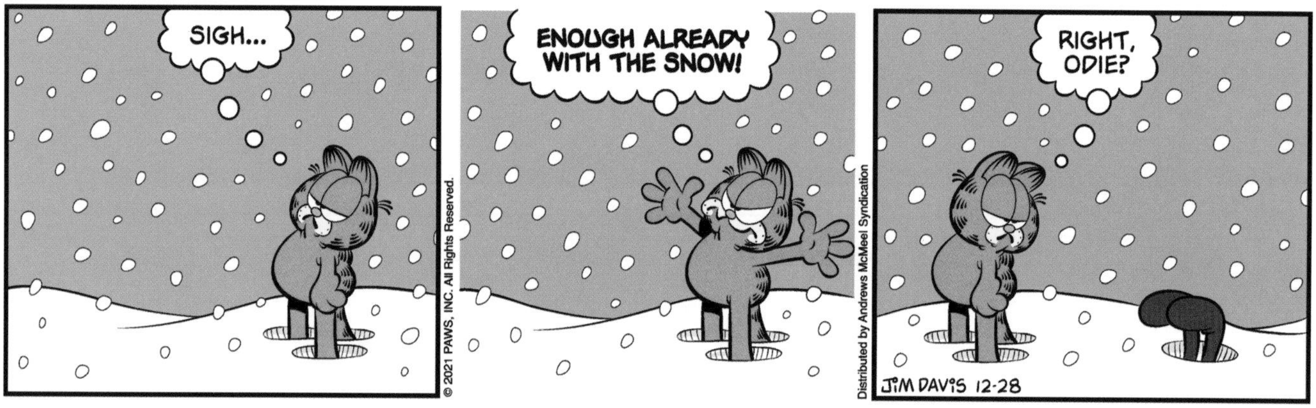
SIGH...
© 2021 PAWS, INC. All Rights Reserved.
ENOUGH ALREADY WITH THE SNOW!
Distributed by Andrews McMeel Syndication
RIGHT, ODIE?
JIM DAVIS 12-28

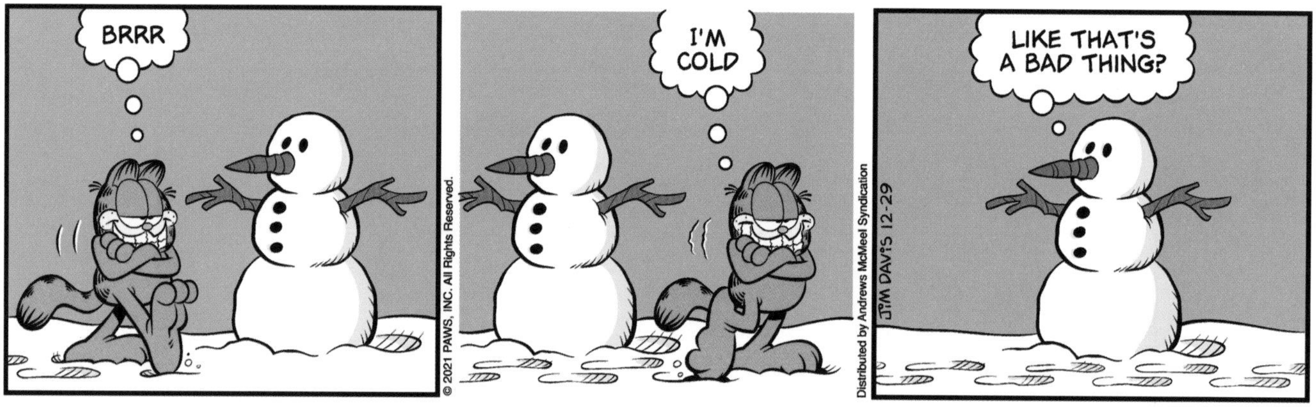
BRRR
© 2021 PAWS, INC. All Rights Reserved.
I'M COLD
Distributed by Andrews McMeel Syndication
JIM DAVIS 12-29
LIKE THAT'S A BAD THING?

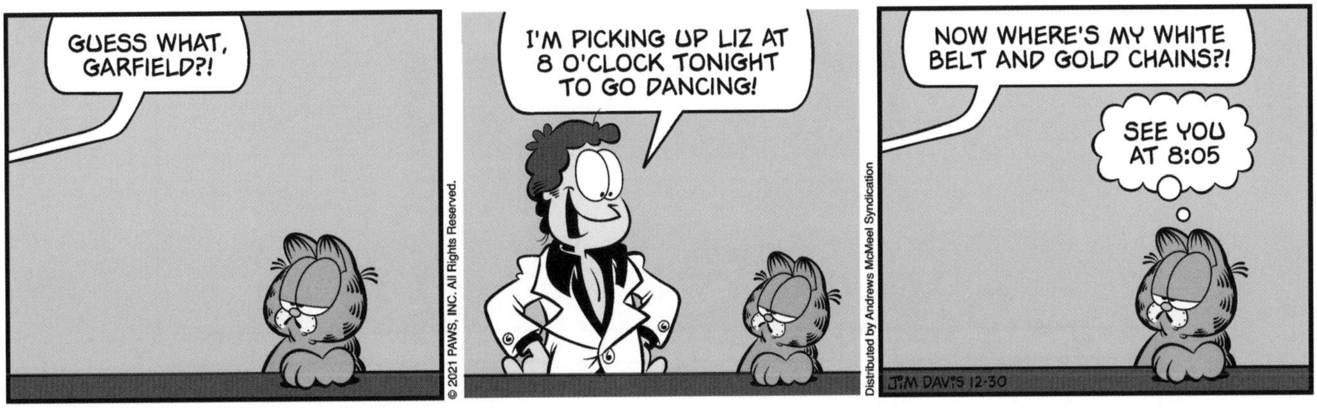
GUESS WHAT, GARFIELD?!
© 2021 PAWS, INC. All Rights Reserved.
I'M PICKING UP LIZ AT 8 O'CLOCK TONIGHT TO GO DANCING!
Distributed by Andrews McMeel Syndication
NOW WHERE'S MY WHITE BELT AND GOLD CHAINS?!
SEE YOU AT 8:05
JIM DAVIS 12-30

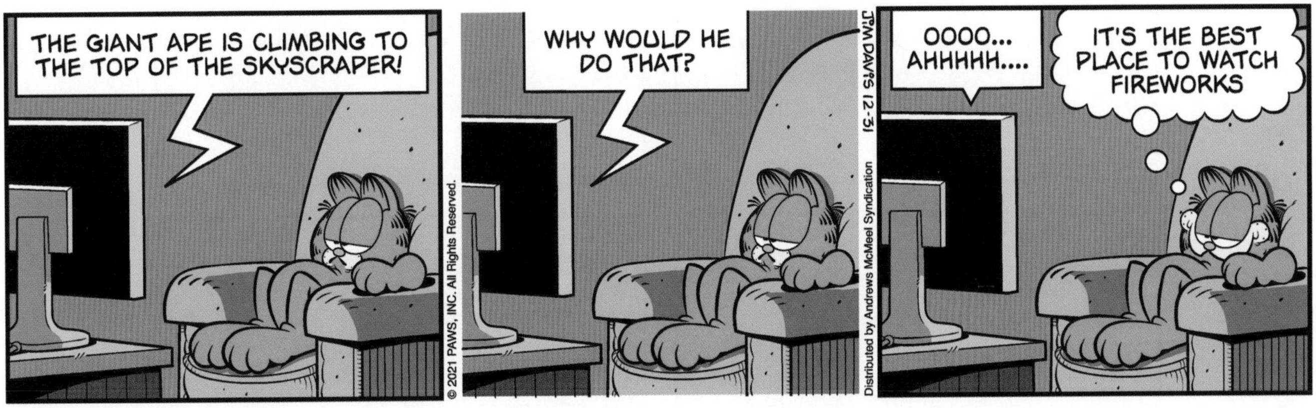
THE GIANT APE IS CLIMBING TO THE TOP OF THE SKYSCRAPER!
© 2021 PAWS, INC. All Rights Reserved.
WHY WOULD HE DO THAT?
JIM DAVIS 12-31
Distributed by Andrews McMeel Syndication
OOOO... AHHHHH....
IT'S THE BEST PLACE TO WATCH FIREWORKS

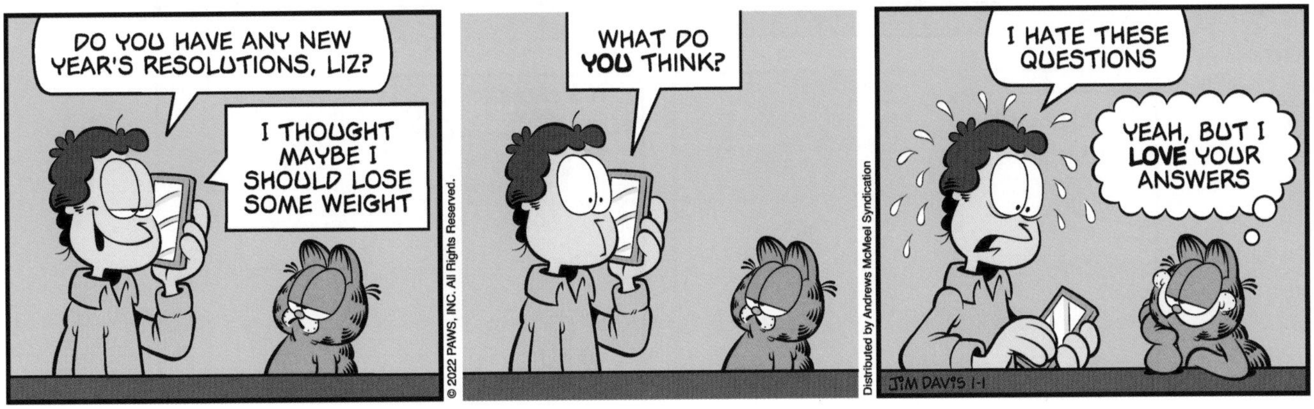
DO YOU HAVE ANY NEW YEAR'S RESOLUTIONS, LIZ?
I THOUGHT MAYBE I SHOULD LOSE SOME WEIGHT
© 2022 PAWS, INC. All Rights Reserved.
WHAT DO **YOU** THINK?
Distributed by Andrews McMeel Syndication
I HATE THESE QUESTIONS
YEAH, BUT I **LOVE** YOUR ANSWERS
JIM DAVIS 1-1

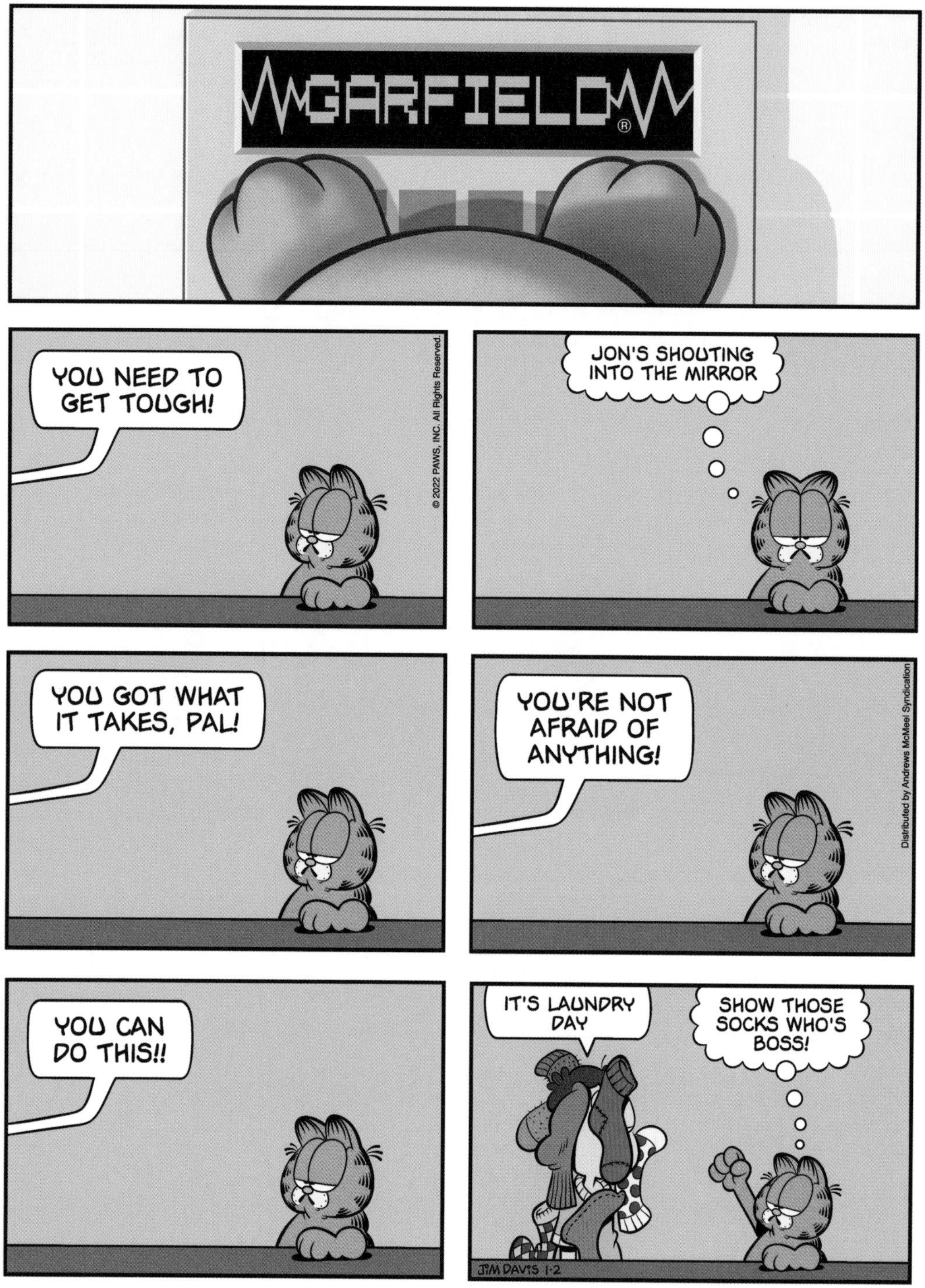
GARFIELD®
YOU NEED TO GET TOUGH!
© 2022 PAWS, INC. All Rights Reserved.
JON'S SHOUTING INTO THE MIRROR
YOU GOT WHAT IT TAKES, PAL!
YOU'RE NOT AFRAID OF ANYTHING!
Distributed by Andrews McMeel Syndication
YOU CAN DO THIS!!
IT'S LAUNDRY DAY
SHOW THOSE SOCKS WHO'S BOSS!
JIM DAVIS 1-2

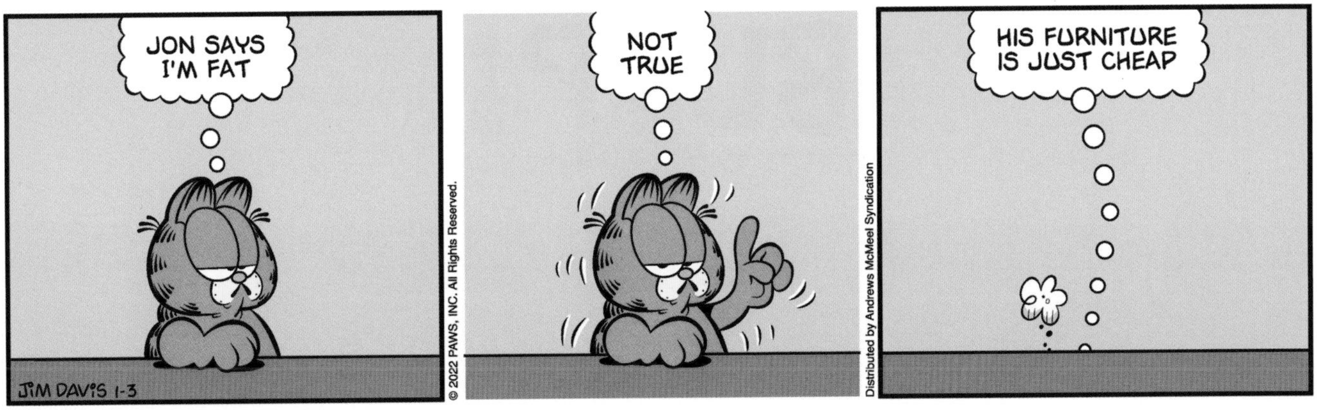
JON SAYS I'M FAT
JIM DAVIS 1-3
NOT TRUE
© 2022 PAWS, INC. All Rights Reserved.
HIS FURNITURE IS JUST CHEAP
Distributed by Andrews McMeel Syndication

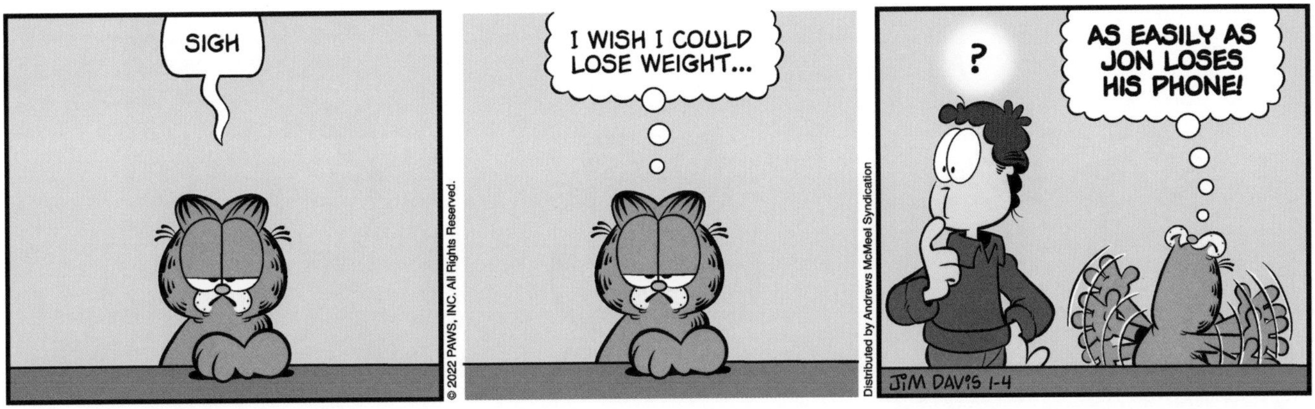
SIGH
I WISH I COULD LOSE WEIGHT...
© 2022 PAWS, INC. All Rights Reserved.
?
AS EASILY AS JON LOSES HIS PHONE!
JIM DAVIS 1-4
Distributed by Andrews McMeel Syndication

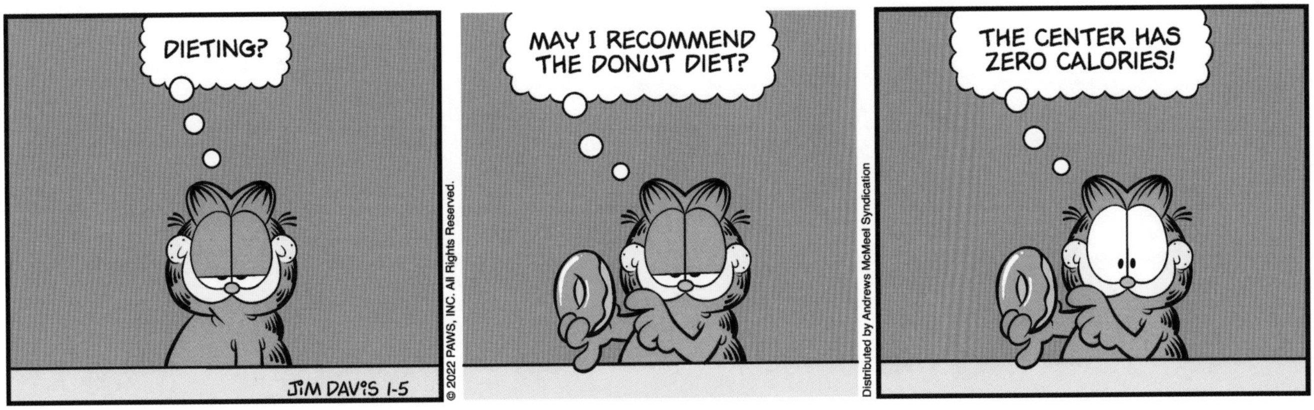
DIETING?
JIM DAVIS 1-5
MAY I RECOMMEND THE DONUT DIET?
© 2022 PAWS, INC. All Rights Reserved.
THE CENTER HAS ZERO CALORIES!
Distributed by Andrews McMeel Syndication

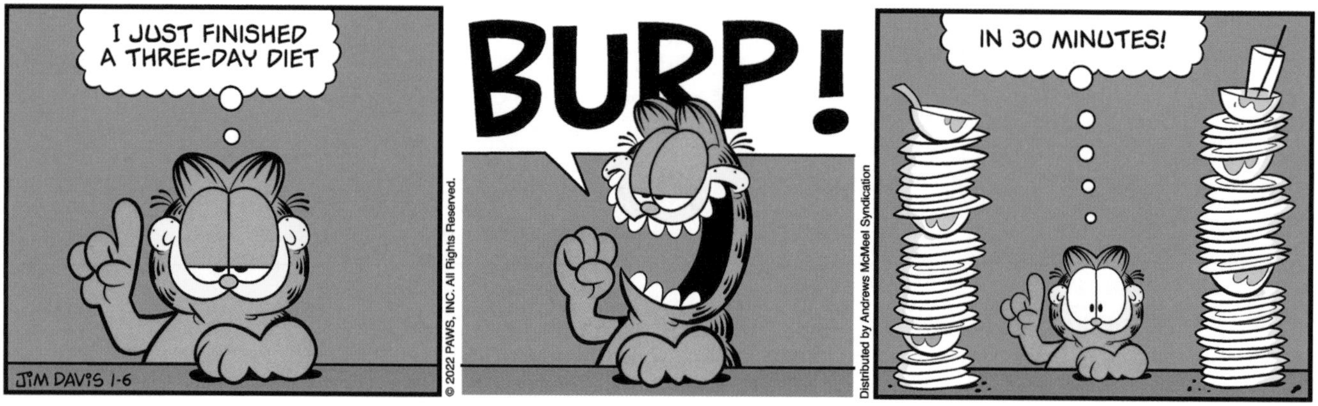

I JUST FINISHED A THREE-DAY DIET
BURP!
IN 30 MINUTES!
JIM DAVIS 1-6
© 2022 PAWS, INC. All Rights Reserved.
Distributed by Andrews McMeel Syndication


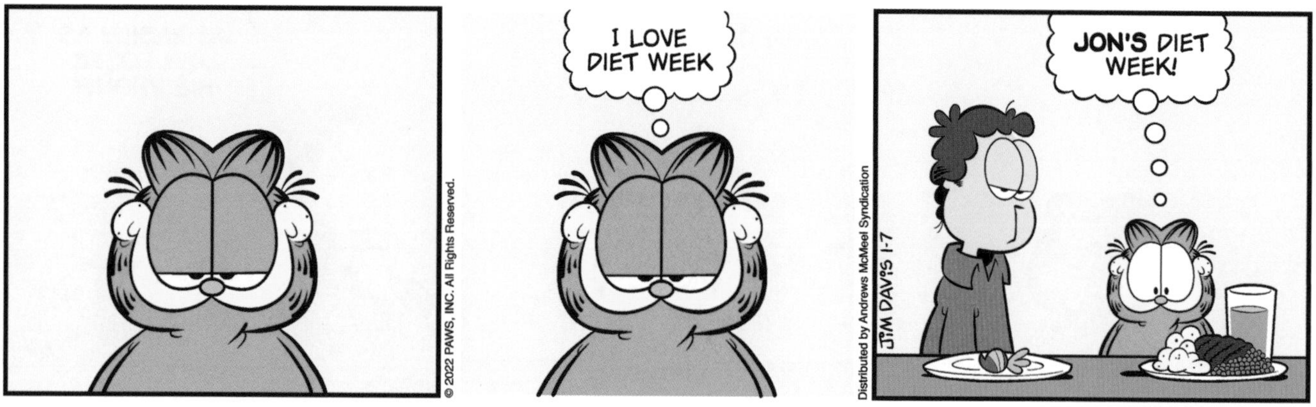

I LOVE DIET WEEK
JON'S DIET WEEK!
JIM DAVIS 1-7
© 2022 PAWS, INC. All Rights Reserved.
Distributed by Andrews McMeel Syndication


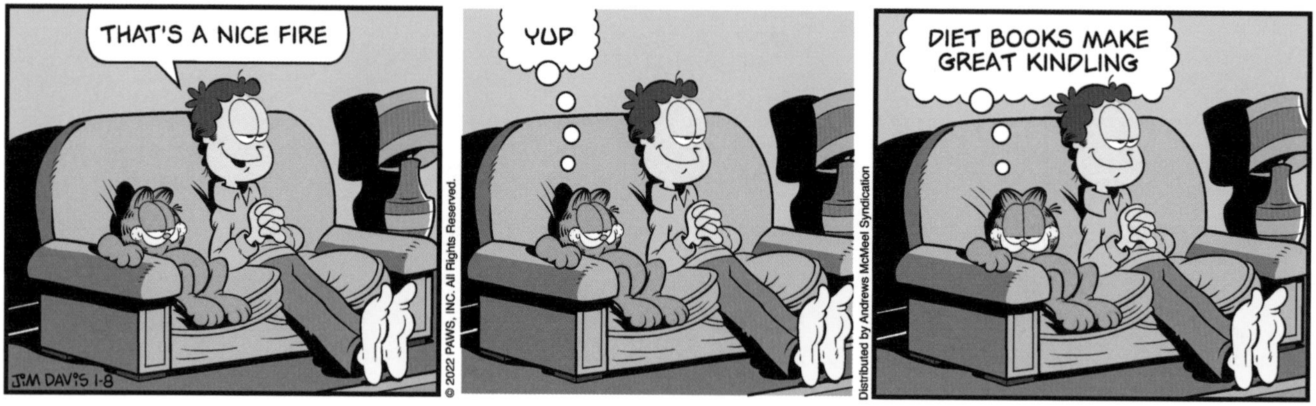

THAT'S A NICE FIRE
YUP
DIET BOOKS MAKE GREAT KINDLING
JIM DAVIS 1-8
© 2022 PAWS, INC. All Rights Reserved.
Distributed by Andrews McMeel Syndication

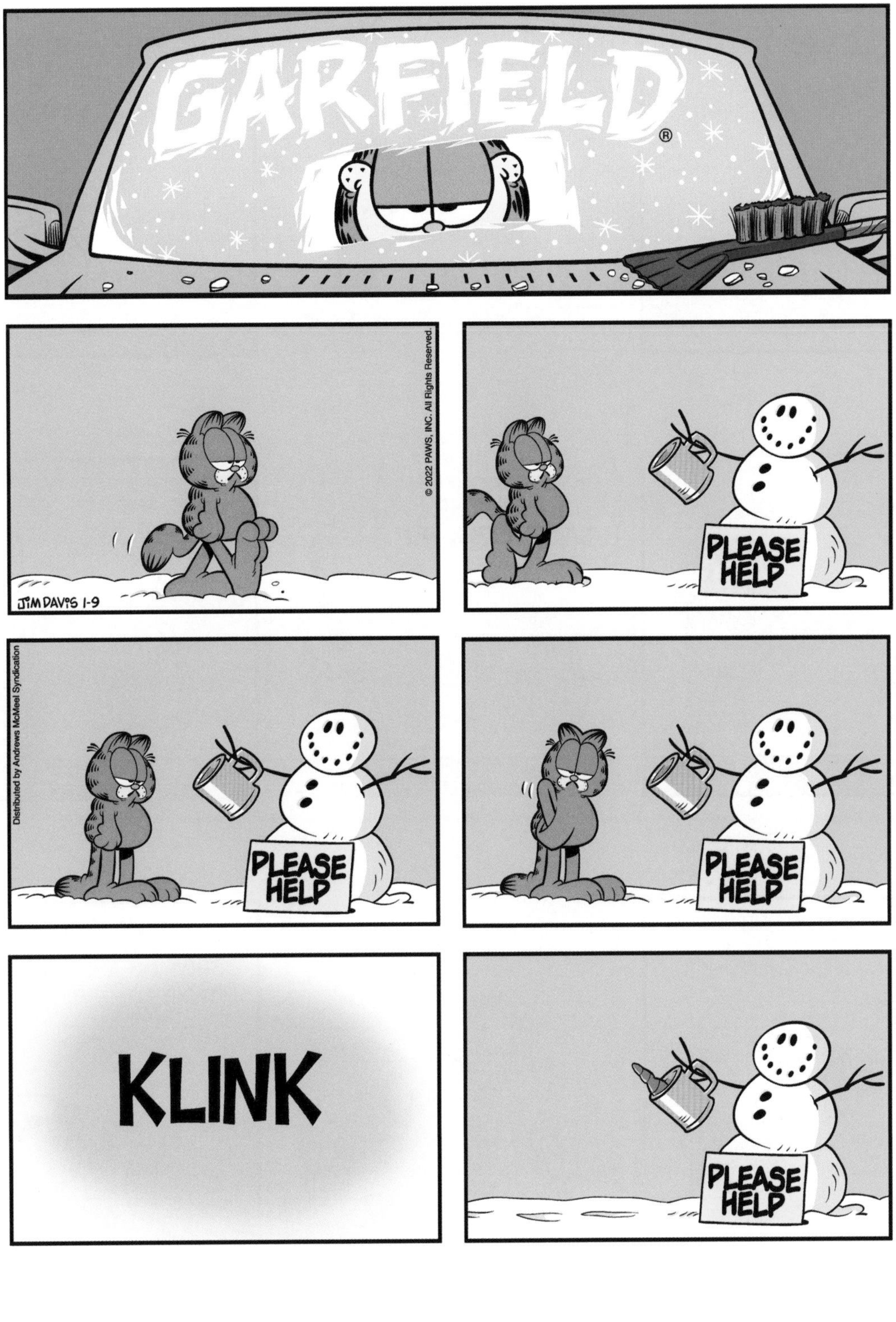
GARFIELD®
© 2022 PAWS, INC. All Rights Reserved.
JIM DAVIS 1-9
PLEASE HELP
Distributed by Andrews McMeel Syndication
PLEASE HELP
PLEASE HELP
KLINK
PLEASE HELP

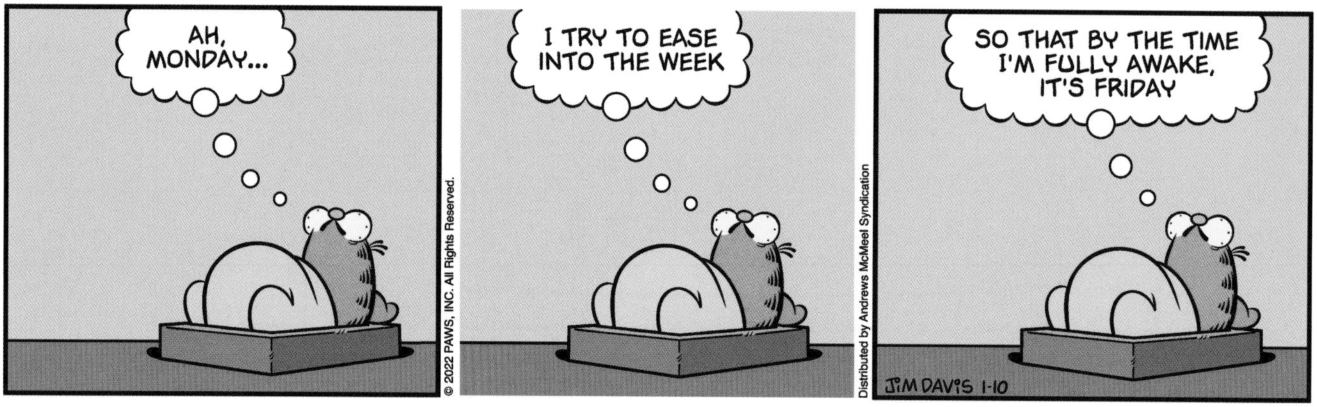
AH, MONDAY...
I TRY TO EASE INTO THE WEEK
SO THAT BY THE TIME I'M FULLY AWAKE, IT'S FRIDAY
© 2022 PAWS, INC. All Rights Reserved.
Distributed by Andrews McMeel Syndication
JIM DAVIS 1-10

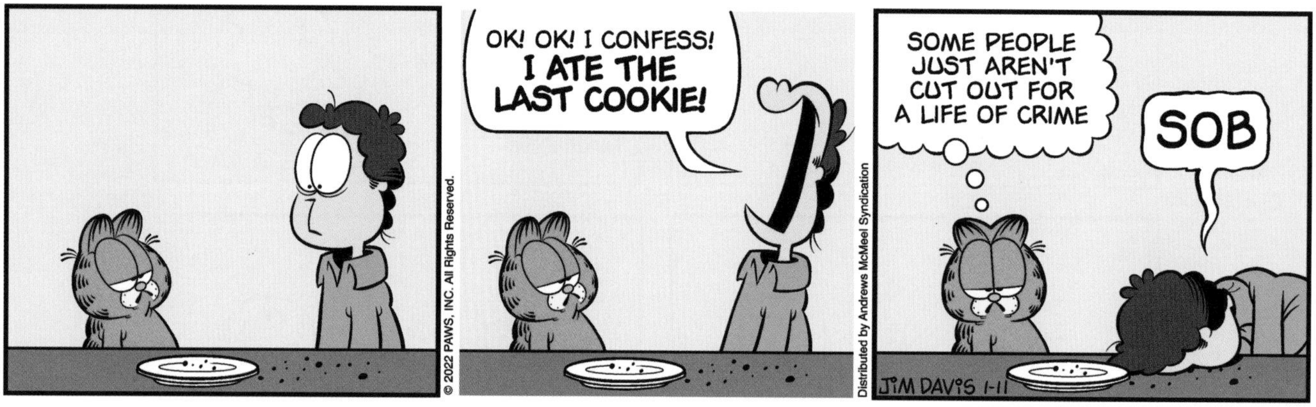
OK! OK! I CONFESS! **I ATE THE LAST COOKIE!**
SOME PEOPLE JUST AREN'T CUT OUT FOR A LIFE OF CRIME
SOB
© 2022 PAWS, INC. All Rights Reserved.
Distributed by Andrews McMeel Syndication
JIM DAVIS 1-11

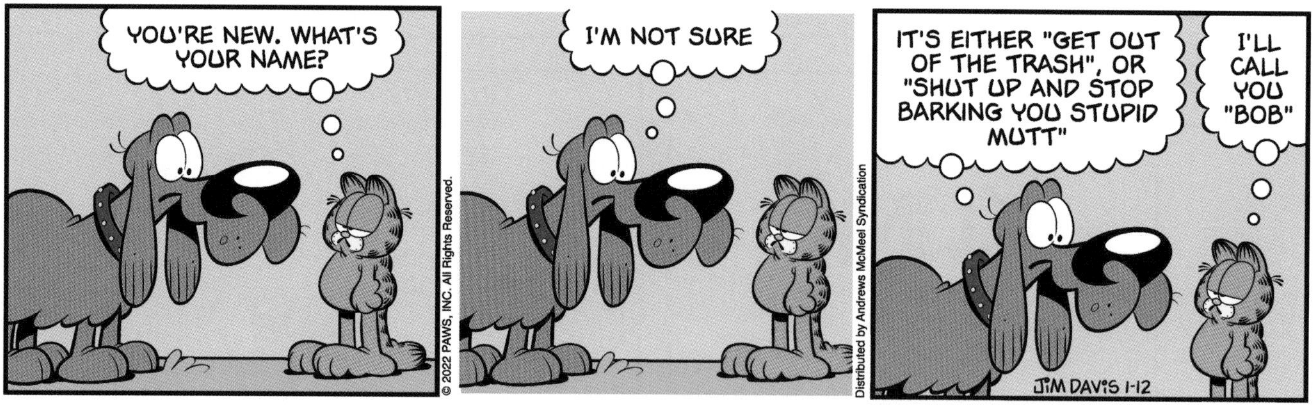
YOU'RE NEW. WHAT'S YOUR NAME?
I'M NOT SURE
IT'S EITHER "GET OUT OF THE TRASH", OR "SHUT UP AND STOP BARKING YOU STUPID MUTT"
I'LL CALL YOU "BOB"
© 2022 PAWS, INC. All Rights Reserved.
Distributed by Andrews McMeel Syndication
JIM DAVIS 1-12

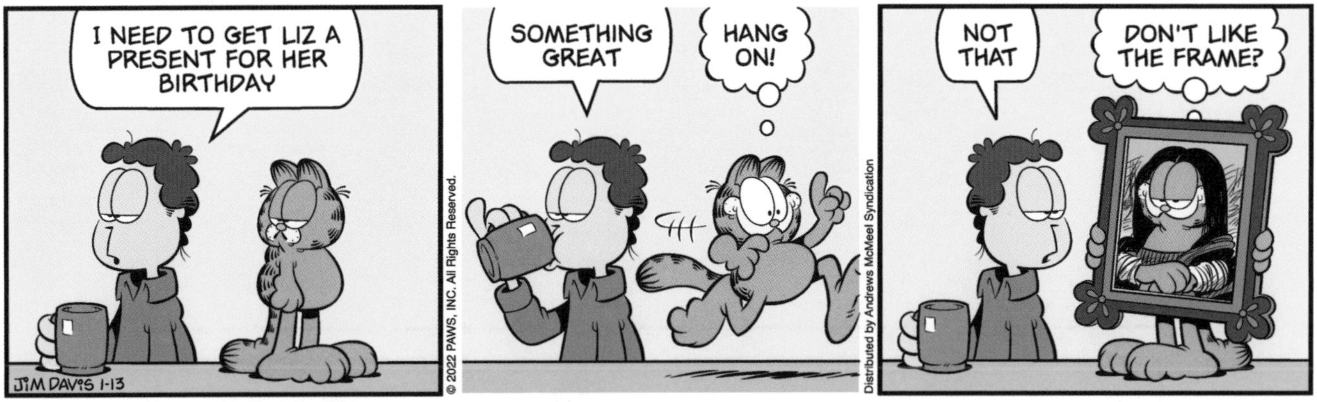
I NEED TO GET LIZ A PRESENT FOR HER BIRTHDAY
JIM DAVIS 1-13
SOMETHING GREAT
HANG ON!
NOT THAT
DON'T LIKE THE FRAME?
© 2022 PAWS, INC. All Rights Reserved.
Distributed by Andrews McMeel Syndication

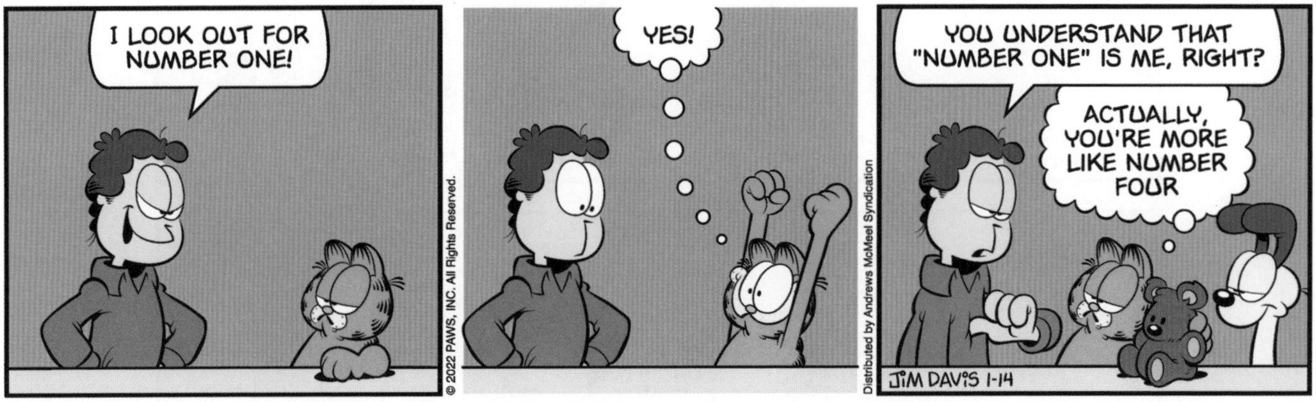
I LOOK OUT FOR NUMBER ONE!
YES!
YOU UNDERSTAND THAT "NUMBER ONE" IS ME, RIGHT?
ACTUALLY, YOU'RE MORE LIKE NUMBER FOUR
JIM DAVIS 1-14
© 2022 PAWS, INC. All Rights Reserved.
Distributed by Andrews McMeel Syndication

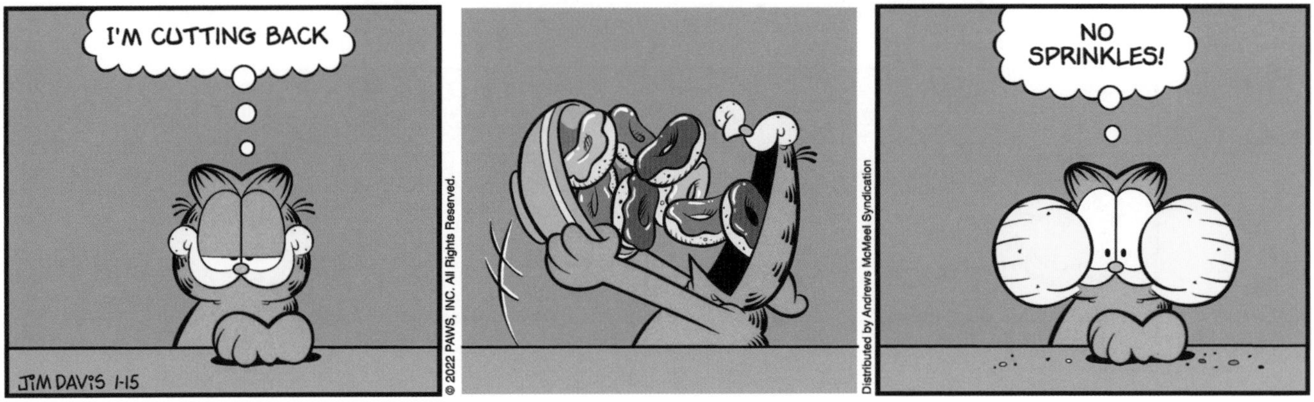
I'M CUTTING BACK
JIM DAVIS 1-15
NO SPRINKLES!
© 2022 PAWS, INC. All Rights Reserved.
Distributed by Andrews McMeel Syndication

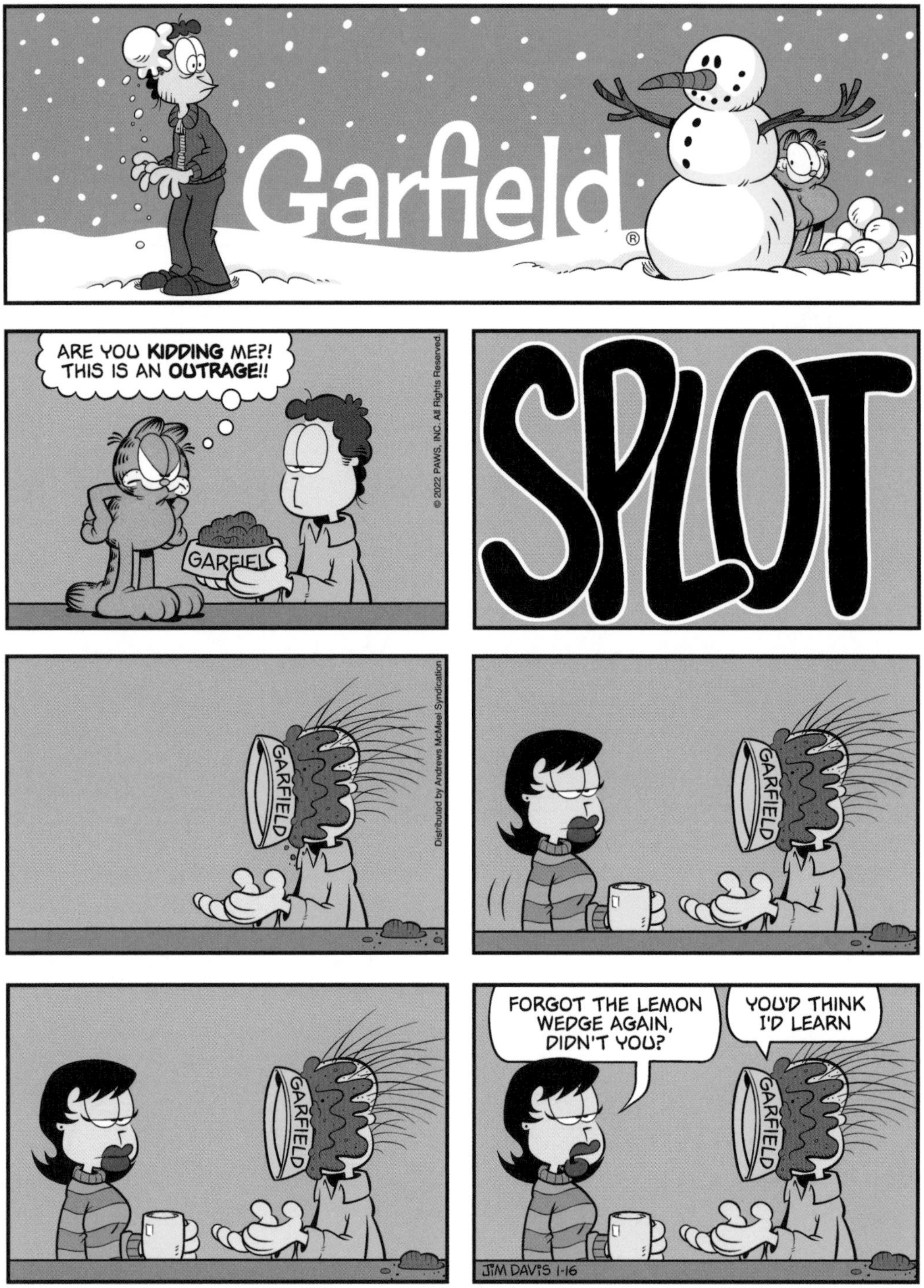
Garfield®
ARE YOU KIDDING ME?! THIS IS AN OUTRAGE!!
GARFIELD
© 2022 PAWS, INC. All Rights Reserved.
SPLOT
Distributed by Andrews McMeel Syndication
FORGOT THE LEMON WEDGE AGAIN, DIDN'T YOU?
YOU'D THINK I'D LEARN
JIM DAVIS 1-16

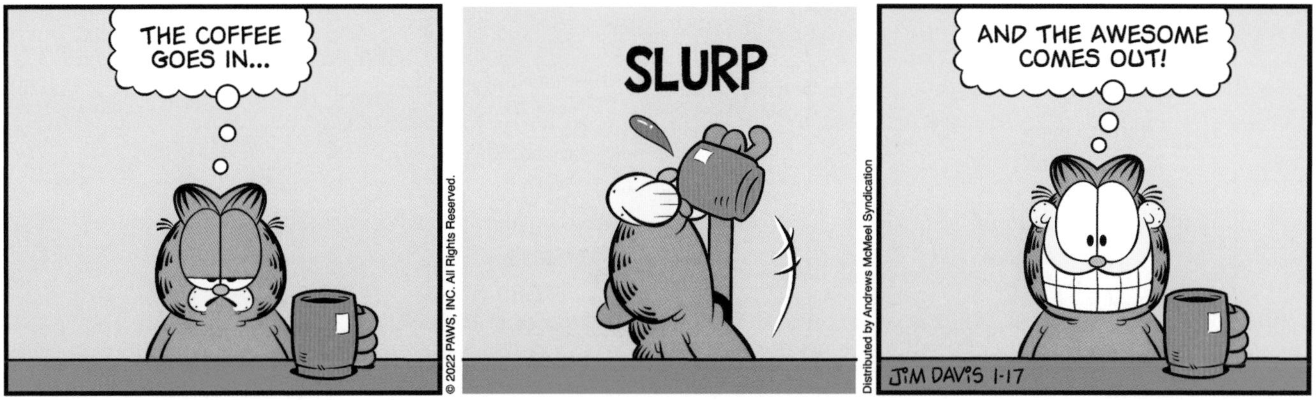
THE COFFEE GOES IN...
SLURP
AND THE AWESOME COMES OUT!
© 2022 PAWS, INC. All Rights Reserved.
Distributed by Andrews McMeel Syndication
JIM DAVIS 1-17

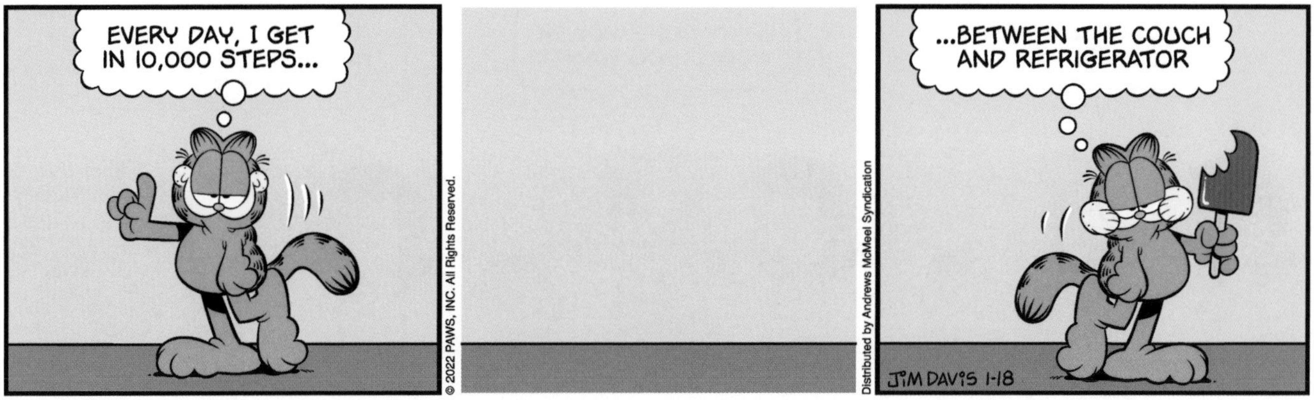
EVERY DAY, I GET IN 10,000 STEPS...
...BETWEEN THE COUCH AND REFRIGERATOR
© 2022 PAWS, INC. All Rights Reserved.
Distributed by Andrews McMeel Syndication
JIM DAVIS 1-18

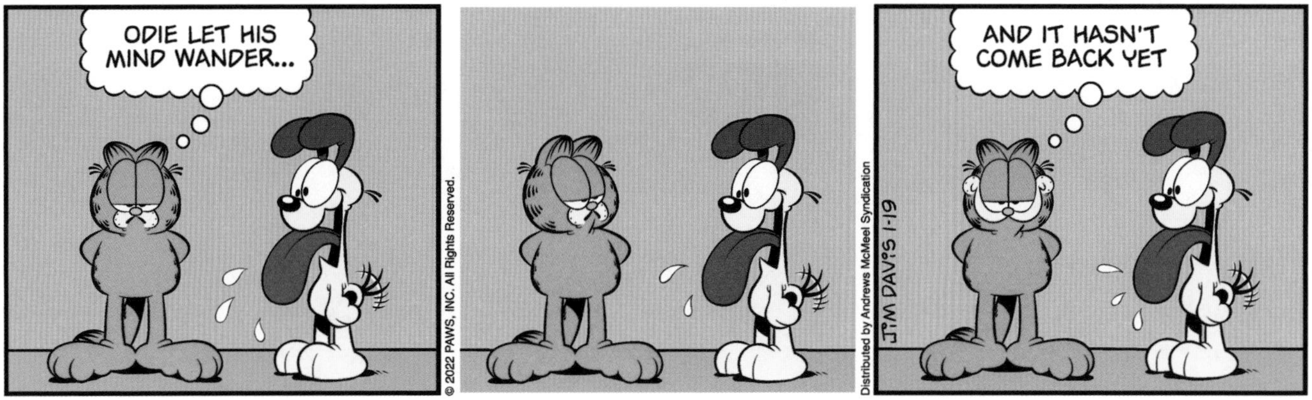
ODIE LET HIS MIND WANDER...
AND IT HASN'T COME BACK YET
© 2022 PAWS, INC. All Rights Reserved.
Distributed by Andrews McMeel Syndication
JIM DAVIS 1-19

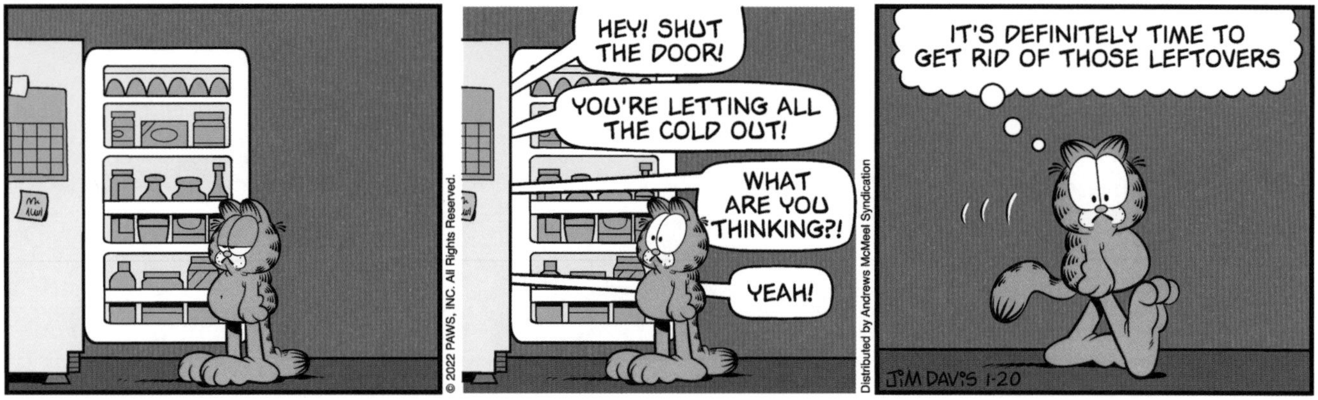
HEY! SHUT THE DOOR!
YOU'RE LETTING ALL THE COLD OUT!
WHAT ARE YOU THINKING?!
YEAH!
IT'S DEFINITELY TIME TO GET RID OF THOSE LEFTOVERS
JIM DAVIS 1-20
© 2022 PAWS, INC. All Rights Reserved.
Distributed by Andrews McMeel Syndication

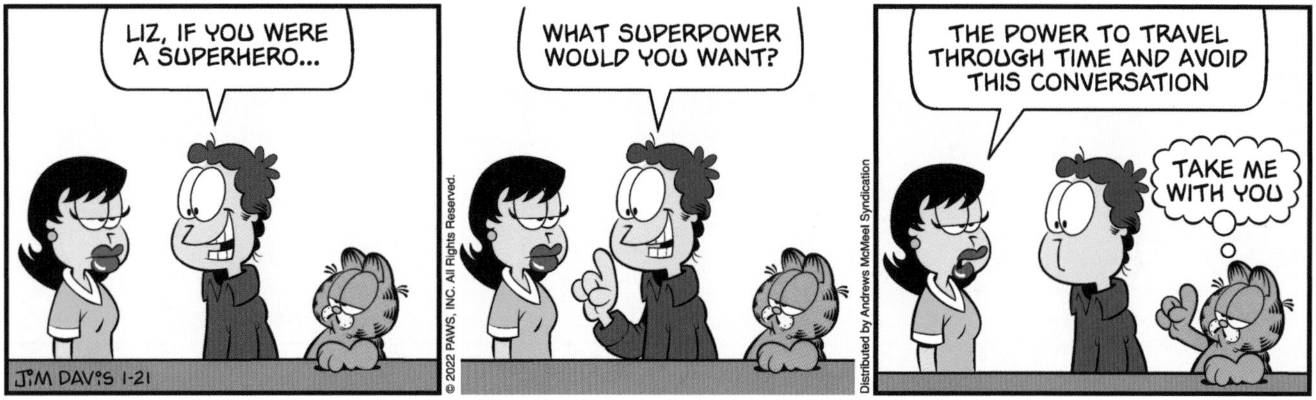
LIZ, IF YOU WERE A SUPERHERO...
WHAT SUPERPOWER WOULD YOU WANT?
THE POWER TO TRAVEL THROUGH TIME AND AVOID THIS CONVERSATION
TAKE ME WITH YOU
JIM DAVIS 1-21
© 2022 PAWS, INC. All Rights Reserved.
Distributed by Andrews McMeel Syndication

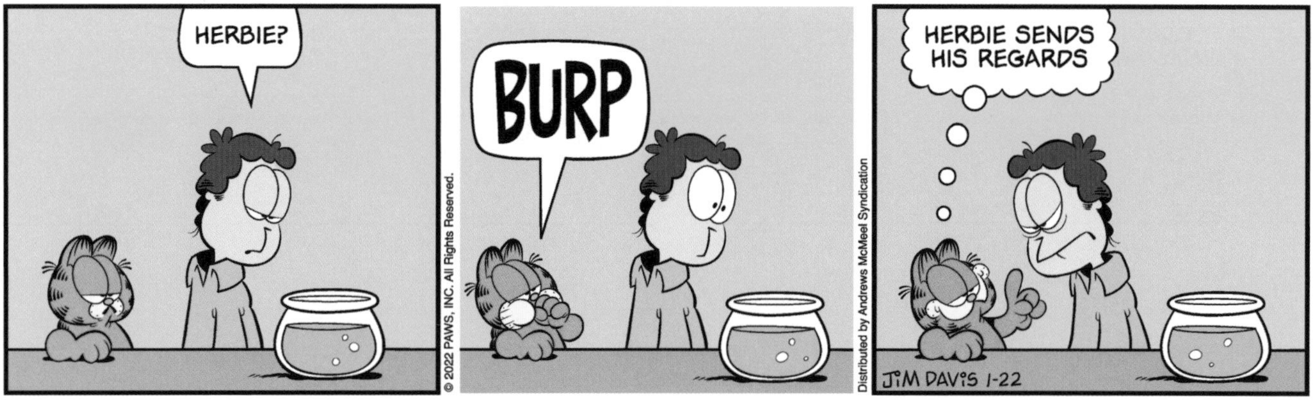
HERBIE?
BURP
HERBIE SENDS HIS REGARDS
JIM DAVIS 1-22
© 2022 PAWS, INC. All Rights Reserved.
Distributed by Andrews McMeel Syndication

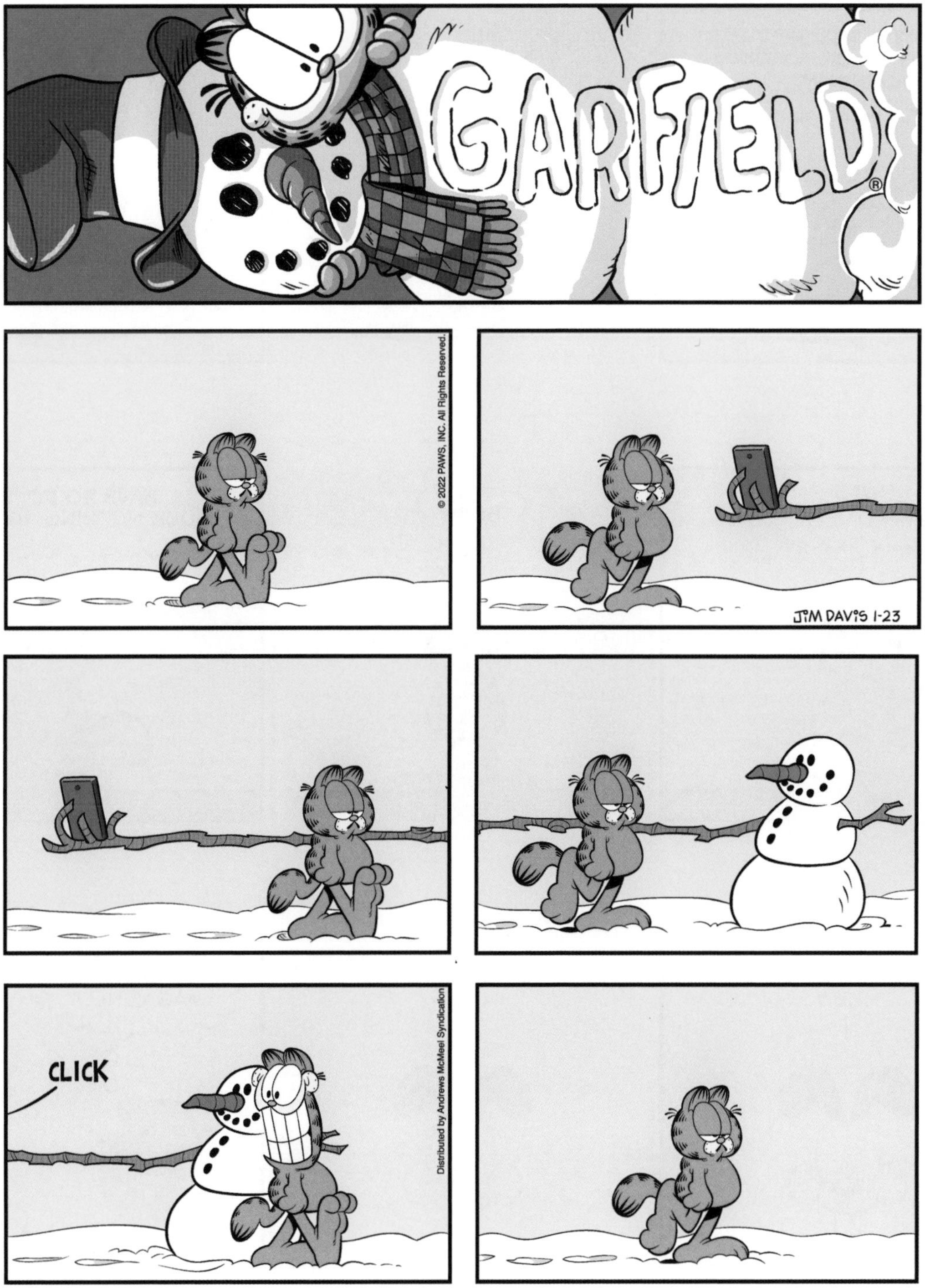
GARFIELD®
© 2022 PAWS, INC. All Rights Reserved.
JIM DAVIS 1-23
CLICK
Distributed by Andrews McMeel Syndication

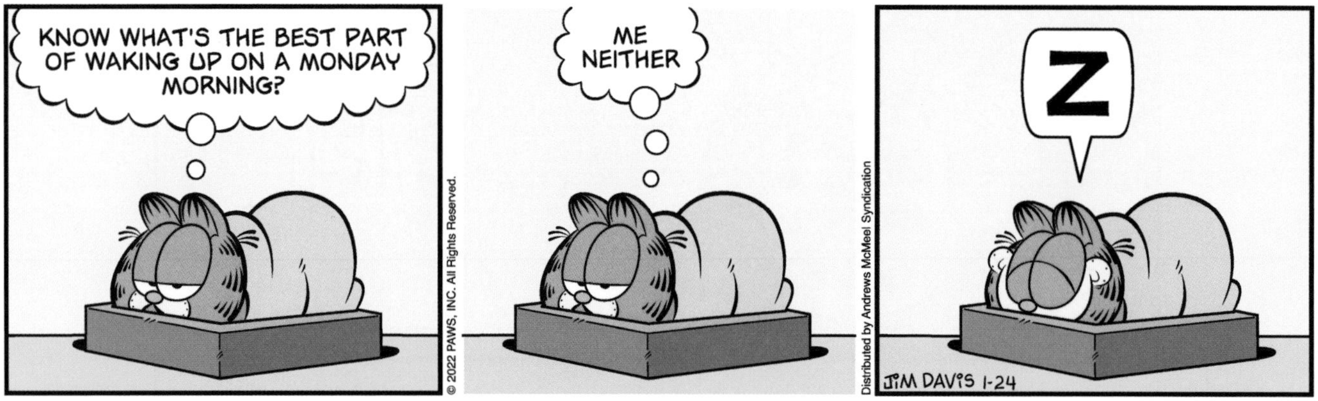
KNOW WHAT'S THE BEST PART OF WAKING UP ON A MONDAY MORNING?
ME NEITHER
Z
© 2022 PAWS, INC. All Rights Reserved.
Distributed by Andrews McMeel Syndication
JIM DAVIS 1-24

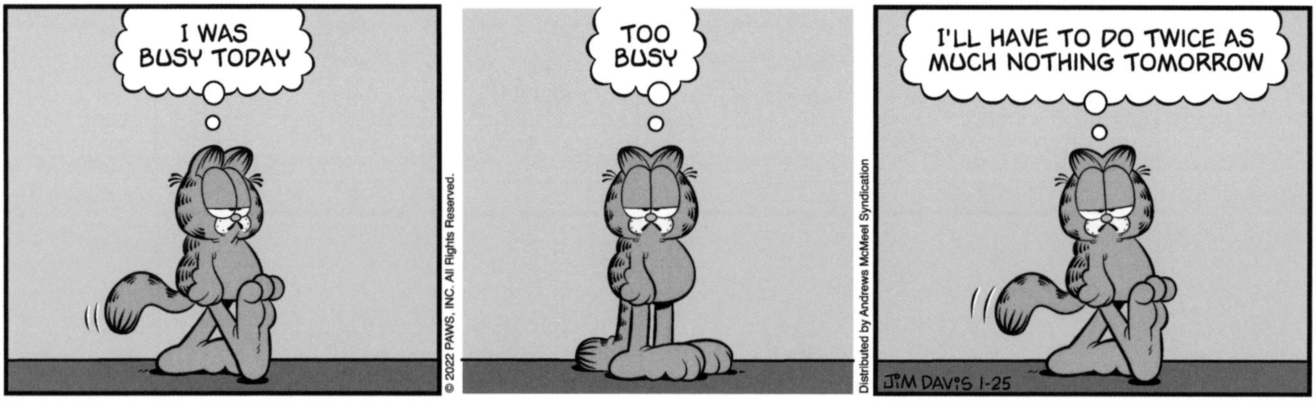
I WAS BUSY TODAY
TOO BUSY
I'LL HAVE TO DO TWICE AS MUCH NOTHING TOMORROW
© 2022 PAWS, INC. All Rights Reserved.
Distributed by Andrews McMeel Syndication
JIM DAVIS 1-25

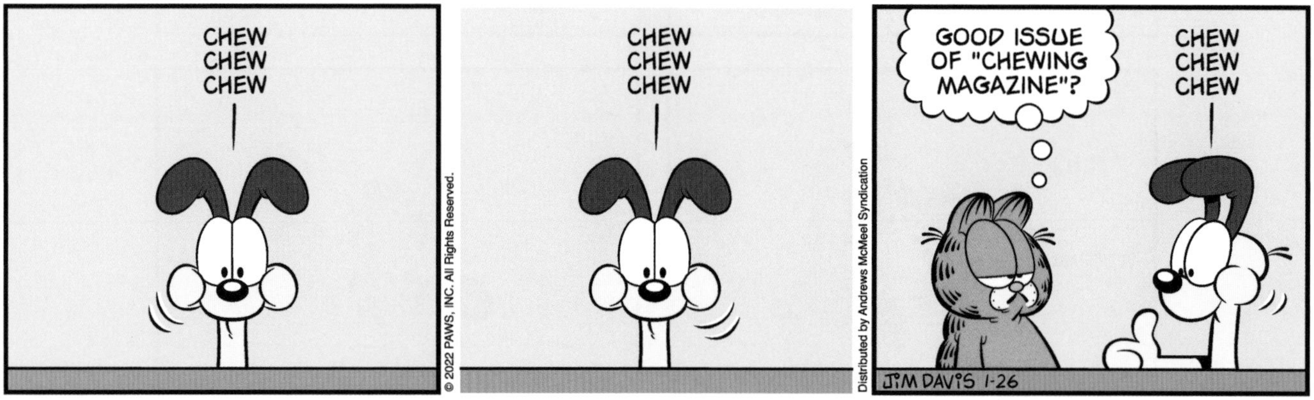
CHEW CHEW CHEW
CHEW CHEW CHEW
GOOD ISSUE OF "CHEWING MAGAZINE"?
CHEW CHEW CHEW
© 2022 PAWS, INC. All Rights Reserved.
Distributed by Andrews McMeel Syndication
JIM DAVIS 1-26

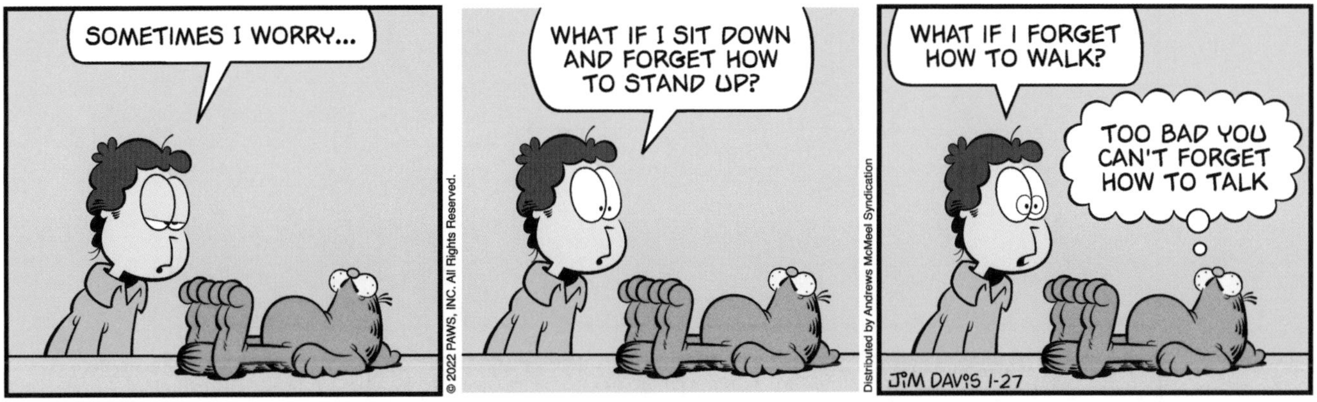
SOMETIMES I WORRY...
WHAT IF I SIT DOWN AND FORGET HOW TO STAND UP?
WHAT IF I FORGET HOW TO WALK?
TOO BAD YOU CAN'T FORGET HOW TO TALK
© 2022 PAWS, INC. All Rights Reserved.
Distributed by Andrews McMeel Syndication
JIM DAVIS 1-27

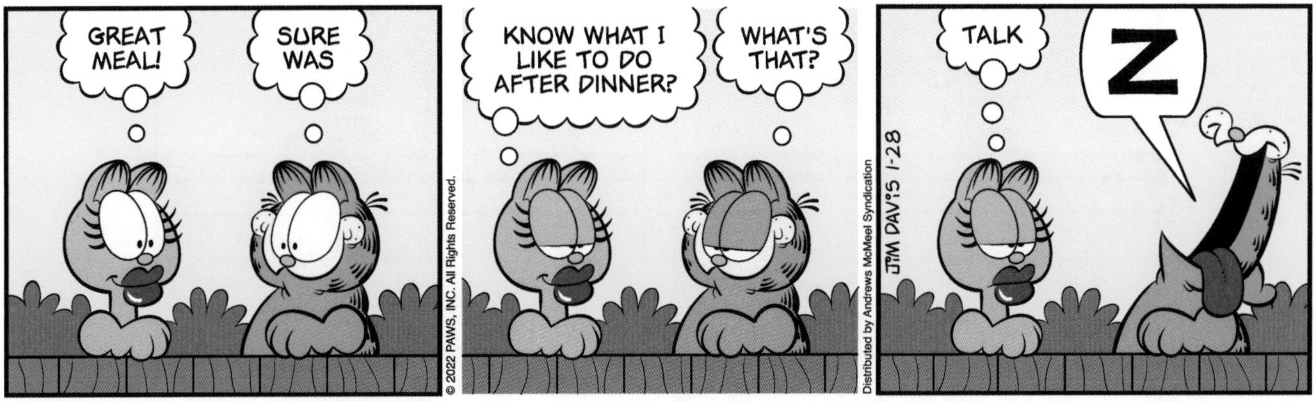
GREAT MEAL!
SURE WAS
KNOW WHAT I LIKE TO DO AFTER DINNER?
WHAT'S THAT?
TALK
Z
© 2022 PAWS, INC. All Rights Reserved.
Distributed by Andrews McMeel Syndication
JIM DAVIS 1-28

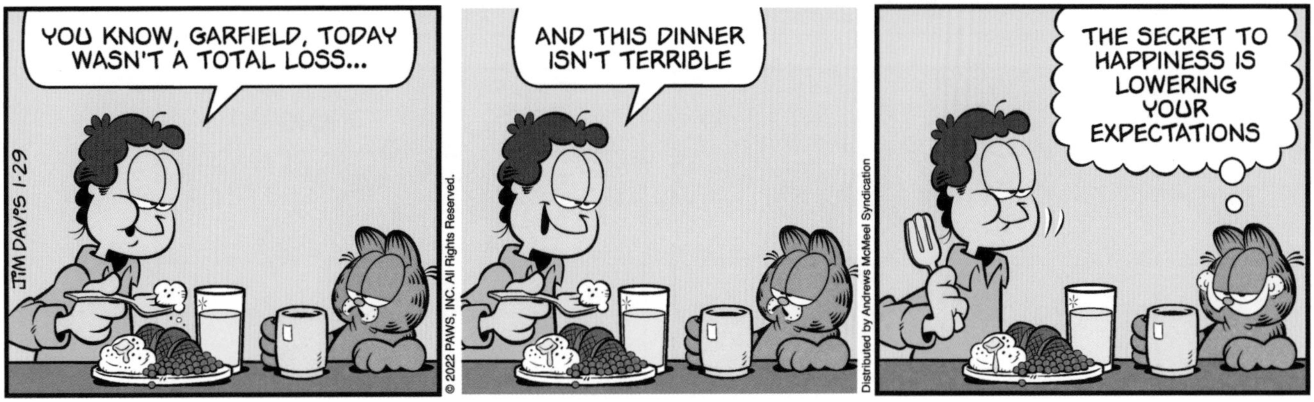
YOU KNOW, GARFIELD, TODAY WASN'T A TOTAL LOSS...
AND THIS DINNER ISN'T TERRIBLE
THE SECRET TO HAPPINESS IS LOWERING YOUR EXPECTATIONS
JIM DAVIS 1-29
© 2022 PAWS, INC. All Rights Reserved.
Distributed by Andrews McMeel Syndication

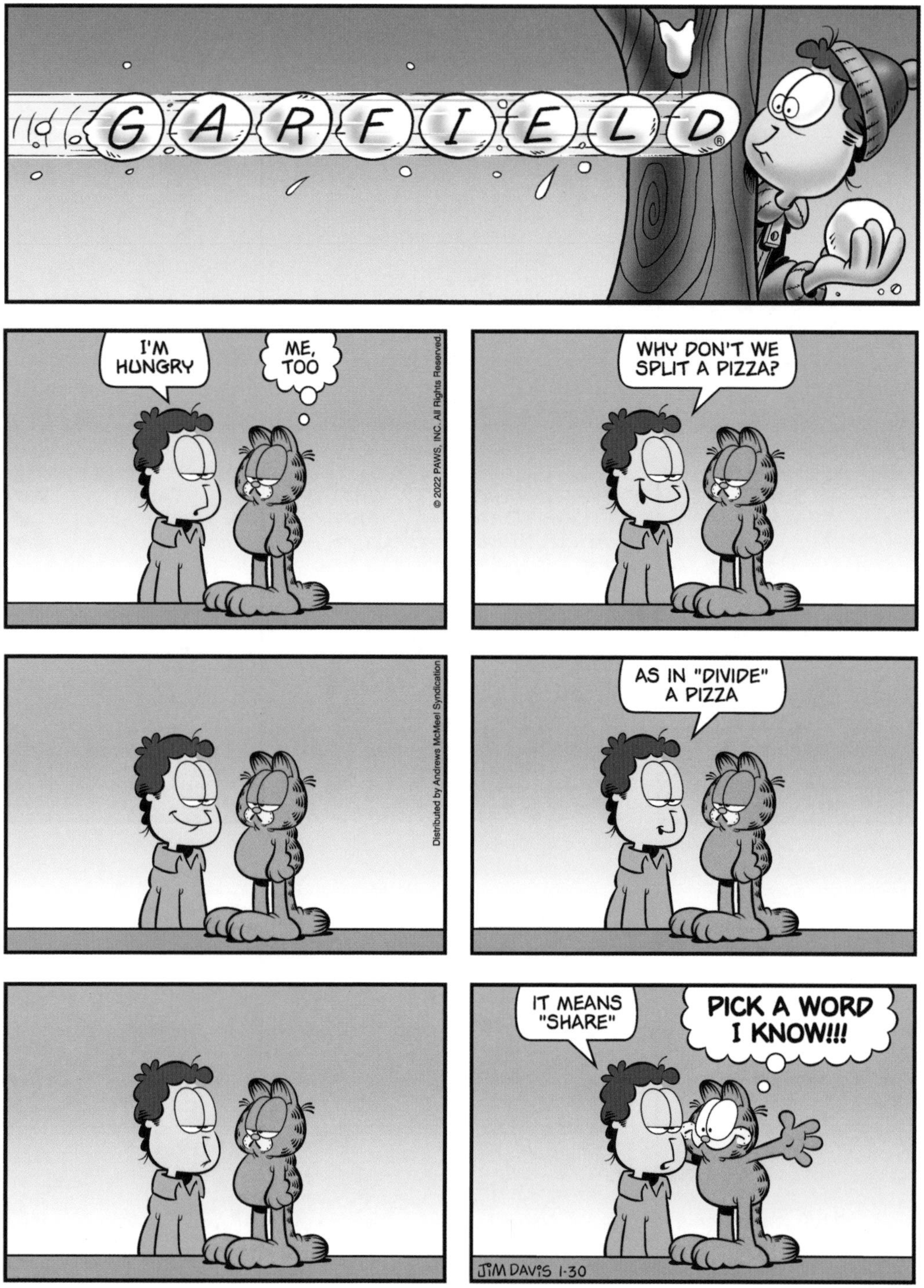
GARFIELD®
I'M HUNGRY
ME, TOO
© 2022 PAWS, INC. All Rights Reserved.
WHY DON'T WE SPLIT A PIZZA?
Distributed by Andrews McMeel Syndication
AS IN "DIVIDE" A PIZZA
IT MEANS "SHARE"
PICK A WORD I KNOW!!!
JIM DAVIS 1-30

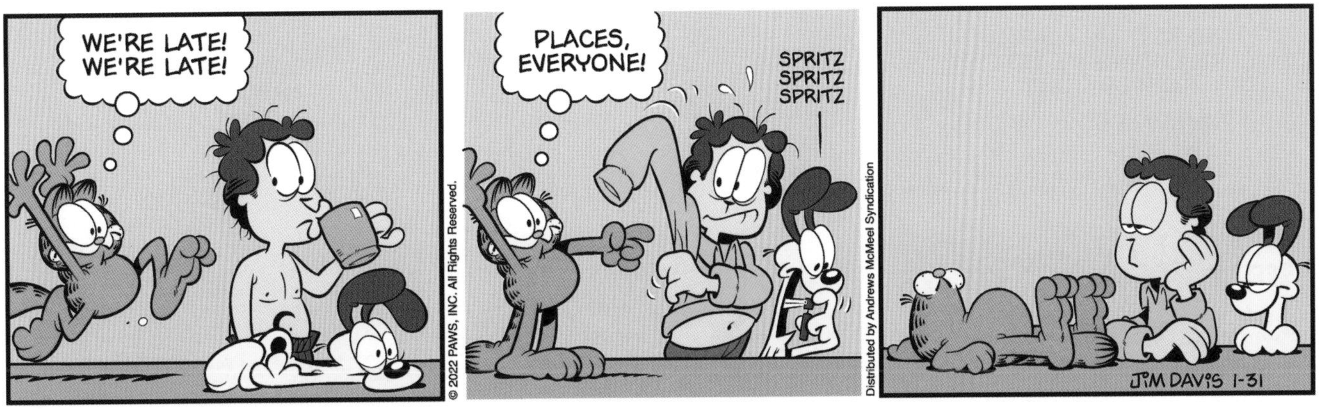
WE'RE LATE! WE'RE LATE!
PLACES, EVERYONE!
SPRITZ SPRITZ SPRITZ
© 2022 PAWS, INC. All Rights Reserved.
Distributed by Andrews McMeel Syndication
JIM DAVIS 1-31

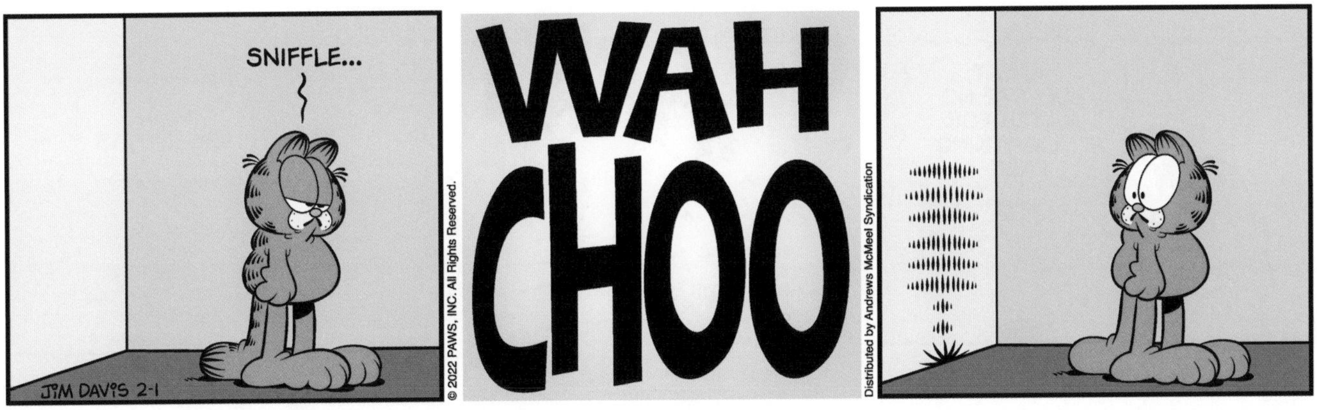
SNIFFLE...
JIM DAVIS 2-1
WAH CHOO
© 2022 PAWS, INC. All Rights Reserved.
Distributed by Andrews McMeel Syndication

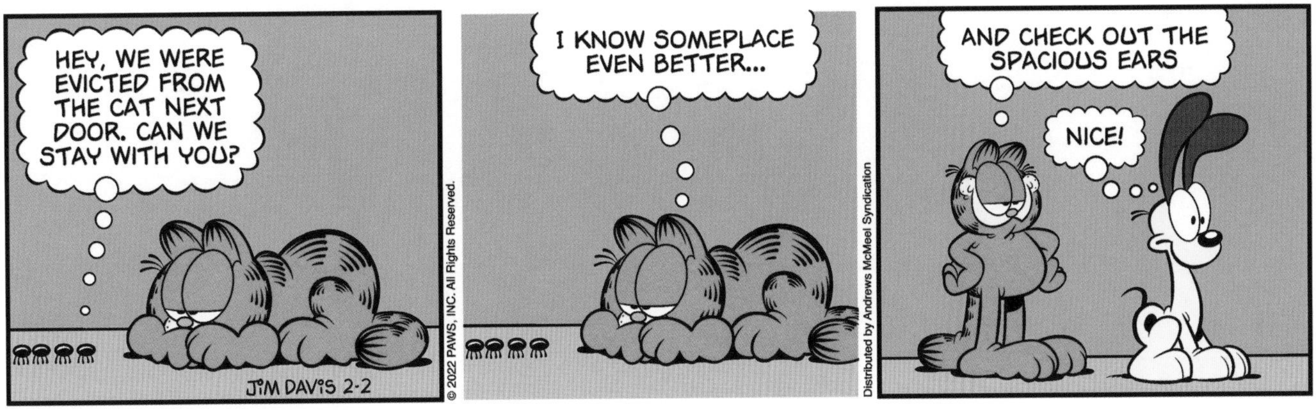
HEY, WE WERE EVICTED FROM THE CAT NEXT DOOR. CAN WE STAY WITH YOU?
JIM DAVIS 2-2
I KNOW SOMEPLACE EVEN BETTER...
AND CHECK OUT THE SPACIOUS EARS
NICE!
© 2022 PAWS, INC. All Rights Reserved.
Distributed by Andrews McMeel Syndication

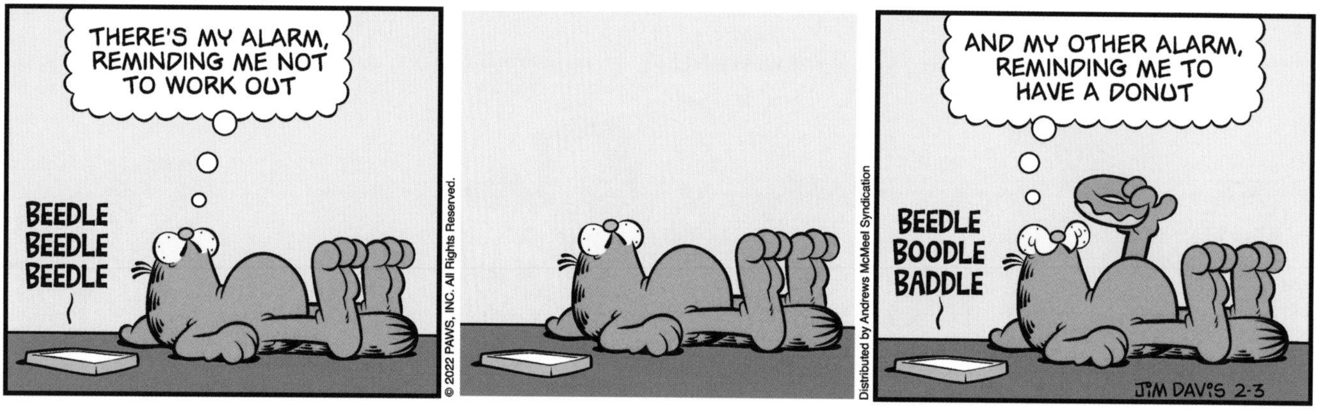
BEEDLE BEEDLE BEEDLE
THERE'S MY ALARM, REMINDING ME NOT TO WORK OUT
© 2022 PAWS, INC. All Rights Reserved.
Distributed by Andrews McMeel Syndication
BEEDLE BOODLE BADDLE
AND MY OTHER ALARM, REMINDING ME TO HAVE A DONUT
JIM DAVIS 2-3

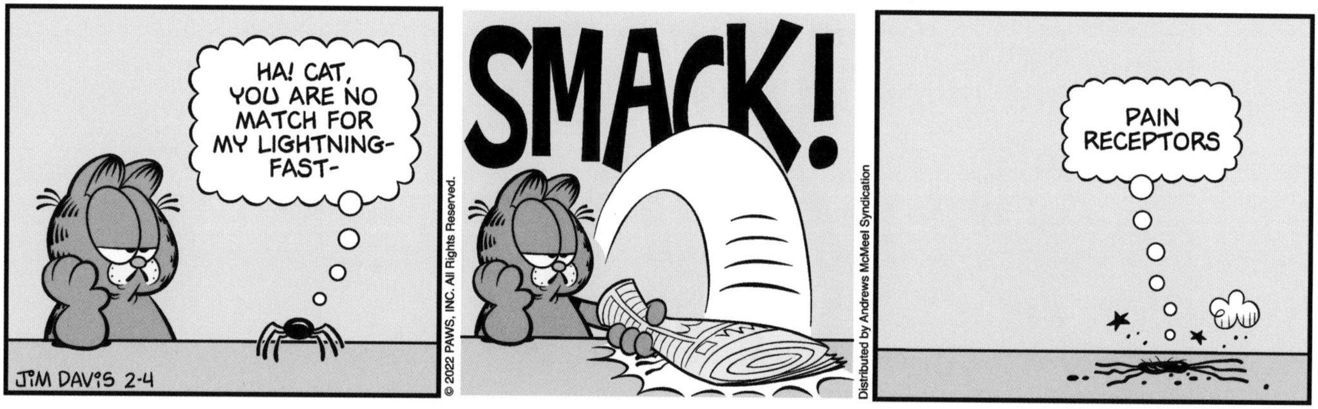
HA! CAT, YOU ARE NO MATCH FOR MY LIGHTNING-FAST-
JIM DAVIS 2-4
SMACK!
© 2022 PAWS, INC. All Rights Reserved.
Distributed by Andrews McMeel Syndication
PAIN RECEPTORS

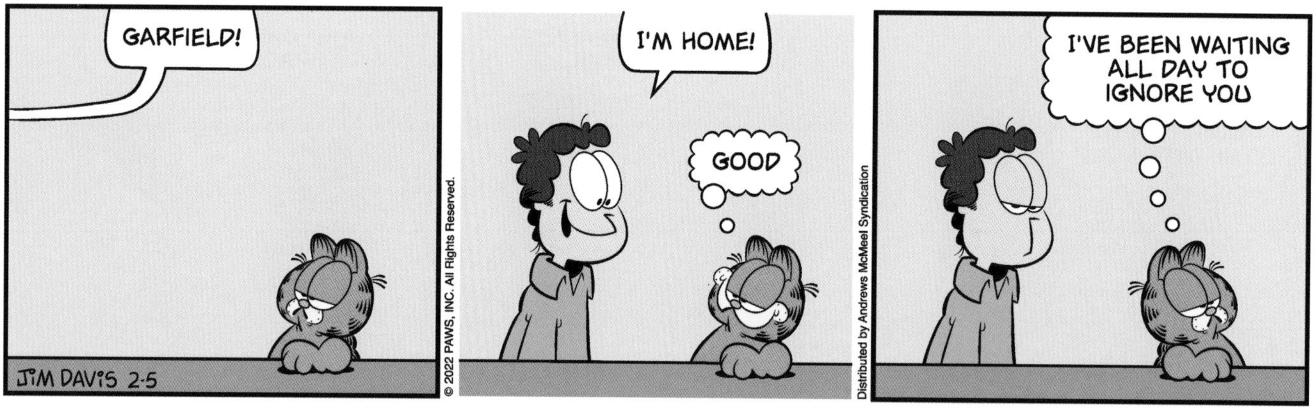
GARFIELD!
JIM DAVIS 2-5
I'M HOME!
GOOD
© 2022 PAWS, INC. All Rights Reserved.
Distributed by Andrews McMeel Syndication
I'VE BEEN WAITING ALL DAY TO IGNORE YOU

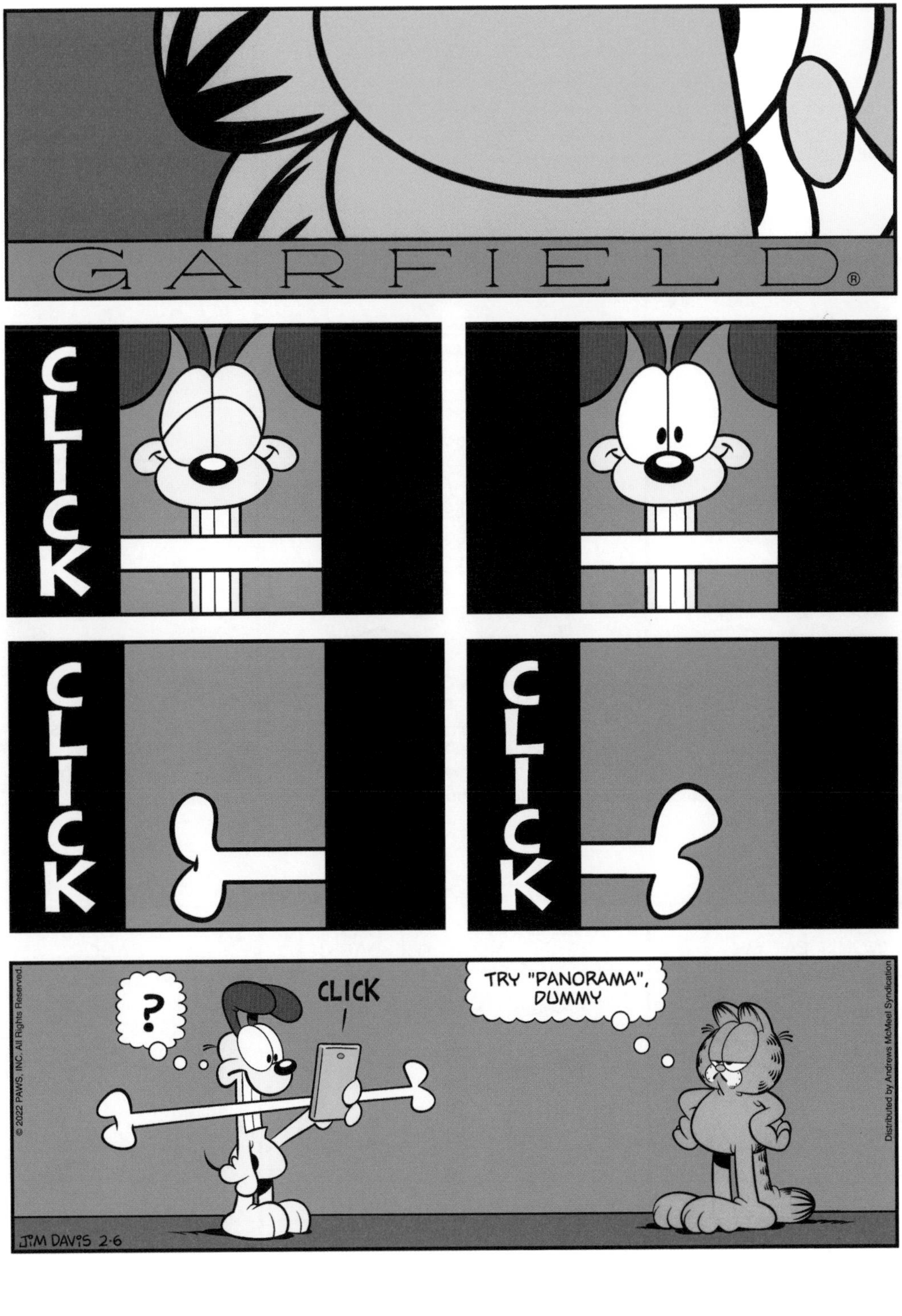
GARFIELD®
CLICK
CLICK
CLICK
?
CLICK
TRY "PANORAMA", DUMMY
JIM DAVIS 2-6
© 2022 PAWS, INC. All Rights Reserved.
Distributed by Andrews McMeel Syndication

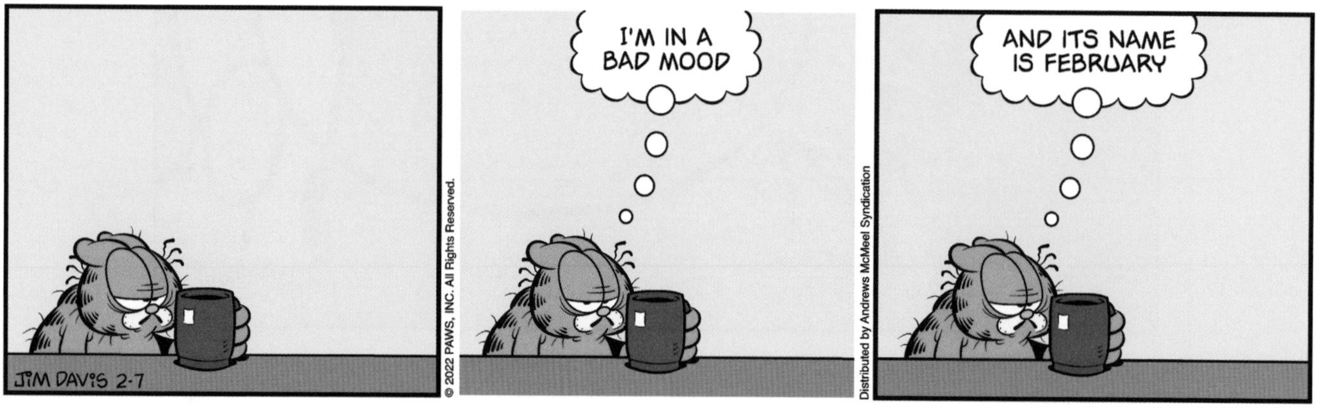
JIM DAVIS 2-7
I'M IN A BAD MOOD
AND ITS NAME IS FEBRUARY
© 2022 PAWS, INC. All Rights Reserved.
Distributed by Andrews McMeel Syndication

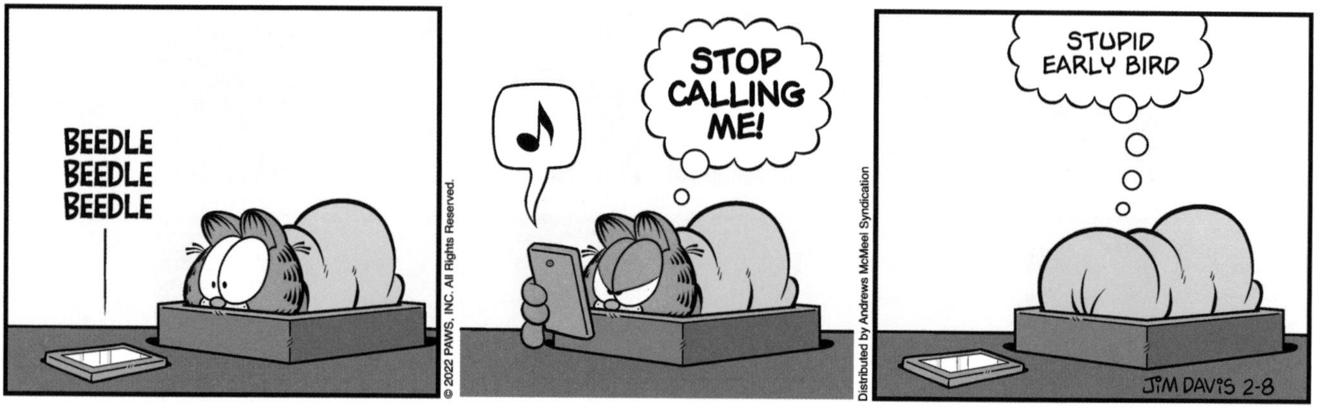
BEEDLE BEEDLE BEEDLE
♪
STOP CALLING ME!
STUPID EARLY BIRD
JIM DAVIS 2-8
© 2022 PAWS, INC. All Rights Reserved.
Distributed by Andrews McMeel Syndication

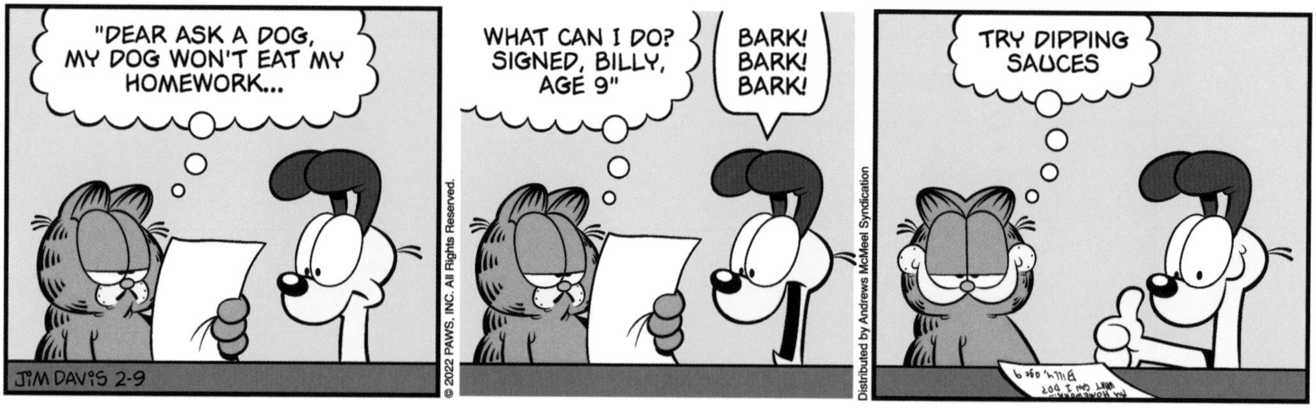
"DEAR ASK A DOG, MY DOG WON'T EAT MY HOMEWORK...
WHAT CAN I DO? SIGNED, BILLY, AGE 9"
BARK! BARK! BARK!
TRY DIPPING SAUCES
JIM DAVIS 2-9
© 2022 PAWS, INC. All Rights Reserved.
Distributed by Andrews McMeel Syndication

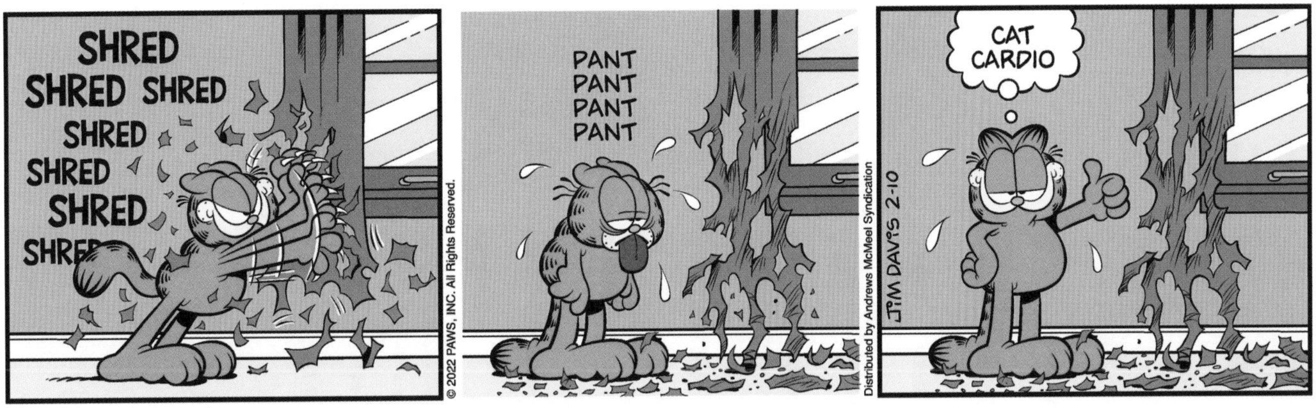
SHRED
SHRED SHRED
SHRED
SHRED
SHRED
SHRED
© 2022 PAWS, INC. All Rights Reserved.
PANT
PANT
PANT
PANT
Distributed by Andrews McMeel Syndication
JIM DAVIS 2-10
CAT CARDIO

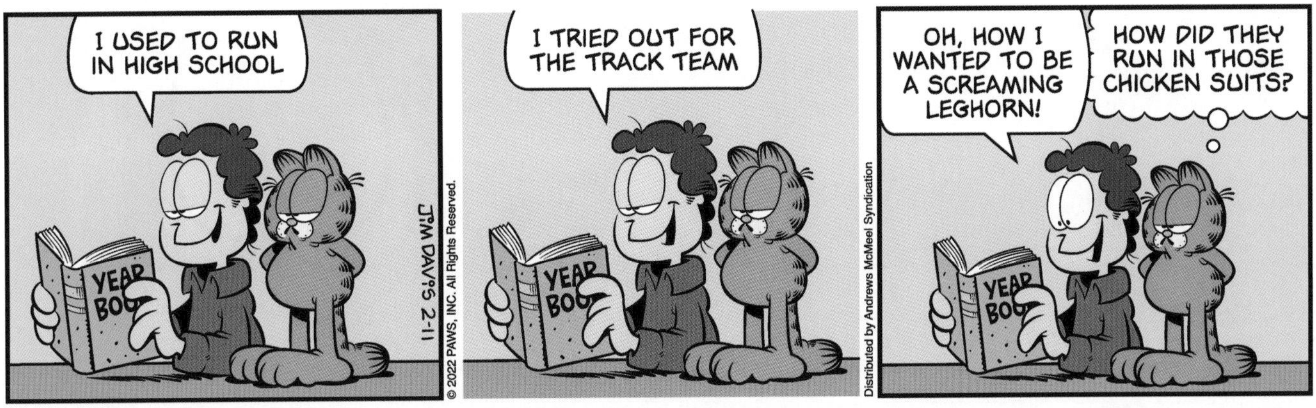
I USED TO RUN IN HIGH SCHOOL
YEAR BOO
JIM DAVIS 2-11
© 2022 PAWS, INC. All Rights Reserved.
I TRIED OUT FOR THE TRACK TEAM
Distributed by Andrews McMeel Syndication
OH, HOW I WANTED TO BE A SCREAMING LEGHORN!
HOW DID THEY RUN IN THOSE CHICKEN SUITS?

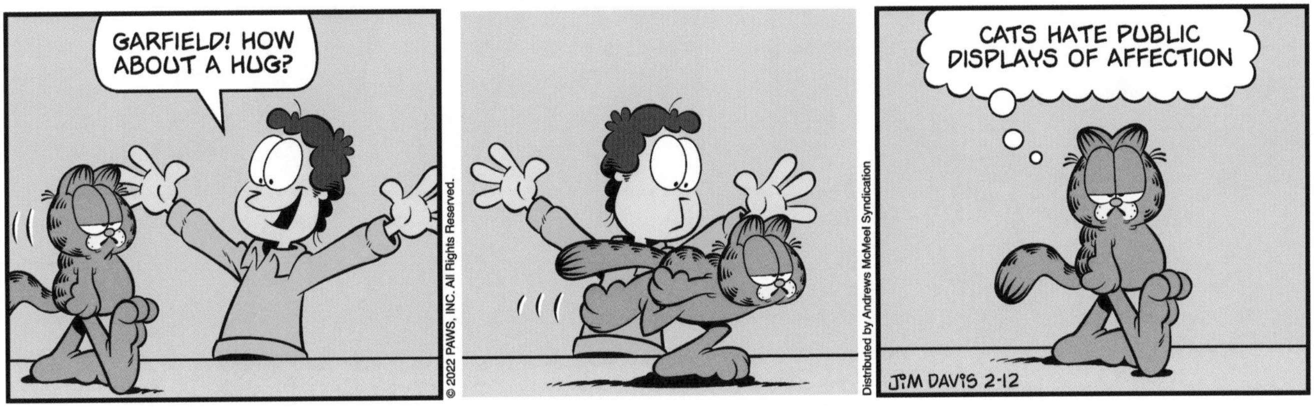
GARFIELD! HOW ABOUT A HUG?
© 2022 PAWS, INC. All Rights Reserved.
Distributed by Andrews McMeel Syndication
CATS HATE PUBLIC DISPLAYS OF AFFECTION
JIM DAVIS 2-12

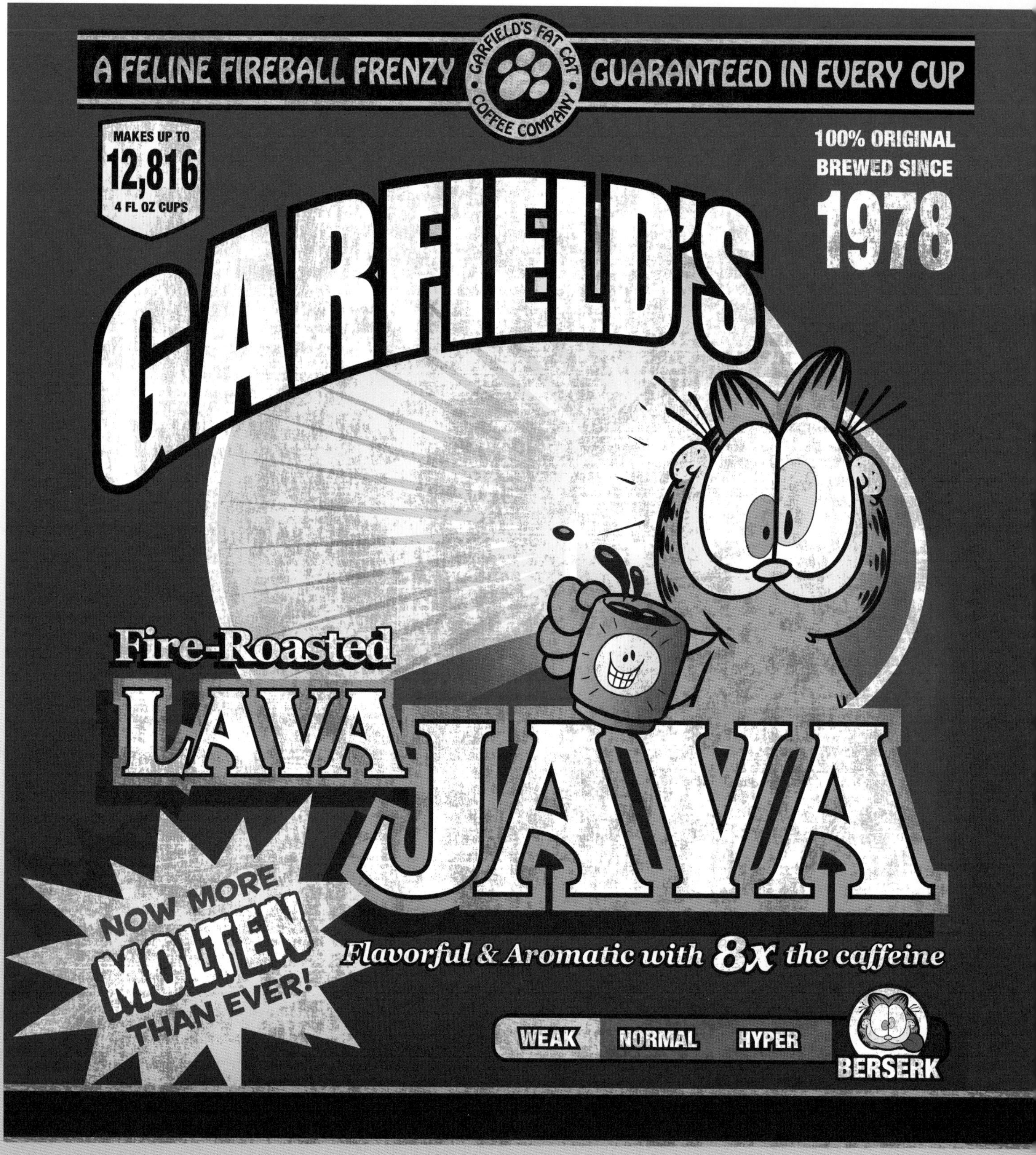
A FELINE FIREBALL FRENZY
GARFIELD'S FAT CAT COFFEE COMPANY
GUARANTEED IN EVERY CUP
MAKES UP TO 12,816 4 FL OZ CUPS
100% ORIGINAL BREWED SINCE 1978
GARFIELD'S
Fire-Roasted
LAVA JAVA
NOW MORE MOLTEN THAN EVER!
Flavorful & Aromatic with 8x the caffeine
WEAK
NORMAL
HYPER
BERSERK

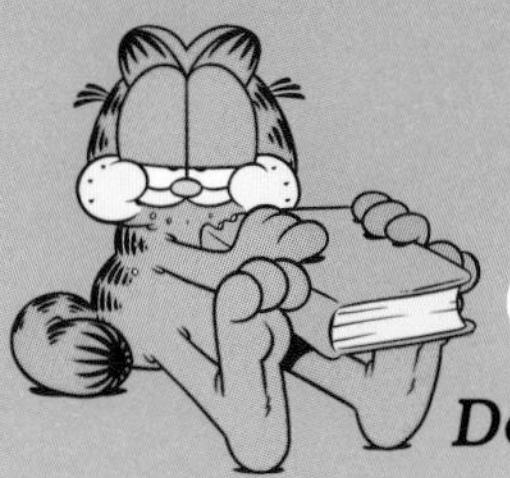

# STRIPS, SPECIALS OR BESTSELLING BOOKS...

# GARFIELD'S ON EVERYONE'S MENU.

***Don't miss even one episode in the Tubby Tabby's hilarious series!***

| Title | No. | ISBN |
|---|---|---|
| GARFIELD AT LARGE | (#1) | 978-0-345-44382-3 |
| GARFIELD GAINS WEIGHT | (#2) | 978-0-345-44975-7 |
| GARFIELD BIGGER THAN LIFE | (#3) | 978-0-345-45027-2 |
| GARFIELD WEIGHS IN | (#4) | 978-0-345-45205-4 |
| GARFIELD TAKES THE CAKE | (#5) | 978-0-345-44978-8 |
| GARFIELD EATS HIS HEART OUT | (#6) | 978-0-345-46459-0 |
| GARFIELD SITS AROUND THE HOUSE | (#7) | 978-0-345-46463-7 |
| GARFIELD TIPS THE SCALES | (#8) | 978-0-345-46909-0 |
| GARFIELD LOSES HIS FEET | (#9) | 978-0-345-46467-5 |
| GARFIELD MAKES IT BIG | (#10) | 978-0-345-46468-2 |
| GARFIELD ROLLS ON | (#11) | 978-0-345-47561-9 |
| GARFIELD OUT TO LUNCH | (#12) | 978-0-345-47562-6 |
| GARFIELD FOOD FOR THOUGHT | (#13) | 978-0-345-47563-3 |
| GARFIELD SWALLOWS HIS PRIDE | (#14) | 978-0-345-91386-9 |
| GARFIELD WORLDWIDE | (#15) | 978-0-345-91754-6 |
| GARFIELD ROUNDS OUT | (#16) | 978-0-345-49169-5 |
| GARFIELD CHEWS THE FAT | (#17) | 978-0-345-49170-1 |
| GARFIELD GOES TO WAIST | (#18) | 978-0-345-49173-2 |
| GARFIELD HANGS OUT | (#19) | 978-0-345-49174-9 |
| GARFIELD TAKES UP SPACE | (#20) | 978-0-345-49178-7 |
| GARFIELD SAYS A MOUTHFUL | (#21) | 978-0-345-49179-4 |
| GARFIELD BY THE POUND | (#22) | 978-0-345-52558-1 |
| GARFIELD KEEPS HIS CHINS UP | (#23) | 978-0-345-52559-8 |
| GARFIELD TAKES HIS LICKS | (#24) | 978-0-345-52587-1 |
| GARFIELD HITS THE BIG TIME | (#25) | 978-0-345-52589-5 |
| GARFIELD PULLS HIS WEIGHT | (#26) | 978-0-345-52594-9 |
| GARFIELD DISHES IT OUT | (#27) | 978-0-345-52595-6 |
| GARFIELD LIFE IN THE FAT LANE | (#28) | 978-0-345-52600-7 |
| GARFIELD TONS OF FUN | (#29) | 978-0-345-52601-4 |
| GARFIELD BIGGER AND BETTER | (#30) | 978-0-345-52605-2 |
| GARFIELD HAMS IT UP | (#31) | 978-0-345-52606-9 |
| GARFIELD THINKS BIG | (#32) | 978-0-425-28516-9 |
| GARFIELD THROWS HIS WEIGHT AROUND | (#33) | 978-0-425-28559-6 |
| GARFIELD LIFE TO THE FULLEST | (#34) | 978-0-425-28564-0 |
| GARFIELD FEEDS THE KITTY | (#35) | 978-0-425-28569-5 |
| GARFIELD HOGS THE SPOTLIGHT | (#36) | 978-0-425-28574-9 |
| GARFIELD BEEFS UP | (#37) | 978-0-345-44109-6 |
| GARFIELD GETS COOKIN' | (#38) | 978-0-345-44582-7 |
| GARFIELD EATS CROW | (#39) | 978-0-345-45201-6 |
| GARFIELD SURVIVAL OF THE FATTEST | (#40) | 978-0-345-46458-3 |
| GARFIELD OLDER AND WIDER | (#41) | 978-0-345-46462-0 |
| GARFIELD PIGS OUT | (#42) | 978-0-345-46466-8 |
| GARFIELD BLOTS OUT THE SUN | (#43) | 978-0-345-46615-0 |
| GARFIELD GOES BANANAS | (#44) | 978-0-345-91346-3 |
| GARFIELD LARGE & IN CHARGE | (#45) | 978-0-345-49172-5 |
| GARFIELD SPILLS THE BEANS | (#46) | 978-0-345-49177-0 |
| GARFIELD GETS HIS JUST DESSERTS | (#47) | 978-0-345-91387-6 |
| GARFIELD WILL EAT FOR FOOD | (#48) | 978-0-345-49176-3 |
| GARFIELD WEIGHS HIS OPTIONS | (#49) | 978-0-345-49181-7 |
| GARFIELD POTBELLY OF GOLD | (#50) | 978-0-345-52244-3 |
| GARFIELD SHOVELS IT IN | (#51) | 978-0-345-52419-5 |
| GARFIELD LARD OF THE JUNGLE | (#52) | 978-0-345-52584-0 |
| GARFIELD BRINGS HOME THE BACON | (#53) | 978-0-345-52586-4 |
| GARFIELD GETS IN A PICKLE | (#54) | 978-0-345-52590-1 |
| GARFIELD SINGS FOR HIS SUPPER | (#55) | 978-0-345-52593-2 |
| GARFIELD CAUTION: WIDE LOAD | (#56) | 978-0-345-52596-3 |
| GARFIELD SOUPED UP | (#57) | 978-0-345-52598-7 |
| GARFIELD GOES TO HIS HAPPY PLACE | (#58) | 978-0-345-52602-1 |
| GARFIELD THE BIG CHEESE | (#59) | 978-0-345-52604-5 |
| GARFIELD CLEANS HIS PLATE | (#60) | 978-0-345-52608-3 |
| GARFIELD CHICKENS OUT | (#61) | 978-0-425-28515-2 |
| GARFIELD LISTENS TO HIS GUT | (#62) | 978-0-425-28557-2 |
| GARFIELD COOKS UP TROUBLE | (#63) | 978-0-425-28562-6 |
| GARFIELD FEEDS HIS FACE | (#64) | 978-0-425-28567-1 |
| GARFIELD EATS AND RUNS | (#65) | 978-0-425-28572-5 |
| GARFIELD NUTTY AS A FRUITCAKE | (#66) | 978-0-425-28576-3 |
| GARFIELD SLURPS AND BURPS | (#67) | 978-1-9848-1773-0 |
| GARFIELD BELLY LAUGHS | (#68) | 978-1-9848-1777-8 |
| GARFIELD EASY AS PIE | (#69) | 978-0-593-15640-7 |
| GARFIELD GOES HOG WILD | (#70) | 978-0-593-15642-1 |
| GARFIELD WHAT LEFTOVERS? | (#71) | 978-0-593-15644-5 |
| GARFIELD LIVIN' THE SWEET LIFE | (#72) | 978-0-593-15646-9 |
| GARFIELD ROAD PIZZA | (#73) | 978-0-593-15648-3 |
| GARFIELD HOME COOKIN' | (#74) | 978-0-593-59919-8 |

**DVD TIE-INS**

| Title | ISBN |
|---|---|
| GARFIELD AS HIMSELF | 978-0-345-47805-4 |
| GARFIELD HOLIDAY CELEBRATIONS | 978-0-345-47930-3 |
| GARFIELD TRAVEL ADVENTURES | 978-0-345-48087-3 |

**AND DON'T MISS . . .**

| Title | ISBN |
|---|---|
| GARFIELD AT 25: IN DOG YEARS I'D BE DEAD | 978-0-345-45204-7 |
| GARFIELD'S JOKE ZONE/INSULTS | 978-0-345-46263-3 |
| GARFIELD FAT CAT 3-PACK/ VOL. 1 | 978-0-345-46455-2 |
| GARFIELD FAT CAT 3-PACK/ VOL. 2 | 978-0-345-46465-1 |
| GARFIELD FAT CAT 3-PACK/ VOL. 3 | 978-0-345-48088-0 |
| GARFIELD FAT CAT 3-PACK/ VOL. 4 | 978-0-345-49171-8 |
| GARFIELD FAT CAT 3-PACK/ VOL. 5 | 978-0-345-49180-8 |
| GARFIELD FAT CAT 3-PACK/ VOL. 6 | 978-0-345-52420-1 |
| GARFIELD FAT CAT 3-PACK/ VOL. 7 | 978-0-345-52588-8 |
| GARFIELD FAT CAT 3-PACK/ VOL. 8 | 978-0-345-52599-4 |
| GARFIELD FAT CAT 3-PACK/ VOL. 9 | 978-0-345-52607-6 |
| GARFIELD FAT CAT 3-PACK/ VOL. 10 | 978-0-425-28558-9 |
| GARFIELD FAT CAT 3-PACK/ VOL. 11 | 978-0-425-28566-4 |
| GARFIELD FAT CAT 3-PACK/ VOL. 12 | 978-0-425-28578-7 |
| GARFIELD FAT CAT 3-PACK/ VOL. 13 | 978-0-345-46460-6 |
| GARFIELD FAT CAT 3-PACK/ VOL. 14 | 978-0-345-49175-6 |
| GARFIELD FAT CAT 3-PACK/ VOL. 15 | 978-0-345-52585-7 |
| GARFIELD FAT CAT 3-PACK/ VOL. 16 | 978-0-345-52592-5 |
| GARFIELD FAT CAT 3-PACK/ VOL. 17 | 978-0-345-52603-8 |
| GARFIELD FAT CAT 3-PACK/ VOL. 18 | 978-0-399-59440-3 |
| GARFIELD FAT CAT 3-PACK/ VOL. 19 | 978-0-425-28561-9 |
| GARFIELD FAT CAT 3-PACK/ VOL. 20 | 978-0-425-28571-8 |
| GARFIELD FAT CAT 3-PACK/ VOL. 21 | 978-1-9848-1775-4 |
| GARFIELD FAT CAT 3-PACK/ VOL. 22 | 978-0-593-15638-4 |
| GARFIELD FAT CAT 3-PACK/ VOL. 23 | 978-0-593-15639-1 |
| GARFIELD FAT CAT 3-PACK/ VOL. 24 | 978-0-593-15650-6 |
| GARFIELD'S 20TH ANNIVERSARY COLLECTION | 978-0-345-42126-5 |
| SEASON'S EATINGS: A VERY MERRY GARFIELD CHRISTMAS | 978-0-345-47560-2 |
| GARFIELD'S GUIDE TO EVERYTHING | 978-0-345-46461-3 |
| ODIE UNLEASHED! | 978-0-345-46464-4 |
| GARFIELD'S BOOK OF CAT NAMES | 978-0-345-48516-8 |
| THE GARFIELD JOURNAL | 978-0-345-46469-9 |
| LIGHTS, CAMERA, HAIRBALLS!: GARFIELD AT THE MOVIES | 978-0-345-49134-3 |
| 30 YEARS OF LAUGHS AND LASAGNA | 978-0-345-50379-4 |
| GARFIELD MINUS GARFIELD | 978-0-345-51387-8 |
| GARFIELD FROM THE TRASH BIN | 978-0-345-51881-1 |
| GARFIELD LEFT SPEECHLESS | 978-0-345-53058-5 |
| MY LAUGHABLE LIFE WITH GARFIELD | 978-0-345-52591-8 |
| GARFIELD'S SUNDAY FINEST | 978-0-345-52597-0 |
| AGE HAPPENS: GARFIELD HITS THE BIG 4-0 | 978-0-345-52609-0 |
| GARFIELD COMPLETE WORKS: VOLUME ONE: 1978 & 1979 | 978-0-425-28712-5 |
| GARFIELD COMPLETE WORKS: VOLUME TWO: 1980 & 1981 | 978-0-425-28713-2 |

**New larger, full-color format!** (marks titles #1–#36)

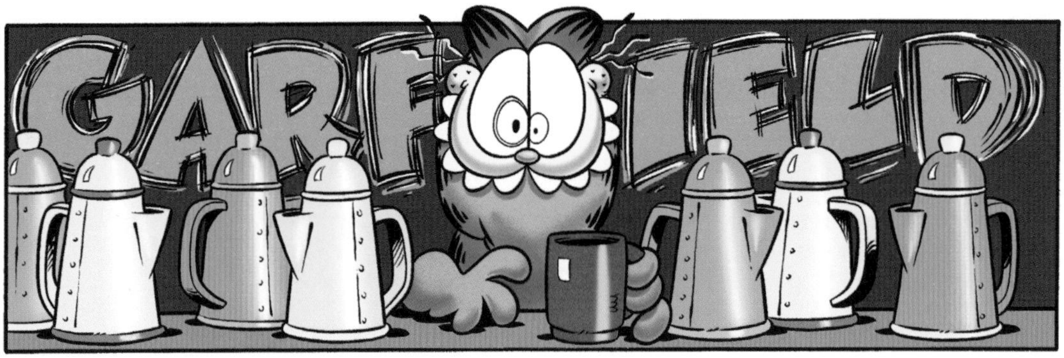
GARFIELD